Virtual Reality Narratives

"With *Virtual Reality Narratives*, Kath Dooley consolidates her status as a leading scholar and practitioner in the field of VR storytelling. Incorporating up-to-date case studies, the book effectively demonstrates how advances in VR technologies have led to uniquely interactive and embodied narrative forms. Dooley explores entertainment-based VR as a medium that alternates between the intimately personalised and the confrontational and participative, with valuable attention paid to what this means for users' agency and their bodies."

—Dr Jennifer O'Meara, *Associate Professor in Film Studies, Trinity College Dublin, The University of Dublin*

"*Virtual Reality Narratives* brings a welcome boost to the study of VR storytelling with thorough analyses and strong readings of well-selected case studies. With expert application to the still-new terrain of VR storytelling, Dooley blends familiar story elements such as plot and game mechanics against a wide range of topics bespoke to the VR environment from body affects to environmental storytelling to user customisation and more. A comprehensive study of the subject and very much recommended!"

—Professor Jenna Ng, *Subject Head of Creative Technologies and Professor of Digital Media and Culture, University of York*

Kath Dooley

Virtual Reality Narratives

Embodied Encounters in Space

palgrave
macmillan

Kath Dooley
UniSA Creative
The University of South Australia
Adelaide, SA, Australia

ISBN 978-3-031-64964-6   ISBN 978-3-031-64965-3 (eBook)
https://doi.org/10.1007/978-3-031-64965-3

This Palgrave Macmillan imprint is published by the registered company Springer Nature Switzerland AG.
The registered company address is: Gewerbestrasse 11, 6330 Cham, Switzerland

In memory of Janet Elizabeth Dooley

Acknowledgements

The research that is presented in this book has been undertaken over several years with the encouragement and support of a range of colleagues, friends and family. It started life as a project aiming to catalogue and explore the innovative work of contemporary virtual reality storytellers and morphed into a more focused examination of VR as a narrative form. This has involved a scholarly journey that has been challenging but hugely rewarding.

I would like to acknowledge the traditional owners of the land on which the book was written, the Kaurna people of the Adelaide plains in South Australia, and pay my respects to their elders, past and present. I recognise the ongoing spiritual connection that the Kaurna people have with this land and their status as the first storytellers of this place.

A number of individuals deserve my special thanks for their contributions and/or collegiality, which has shaped this book in one way or another. I express my gratitude to my UniSA peers—in particular, Kim Munro and Ben Stubbs of the Expanded Storytelling Lab, Professors Craig Batty and Adrian Franklin, and my PhD student, George Martin. I'd also like to thank the extended community of researchers and practitioners working on VR storytelling who have provided general advice and feedback: in particular, Nathan Anderson, Stephen Butchko, Alex Munt, Deirdre V. Lyons, Mirjam Vosmeer and Simon Weaving. For generously granting interviews, I thank Stephen Butchko, Christopher Lane Davis, Deirdre V. Lyons and Lyndsie Scoggin. For granting permission for the use of images, I additionally thank Sparsh Ahuja (Project Dastaan), Nathan Anderson (New Canvas), Mike Brett (38 Minutes), Stephen Butchko

(Ferryman Collective), Daniel Cannizzaro (Tender Claws), Nonny de la Peña (Emblematic Group), Yasmin Elayat (Changing Same Collaborative), Peter Hegedus (Soul Vision Films), Leonardo Lami (Anagram) and Chin Hsuan Sung (The Walkers Films).

Most importantly, I wish to acknowledge the ongoing support of my partner Jamnes and my son Ren. Thank you for tolerating my extended writing sessions and for providing distractions along the way.

Portions of Chap. 5 appeared in 'Traversing Space in The Under Presents' (2019), a VR Game, in *International Conference on Interactive Digital Storytelling* (pp. 442–453), Cham, Springer Nature Switzerland. Material from Chap. 2 was presented as part of the 2024 Interactive Film and Media Conference (online).

I have no competing interests to declare regarding this publication.

Human Ethics Approval for interviews conducted as part of this book's research was granted by Curtin University (HREC number 2017-0032).

Contents

1	**Introduction**	1
	The Qualities of VR and Its Evolution as an Entertainment Medium	8
	Exploring Virtual Reality Narratives	10
	Key Research Questions and Methodology	27
	Chapter Breakdown	30
	References	32
2	**A Body in the Story: Exploring Body Representation, Presence and Embodiment in Virtual Reality Narratives**	39
	Introduction	39
	Presence and Embodiment in Virtual Reality	43
	Case Study Analysis	47
	Conclusion	63
	References	65
3	**Virtual Reality Narration: Listening to and Reliving Stories Through First-Person Testimony**	69
	Introduction	69
	User Positioning in VR	72
	The Position of the Narrator	77
	Case Studies	78
	Conclusion	90
	References	92

4 Exploring Environmental Storytelling Techniques in Expressive, Virtual Reality Documentary 95
Introduction 95
Virtual Reality Documentary 99
Environmental Storytelling in Virtual Reality 101
Case Study Analysis 104
Conclusion 121
References 123

5 Time, Space and the Body in *The Under Presents* (2019), a Multiplayer Virtual Reality Game 127
Introduction 127
The Growth of VR Games 128
The Under Presents—*An Overview* 130
Narrative Structures Within The Under Presents 134
Traversing Time Loops and 'Corporeal Space' 138
A 'Real-Time' Experience of Narrative Events 144
Live Actors, Players and Intimate Experience 147
Conclusion 152
References 153

6 Between Storytelling and Storyliving: User Customisation of Virtual Reality Narratives 157
Introduction 157
Storytelling and Storyliving in VR 160
Narrative Theories and Models for IDNs 162
Case Study Analysis 167
Discussion and Conclusion 180
References 182

7 Virtual Reality Narratives Live Online: Immersive Theatre in VRChat Worlds 185
Introduction 185
On 'Liveness' in Immersive, Digital and VR Theatre 187
A Brief History of VR in Theatre and Performance Contexts 189
Live Theatre in VRChat 194
Narrative Structures: The Participant's Journey 204

The Virtual Body as Storytelling Tool 206
Conclusion 209
References 210

8 Conclusion: Virtual Reality Narratives as Embodied Encounters in Space 213
Introduction 213
Virtual Reality as Spatialised Storytelling 214
Virtual Reality Narrators, User Positioning and Point of View 217
Virtual Reality as Interactive Digital Narrative (IDN) 219
Diversity and Inclusion 229
Future Directions 231
References 234

Correction to: Virtual Reality Narratives C1

Index 239

About the Author

Kath Dooley Associate Professor is a researcher and writer/director of film and virtual reality projects based at the University of South Australia (UniSA). Her creative work has been screened at events such the Busan International Short Film Festival and the International Festival of Virtual and Augmented Reality Stories (FIVARS), Toronto. Kath is the author of *Cinematic Virtual Reality- A Critical Study of 21st Century Approaches and Practices* (Palgrave Macmillan, 2021) and co-editor of *Screenwriting for Virtual Reality: Story, Space and Experience* (Palgrave Macmillan, 2024). Her research interests include embodiment in the context of screen media, virtual reality and screenwriting, women's screen industry practice, and diversity in the screen industries. Kath is a member of the Expanded Storytelling Lab (XSL) at UniSA.

Abbreviations

3DoF	Three degrees of freedom
6DoF	Six degrees of freedom
AI	Artificial Intelligence
AR	Augmented Reality
CAVE	Cave Automatic Virtual Environment
CG	Computer Graphics
CGI	Computer-Generated Images
CVR	Cinematic Virtual Reality
HCI	Human Computer Interaction
HMD	Head Mounted Display
IDN	Interactive Digital Narrative
IDS	Interactive Digital Storytelling
LARP	Live Action Role Playing Games
MR	Mixed Reality
UI	User Interface
UX	User Experience
VE	Virtual Environment
VR	Virtual Reality
XR	Extended Reality

List of Figures

Fig. 2.1	A screenshot from the trailer for *The Man Who Couldn't Leave* (2022). (Courtesy of The Walkers Films Ltd.)	49
Fig. 2.2	A screenshot from the trailer for *The Man Who Couldn't Leave* (2022). (Courtesy of The Walkers Films Ltd.)	52
Fig. 2.3	Screen capture from *Please, Believe Me*, directed and produced by Emblematic Group founder Nonny de la Peña and made in collaboration with Paper Crane games	59
Fig. 2.4	Screen capture from *Please, Believe Me*, directed and produced by Emblematic Group founder Nonny de la Peña and made in collaboration with Paper Crane games	61
Fig. 3.1	The user plays a retro arcade game that illustrates Goliath's early life experience in *Goliath: Playing with Reality* (2021). (Courtesy of Anagram)	80
Fig. 3.2	Sorella makes eye contact with the camera/viewer in *Sorella's Story* (2022). (Courtesy of Soul Vision Films)	87
Fig. 4.1	*The Changing Same: The Dilemma,* Directed by Joe Brewster, Yasmin Elayat, Michèle Stephenson. (Produced by Rada Studio and Scatter. © Changing Same Collaborative LLC)	107
Fig. 4.2	*The Changing Same: The Dilemma,* Directed by Joe Brewster, Yasmin Elayat, Michèle Stephenson. (Produced by Rada Studio and Scatter. © Changing Same Collaborative LLC)	109
Fig. 4.3	*Child of Empire.* (*© Project Dastaan*)	112
Fig. 4.4	*Child of Empire.* (*© Project Dastaan*)	113
Fig. 4.5	A landscape take shape in *On the Morning You Wake (to the End of the World). (© 2022 ARTE France, The British Film Institute and 38 Minutes Ltd)*	117

Fig. 4.6 The landscape is reduced to particles in *On the Morning You Wake (to the End of the World)*. (*© 2022 ARTE France, The British Film Institute and 38 Minutes Ltd*) 119

Fig. 5.1 Two players engage with a live actor avatar (screen capture from the author's game play). *The Under Presents* (2019), Tender Claws, LLC 131

Fig. 5.2 One of several photo booths located in the multiplayer area that transport the player to the Time Boat experience (screen capture from the author's game play). *The Under Presents* (2019), Tender Claws, LLC 132

Fig. 5.3 The MC presents a slideshow on the Aickman's doomed voyage. (*The Under Presents* (2019), Tender Claws, LLC) 136

Fig. 6.1 Onboarding instructions and user interface for *Lustration* (screen capture taken by the author). (Courtesy of New Canvas) 168

Fig. 6.2 Bardolph and Gallus wait for a target to appear. Screen capture from *Lustration*, Episode One. (Courtesy of New Canvas) 170

Fig. 6.3 Aliria explores Detective Pine's apartment in The Between. Screen capture from *Lustration* Episode Two. (Courtesy of New Canvas) 175

Fig. 7.1 The bedroom onboarding space. (Courtesy of the Ferryman Collective) 199

Fig. 7.2 Behind the scenes of *Welcome to Respite*—the audience member playing the character of Alex can choose the skin tone of their avatar. (Courtesy of the Ferryman Collective) 201

List of Tables

Table 3.1 User roles within VR narratives 75

Table 6.1 Protostory elements in *Lustration* based on SPP analysis model (Koenitz, 2023, p. 87) 172

Table 6.2 Protostory elements in *Fire Escape* based on SPP analysis model (Koenitz, 2023, p. 87) 178

CHAPTER 1

Introduction

In November 2022, as a remote attendee of the Raindance Film Festival, I experienced *Gumball Dreams* (Ferryman Collective 2022) an approximately one-hour-long virtual reality (VR) experience that was delivered through the online social VR platform, VRChat. Wearing an Oculus Quest 2 headset and holding hand controllers, I became immersed in a fictional, animated universe full of psychedelic colours and dazzling lights. The narrative of this work revolved around Onyx, a blue, non-gendered alien with large eyes and antlers, who was approaching the end of their life. Like another audience member in this participatory drama, I was cast in the role of a fellow alien who was called to assist in Onyx's transition to the next world.[1] After adopting an avatar and completing a number of game-like challenges designed to acclimate me to my new body and world, I passed through an obelisk and found Onyx housed within a castle constructed from a giant gumball machine. My mission, it seemed, was to retrieve batteries that would power the protagonist's space mission. The most remarkable aspect of the experience was that the character of Onyx was played by a live actor who engaged me in one-on-one conversation. 'What is your dream?' the alien asked after separating me from the other participant. While somewhat confronting, I found this intimate discussion

[1] *Gumball Dreams* is designed to be experienced by an audience of three participants; however my own experience of the project involved only two audience members. For more information on the project see: https://www.ferrymancollective.com/gumball-dreams

K. Dooley, *Virtual Reality Narratives*,
https://doi.org/10.1007/978-3-031-64965-3_1

to be the most memorable part of the experience, which ended with Onyx's peaceful transition to another realm. Drawing on the conventions of immersive theatre, the project's fantastical world and participatory narrative presented a personalised and intimate experience for the remote participant.

Upon later contemplation of the project, I recalled VR pioneer Jaron Lanier's assertion that virtual reality can

> take away a room and replace it with Seattle. Then take away your body and replace it with a giant body. All of the pieces are gone and yet there you are, still experiencing what is left. [...] Your centre of experience persists even after the body changes and the rest of the world changes. Virtual reality peels away phenomena and reveals that consciousness remains and is real. Virtual reality is the technology that exposes you to yourself. (Lanier, 2017, p. 55)

The notion of 'exposure' that Lanier writes about resonated with my experience of *Gumball Dreams* on multiple levels, but most notably in regard to my feelings of vulnerability when directly questioned by the ancient alien, Onyx. Despite my inhabitation of a fictional alien avatar, and my freedom to respond in any manner conceivable, I found myself compelled to tell the truth. As the narrative moved on to the next sequence, I was stuck thinking, *Why did I do that?* My experience as the work played out was thus one of deep introspection, which left me with many questions as to the power of the project's artistic approach, immersive qualities and my role within the narrative.

Gumball Dreams is one of numerous entertainment-focused and narrative-based VR experiences that has been offered to a global audience in recent years. I use the term 'entertainment-focused' here to describe creative works that have the primary goal of engaging users in stories for pleasure, amusement or to expand their worldview, as separate from VR narratives produced in other contexts, such as for healthcare or defence. Such entertainment-focused works may have experimental, artistic and/or commercial drivers. Contemporary VR experiences are dynamic and multifarious, adopting a range of production technologies and delivery platforms. While VR, as an entertainment technology, has existed for some time, developments in the second decade of the twenty-first century led to the release of consumer-grade products, giving rise to a 'third wave' of VR (Heim, 2017), fostered by a convergence of art forms, evolving digital technologies and an expanding global consumer base. Writing on electronic narrative forms in 2006, narratologist Marie-Laure Ryan suggested that 'the jury is still out on whether digital technology has bred/will breed major new forms of narrative' (p. xii). In this book I suggest that more than 15 years later, advances in VR technologies have given rise to an embodied narrative form that can be considered unique, and that this requires further scrutiny. Narrative-based VR experiences draw upon, or in some cases, reconfigure the conventions and properties of older media such as theatre, cinema and/or games. As a form of moving image that might be experienced via head mounted display (HMD) goggles, a dome screen or CAVE environment,[2] VR dissolves the rectangular frame associated with the cinema, television or computer screen, immersing the viewer in a 360-degree environment that is experienced as a replacement for their real-world surroundings. This 'engulfment' that 'eradicates any perceptible presence of its screen boundaries' (Ng, 2021, p. 108) demands the participation of the interactor's whole body.[3] I argue that as an inherently interactive medium that places the user *inside* a storyworld in a visible or invisible virtual body, virtual reality offers a means for the creation of narratives that incorporate the user's body as a storytelling tool, fostering user-centred stories that unfold in three-dimensional space.

This monograph offers an in-depth exploration of recent evolutions in virtual reality storytelling, specifically looking at entertainment-based works created or launched within the last five years. Through the analysis of a range of case studies, this exploration will evidence the increasing diversity and sophistication of narrative-based projects that have been created and exhibited around the world during this time. The majority of the case studies that receive analysis in the book date from 2020 onwards. This milestone year, in which COVID-19 led to widespread lockdowns around the world, marked eight years since a 2012 Kickstarter crowdfunding campaign to fund development of the Oculus Rift HMD generated US$2.4 million in pledges from VR enthusiasts and other stakeholders. Two years later, after the release of Oculus' second iteration HMD, the DK2, the company was acquired by Facebook (now rebranded as Meta) for US $2 billion. These events created market conditions that gave rise to

[2] A Cave Automatic Virtual Environment (CAVE) is constructed of a set of screens that cover the walls, ceiling and floor of a cube-shaped room, allowing for a 360-degree environment to be projected.

[3] Jenna Ng argues that virtual reality can be considered the first instantiation of the 'post-screen' due to its confinement of the interactor's field of view and engulfment of the interactor via large screens, which dissolves screen boundaries. See Ng, J. (2021). *The post-screen through virtual reality, holograms and light projections: where screen boundaries lie* (p. 282). Amsterdam University Press.

the current wave of activity in virtual reality entertainment. Aided by advances in smartphone technologies, consumer grade headsets, ranging from low cost 'Google cardboard' models to the high-end Oculus Rift HMD, entered the mass market for use in the home around 2015.[4] One can observe a flurry of activity in the years that followed, as practitioners and investors explored the new potentials of VR. While take up of headsets by consumers was limited in these years, the COVID-19 pandemic created a new drive for virtual experiences. With a significant portion of the world's population in lockdown, sales of Oculus' then latest model, the Oculus Quest, surged in 2020, leaving the company unable to meet consumer demand (Johnson, 2020). This time of increased user uptake stands as a useful point from which to explore the changing nature of narrative-based VR experiences. But further to the increased use of VR in the home, one must note that the technological advances featured in the Oculus Quest headset (and the Quest 2, which was released in October 2020), reflects the increased creation and distribution of VR entertainment offering users six degrees of freedom (abbreviated to 6DoF—the ability to move around within a virtual environment as well as to turn one's head from side to side, and to interact with objects using hand controllers), further to earlier iterations with more limited capabilities. The Quest headset was the first to allow untethered users the capability to interact with content offering 6DoF for an affordable price.[5] In October 2022 Meta revealed that more than US 1.5 billion had been spent by consumers on games and apps in its Quest store (Matney, 2022). This availability of new VR technologies and apps, an increased customer base for VR entertainment and evolving user expectations has created the conditions for new narrative possibilities.

Moreover, COVID-19 lockdowns in 2020 impacted upon the development and exhibition of VR-based entertainment in several other significant ways. Widespread lockdowns resulted in a boom for online VR social platforms such as VRChat and the now defunct AltSpace, both of which have been sites for the creation of narrative-based experiences. As Chap. 7

[4] Google Cardboard-style viewers retailed from around US$10 and worked in conjunction with a mobile phone screen to offer monoscopic or stereoscopic 360-degree experiences. The prototype was developed by Google and made of cardboard, with the aim of providing a cheap entry point to VR viewing. By contrast the Oculus Rift cost US$599 to purchase on its initial release in 2016.

[5] The Oculus Rift and HTC Vive need to be tethered to a computer, unlike the Oculus Quest HMD.

of this book explores, innovative artists and theatre makers looked to these platforms as a new venue for live theatre production in the wake of physical venue shutdowns, producing an array of experimental works that could be accessed from consumers' and performers' homes. In parallel, the loss of physical venues for high-profile film festivals with VR streams, such as Sundance and Tribeca, meant that whole catalogues of entertainment-based VR that may have received limited viewing at a physical site, found larger worldwide audiences through online portals. For example, Loren Hammonds, film and immersive programmer of the 2020 Tribeca Film Festival, offered selected VR experiences to viewers via the Oculus TV app after a physical version of the festival was cancelled. She observed that these projects received approximately 43,000 views whereas no more than 4000 views would likely have occurred during an in-person festival (Kohn, 2020). As the pandemic continues to wane and society moves to a new normal it is useful to consider how these events have affected the evolution of narrative-based VR entertainment.

To date, a considerable number of academic studies of virtual reality storytelling have been conducted by researchers in screenwriting, screen studies, journalism and other disciplines. Many of these have focused on a subgenre of work labelled as 'cinematic virtual reality' (CVR) (see Dooley, 2021; Mateer, 2017; Nielsen et al., 2016; Reyes, 2018; Ross & Munt, 2018; and many others). In my earlier monograph dedicated to this subgenre, I define CVR as encompassing

> narrative works that unfold in a 360-degree environment with a fixed story outcome, in which viewer participation is largely constrained to choosing the vantage point of the story, as distinct from open-ended, fully interactive VR applications and 'game' like experiences with limited or no narrative elements. (Dooley, 2021, p. 6)

This earlier study acknowledges the slipperiness of the CVR term, which in the infancy of VR's latest wave of activity was used in varying industrial contexts. Most commonly, however, the term refers to a format that continues to be associated with cinematic codes and conventions or methods of productions (such as live action filmmaking). While 'VR is not cinema' (Lanier p. 236), there is no doubt that CVR draws upon cinematic approaches. These experiences usually offer the viewer three degrees of freedom (abbreviated to 3DoF—the ability to look up and down, and left or right from a fixed position) and encompass pre-rendered 360-degree video. Academic interest in CVR is not surprising considering the wave of practitioner experimentation that occurred in the second half of the 2010s, much of which was driven by investment from film and journalism organisations. The development of cheap omnidirectional cameras fostered a wave of 360-video content featuring live action and/or computer-generated imagery. Following Facebook's earlier mentioned acquisition of Oculus, film entertainment companies such as 20th Century Fox and Disney invested heavily in the medium, the latter bankrolling VR 'Film' startup Jaunt VR, which pioneered CVR content (Matney, 2019). In parallel Facebook launched its Oculus Story Studio while Google set up Spotlight Stories to explore the narrative possibilities of the medium. VR was subsequently taken up by several high-profile film directors (e.g. Hollywood veterans Doug Liman and Kathryn Bigelow), who experimented with the creation of 'VR films' (Dooley, 2021). High-profile film festivals such as Sundance, Tribeca, SXSW and Venice launched VR streams, showcasing an array of short works. Alongside this, Newspapers *The New York Times* and *The Guardian* launched 'The Daily 360' (2016–2017) and 'The Guardian VR Studio' (2016–2018) online respectively, to experiment with VR from a journalistic perspective (Dooley, 2021). After the completion of innovative programs that played with the capabilities of the new technologies, these programs ended, a move that perhaps signalled a lack of interest from mass audiences. On a similar note, having failed to establish a sustainable business model, Jaunt VR pivoted in the direction of augmented reality (AR) in 2018. The Oculus Story Studio folded in 2017, followed by the axing of Spotlight Stories in 2019. Film festivals (both established and new standalone offerings), however, have continued to showcase an abundance of VR work, with the prestigious Cannes film festival unveiling an official selection of immersive works in 2024.

In more recent times, as hyperbolic claims about the potential of VR technology subside, one can note a continued interest in VR's cinematic potential by practitioners and researchers (see for example, Arcagni & D'Aloia, 2021; Sagot-Duvauroux et al., 2022; Zhang & Weber, 2023); however, VR experiences are now observably more diverse than they were prior to 2020, often blurring the boundaries between the media formats of film, game and theatre. This shift towards cross-disciplinary and transdisciplinary media approaches has resulted in narrative-based experiences realised via a range of technologies and platforms. As such, they may be featured in festivals under the banner of 'Extended Reality (XR)' or

'Immersive' programs, alongside work driven by AR or mixed reality (MR) technologies. To take one example, the 2022 program for Venice Immersive, one of the world's leading yearly showcases of innovation in VR storytelling, featured 75 works in 'competition' or 'non-competition' categories. These included 360-video productions, more interactive works offering 6DoF, a VR feature film, and 30 VRChat worlds (some of which incorporated live theatre and other performance). On this selection, co-curator Michel Reilhac commented that 'we have completely stepped away from categorising between story and interactivity on the other side. [...] It's all always mixed, so we do not have now any distinction between genres. A 360-documentary experience will be judged on the same level as a sophisticated game-based story' (quoted in Bye, 2022). In the same interview, co-curator Liz Rosenthal described the festival's decision to return to in-person (as opposed to online) exhibition as reflecting that VR is 'all about the social. [...] I think it's a completely new art form or new experiential form, and that's why we wanted to find a way in real life of bringing people into it (in person)' (quoted in Bye, 2022). These comments, on the variety of work that is now categorised as VR entertainment, and its marketability as a social rather than individual experience, demonstrate developments that have manifested in recent years. This book seeks to investigate these directions, drawing attention to the evolution of VR narratives in a range of formats, including 360-degree video.

While earlier CVR works have now received significant academic attention, less work has interrogated VR experiences produced in more recent years, including those with more varied interactive or hybrid elements. The aforementioned platform shift towards more interactive VR experiences that offer 6DoF fostered by the increasing take up of headsets such as the Oculus Quest has meant that many earlier VR works produced for now defunct headsets, are no longer able to be accessed. Meanwhile, the development of software applications that allow for the native authoring of VR experiences in 360-degree space (e.g. *Quill* and *Gravity Sketch*) has allowed creators to design virtual environments with a new understanding of the medium's affective abilities. Thus, new content demonstrates a greater awareness of VR as an embodied medium and reflects a more mature creative approach to storytelling from the XR community. A number of innovative works that combine documentary-based or fictional storytelling with game design, live theatre and other elements works will be profiled in this book, demonstrating a maturity regarding their use of 360-degree space and interactive devices. I argue that, in the wake of the initial hype associated with the latest wave of VR, these interdisciplinary works that move beyond the individual practices of older media have much to tell us about the future of VR storytelling.

Before moving on to outline key research questions and methodology, this introductory chapter will chart a short history of VR as a medium that can entertain and expand our worldview. I will then address the term 'narrative' and discuss its usage across media and disciplinary contexts. In doing so, I'll demonstrate the need for virtual reality narratives to be considered as unique.

The Qualities of VR and Its Evolution as an Entertainment Medium

Virtual reality, as a technology, has a long history of development and application in fields such as medicine, defence, and architecture (to name a few), as well as in arts and entertainment. Shin defines it as a 'computer-generated experience that can simulate physical presence in real or imagined environments' (2018, p. 65) while Laurel describes it as 'a medium in which the human sensorium is surrounded by (or immersed in) stimuli that are partially or wholly generated or represented by artificial means and in which all imagery is displayed from the point of view of an individual participant, even as he or she moves around' (2013, p. 184). On a similar note Jerald suggests that VR involves 'psychologically being in a place different than where one is physically located, where that place may be a replica of the real world or may be an imaginary world that does not exist and could never exist' (2015, p. 45). These definitions foreground the immersive experience of VR, which involves a feeling of presence in a synthetic environment, 'a complex, multidimensional perception, formed through an interplay of raw (multi-) sensory data and various cognitive processes' (Riva et al., 2007, p. 46). The terms 'presence' and 'immersion' are sometimes used interchangeably but are distinct though related concepts (Slater, 2003). The latter, according to Slater, is 'what the technology delivers from an objective point of view' regarding the preservation of fidelity in relation to a user's equivalent real-world sensory modalities (2003, p. 1). Presence is thus 'a human reaction to immersion' (Slater, p. 2). In the context of VR narratives, a sense of presence in a virtual storyworld gives rise to an embodied experience for the interactor and is arguably what defines VR as a distinct medium. These concepts receive further attention in Chap. 2 of this book.

Several key inventions and developments over time have given rise to the VR experiences that exist today. As I've noted elsewhere (Dooley, 2021), Sir Charles Wheaton's innovative design of the stereoscope in 1838 created the means for the individual stereoscopic view that underpins three-dimensional VR (Tricart, 2018, pp. 7–8). More than 120 years later, a 'Telesphere Mask' was patented by filmmaker and philosopher Morton Heiling in 1960. This device offered stereoscopic viewing in an early model HMD but was limited in its ability to respond to the user (Flynn, 2019). Following experimentation with more advanced computer graphics, sensors and head tracking technologies, VPL Research, a Californian start-up company, launched the 'Eye Phone' HMD in 1989 (Lanier, 2017). This product bears some resemblance to the HMDs of more recent times; however, its expensive price tag prohibited widespread sales at the time. While VPL Research dissolved after it was declared bankrupt in 1990, the new decade saw the development and launch of HMDs for computer gaming, such as the 'VR-1' Arcade Attraction by SEGA in 1994 and Nintendo's portable tabletop HMD, 'Virtual Boy' in 1995 (Mowbray, 2022). These devices were considerably more advanced than those that had come before; however, poor optics and visuals resulted in widespread motion sickness and other problems, once again leading to a lack of commercial success.

From the late 1990s until the 2010s, virtual reality more or less disappeared from commercial contexts although experimentation with motion tracking and tactile interfaces in university settings brought advances to the field during these years (Laurel, 2013, p. 185). Moreover, the 1990s saw experimentation with VR's artistic possibilities by several practitioners and academics. In his survey of performative applications of VR in the 1990s, Dixon recalls a number of innovative projects, such as Brenda Laurel and Rachel Strickland's *Placeholder* (1993), the first of nine experimental VR works funded by the Bannf Center's Art and Virtual Environments scheme (2006, p. 27). He describes this work as 'driven by eleven computers from a Silicon Graphics reality engine to a Macintosh powerbook, and using over 25,000 lines of code' opening up 'the potential for virtual "flight" (through the character of a crow)' (p. 28). Also highly influential was Char Davies' *Osmose* (1994–1995), which offered the user an 'advanced sense of fully embodied immersion through the use of a (then) sophisticated datasuit' (Dixon, 2006, p. 31).[6] These embodied VR performances that appeared in parallel with advances in 3D cinema, and role-playing, simulation and open-world games, can be viewed as the antecedents to current-day VR as entertainment.

Exploring Virtual Reality Narratives

My quest to articulate the specificity of contemporary VR narratives begins with a search for terms of reference as well as theoretical models that might guide the analysis that is featured in the following chapters. The question of what comprises a narrative is complex and contested by numerous scholars of media and/or narratology (the study of narrative structures, conventions and functions). Writing more than 20 years ago, Richardson observed that 'now, narrative is everywhere' (2000, p. 68), a comment on the expansion of narrative theory and analysis across literary, cultural, performance and film studies at the end of the twentieth century, which has complicated understandings of the term. With this in mind, I will now unpack the notion of 'narrative' across media and disciplinary lines, noting theories that have relevance for VR.

I begin with an attempt to pinpoint a general definition of the term, drawing on the understandings of several narrotologists and theorists. Richardson observes that basic definitions of narrative stress its 'temporal, causal, minimal, and transactional' nature (p. 169). This suggests 'the representation of events in a time sequence as the defining feature of narrative' and that 'some causal connection, however oblique, between the event is essential' (p. 169). Considering the position of Gerard Genette, he further observes that 'any statement of an action or event is ipso facto a narrative, since it implies a transformation or transition from an earlier to a later state' (p. 169). Richardson's definition accords with Landa's understanding of narrative as 'a semiotic representation of a series of events connected in a temporal and causal way', which can be constructed using images, written or spoken language, or through gest (2005). This second definition stresses that narrative 'is only a sign', in other words, not a series of events, but a representation of events that can be interpreted by the receiver.

On a related note, Richardson notes a definition of narrative as 'a way of reading a text, rather than a feature or essence found in a text' (p. 169).

[6] I'll offer further exploration of these, and other performance-based VR works, in Chap. 6.

This definition is typical of a 'cognitive turn' in narratology in the twenty-first century, which stresses the role of the reader in the construction of narrative. In regard to a written or visual text, this reading depends on the receiver's mental representation of elements that are read as signs. As Fludernik notes, 'Cognitive narratology demonstrates that readers do not see texts as having narrative features but read texts as narrative by imposing cognitive narrative frames on them—for instance, by interpreting animals as quasi- human protagonists in fables' (2010, p. 926). This definition raises questions in regard to links between a reader's cultural framework, interpretation and emotional response to narrative material.

Narratologist Marie Laure Ryan writes on the elements that constitute a narrative within the realm of digital media, suggesting that these include 'a world (setting), populated by individuals (characters), who participate in actions and happenings (events, plot), through which they undergo change (temporal dimension)' (2002, p. 583). A mental representation of these elements can be conjured by a variety of media and a multitude of signs. This definition can be applied to a range of linear and non-linear narratives and is useful when considering the digital and interactive nature of VR. I therefore take it as a starting point in my analysis of VR narratives. In doing so I avoid an ideological perspective that Koenitz labels as narrative fundamentalism', where the phenomenon of narrative is artificially restricted to 'certain traditionalistic Eurocentric forms (the novel and the Hollywood-style movie' (2023, p. 53).

Going forward, I acknowledge that depending on their disciplinary background, narratologists take a range of positions on narrative, ranging from what Ryan describes as 'stiflingly traditionalist' to 'wildly expansionist' approaches (2006, p. xviii). Likewise, narratological models are varied, offering a range of perspectives on the structures that underpin narrative texts (Landa, 2005). Richardson suggests that modern narrative theory involves 'far too many story strands, loose ends, abrupt turns, and unmotivated re-appearances of forgotten figures and theoretical approaches to fit easily within any one narrative structure' (p. 172). On this he cites the persistence of Marxist and Freudian paradigms of narrative analysis, as well as more recent feminist and postcolonial approaches to narrative analysis. This observation on the variety of approaches to the study of narrative evidences Bordwell's claim that 'Narratology is a paradigm case of interdisciplinary inquiry' (2012, p. 2).

Drawing upon Ryan's definition, my own understanding of narrative leans towards a traditionalist approach that considers narrative as 'an invariant core of meaning, a core that distinguishes narrative from other types of discourse and gives it a transcultural, transhistorical, and transmedial identity' (2006, p. xvi). As Ryan points out, while regarding narrative as 'a stable foundation of human cognition', this approach does not exclude diverse forms of storytelling or confine digital narrative solely to the emulation of literary forms (p. xviii). Scholars and practitioners adopting this approach have sought to account for user participation within a fictional storyworld, which Ryan notes as a difficult project (p. xvii). Recent evolutions in VR storytelling that involve AI algorithms and open worlds featuring live actors present new possibilities on this front, and thus call for further explorations of tensions between narrative form, interactivity and immersion.

In my quest to articulate the specific features of entertainment-based VR narratives, I look to narrative theories and models associated with some of its antecedents—cinema, theatre and games—as well as those applied in the context of digital media more broadly in the field of Interactive Digital Narrative (IDN). Going forward, these theories are adopted as lenses through which to explore the specificity of VR narratives, a process that both exposes the limits of existing theory and highlights the specific embodied experience that the medium conjures.

Film Narratives

In their seminal text exploring cinema analysis, Bordwell et al. describe a narrative as a 'chain of events in cause-effect relationship occurring in space and time' (2016, p. 73). This definition, which aligns with those of Richardson and Landa, stresses the linking together of a number of events into what we might also describe as a 'story'. This term is not to be confused with 'plot', which describes the organisation of narrative events into a particular order or structure (p. 75). This structure guides the viewer through the story and influences their understanding of story events occurring in the film's diegesis (storyworld).

Classical film narratives can be seen to consist of a beginning and end, with a series of occurrences in between, a convention that was established in the early years of cinema. These occurrences generally involve characters who react to a series of conflicts driven by external and/or internal forces. This framework draws upon the notion of a 'dramatic arc' and 'Hero's Journey', which Koenitz et al. describe as 'the two most influential and pervasive narrative structures in the Western narrative tradition, regardless of medium' (2018, p. 3). The former, which is typical of classical Hollywood cinema, stems from Aristotle's Poetics, a narrative theory dating back to 350 BC that stresses a unified plot with a beginning/middle/end. The latter, also known as the 'Monomyth' was popularised by Joseph Campbell in his text *The Hero with a Thousand Faces* (1949). According to this text, the hero's journey takes place in two worlds: the everyday 'normal' world, where the story protagonist resides, and an extraordinary world into which he/she is thrust following the onset of a disturbing force. It is here that several obstacles must be overcome before the hero returns to the normal world, triumphant. This structure has parallels with Todorov's five stage theory of a narrative that involves equilibrium, disruption, recognition of disruption, repair and finally a return to a new equilibrium (see Todorov & Weinstein, 1969). Campbell's narrative structure was later expanded upon by Hollywood screenwriter Christopher Vogler (1992), who proposes 12 stages in the hero's journey. While Campbell proposed the Monomyth as a 'universal' storytelling model, this has rightly been criticised in more recent times. For example, Koenitz et al. note, the structure 'blinds us – scholars, writers, designers – to non-Western forms of narrative (as well as twentieth century avant-garde forms), which come to be seen as "more primitive" and/or "less developed"' (p. 4). Relatedly, Hambly points out that 'Campbell interpreted myths from the sociopolitical-cultural viewpoint of a mid-twentieth-century, white, male American' (2021, p. 137). In parallel with this criticism, one can note a move away from the white male protagonist who has dominated classical Hollywood, in the search for more diverse forms of cinema storytelling in the twenty-first century.

Cinema narratives contain narration, 'the moment-by-moment process that guides viewers in building the story out of the plot' (Bordwell et al., 2016, p. 87). This narration might restrict the audience's understanding of events (for the purpose of creating suspense) or allow them access to more story information than is possessed by the characters that they follow on screen. A seminal theory often invoked in discussion of cinematic narration comes from literary theorist Gerard Genette, who explores the notions of 'voice' and 'focalisation' (1980). With the term 'voice' he refers to the question of who narrates and from where, positing the positions of 'intra-diegetic' (narration located inside the storyworld) and 'extra-diegetic' (narration that located outside of the storyworld). Furthermore, Genette suggests that narrators as characters can be 'homodiegetic' (existing within the storyworld and telling their own story) or 'heterodiegetic' (telling a story in which they do not take part) (p. 245). Focalisation refers to the character whose point of view orders the narrative perspective or as Genette put it, 'who sees?' (1980, p. 186). This latter concept, he posits, determines the mood of a narrative and is not to be confused with the question, who narrates? (p. 186). These concepts in Genette's narratology retain value as a means of analysis that might be applied to virtual reality experiences, shedding light on works featuring the participant as a character.

In contrast to virtual reality, one might consider traditional cinema to be a passive medium that is consumed by a viewer seated before a rectangular screen. However, Bordwell et al. remind us that 'while watching a film, the viewer picks up cues, recalls information, anticipates what will follow, and generally participates in the creation of the film's form' (p. 72). This observation exposes the complexity of film narratives, and the way that contemporary viewers are equipped to read and interpret cinematic codes and conventions. VR has the potential to offer a more interactive narrative experience than cinema, but one might argue that the grammar of this narrative medium is still in flux (Dooley, 2018), meaning that the codes and conventions that convey meaning to an audience member are yet to be established.

Game Narratives

As Aarseth observes, 'computer games generate many questions and challenges for narrative theory' (2012, p. 129). This dominant form of entertainment, which influences and is influenced by adjacent media such as film, television and literature, is one that has received significant attention by scholars in recent decades, many of whom have interrogated the qualities of games as interactive narratives. The first decade or so of the twenty-first century saw the so-called ludology vs. narratology debate, which interrogated the extent to which games could be analysed as a narrative form, due to their underlying narrative structures (characters, settings etc.). On the narratology side, scholars such as Ryan (2001) argued for a move beyond literary notions of narrativity to account for the experience of playing games. This position suggests that games 'embody a virtualized, or potential dramatic narrativity, which itself hinges on the virtual diegetic narrativity of a retelling that may never take place' (Ryan, 2001, n.p.). Ludologists, on the other hand, argued that a game's meaning is constructed through its rules and mechanics, and that these elements must be foregrounded. Frasca, for example (1999, n.p.) asserted the need to analyse games as distinct from narrative, proposing the term ludology 'to refer to the yet non-existent "discipline that studies game and play activities"'. In 2005 Murray proclaimed that the debate had 'moved on', declaring that 'games are not a subset of stories; objects exist that have qualities of both games and stories' (2005, n.p.).[7]

Writing several years later, Aarseth argues that few scholars approached the debate using a 'properly narratological analysis, using the basic concepts and models of modern narrative theory' (2012, p. 129). He therefore calls for the adoption of a model of analysis that gives neither games or stories priority but rather acknowledges both as mediated representations of human reality (p. 130). His useful framework for analysis, which I will briefly summarise, interrogates four elements that can be seen to exist across both categories of games and stories: places (worlds), things (objects), characters (agents) and events (p. 131). Game worlds, he observes, are 'physical or pseudo-physical (virtual) structures that are clearly delimited and which can be described by geometry or topology' (p. 131). This means that unlike the fictional worlds of a film production, for example, they have a concrete nature, relying not on the imagination, but on measurable space (conjured by computer technology) that can be explored by a player. Furthermore, these works include ludic spaces (gameplay arenas) and non-ludic spaces (non-playable spaces), which vary in scope depending on the type of game (p. 131). One could argue that virtual reality narratives offer a similar concrete representation of space, seeing as a 360-degree environment is represented in full, leaving no 'off-screen' space, as is the case for film and television works.

Aarseth categorises the objects found in a game world according to their malleability. They can be (a) Static, non-interactable objects, (b) Static, usable objects, (c) Destructible, (d) Changeable, (e) Createable or (f) Inventible, these qualities determining the level of agency for a player (p. 132). On character, he notes the importation of figures from other media, and offers a system of classification based on depth/shallowness as well as their malleability (p. 132). On the shallow end of the spectrum, a

[7] The facts of the 'ludology vs. narratology' debate have been questioned by several scholars, and many of the originally involved players have since clarified or changed their positions. For example, Frasca later rejected the separation of narratology and ludology and expressed that the 'debate as presented never really took place because it was cluttered with a series of misunderstandings and misconceptions…' (2003, p. 1).

character might be a robot with no personality, while conversely some characters are designed with complex character traits and back stories. A game might offer a mix of objects and character types across these categories. Lastly, he classifies events in relation to the presence of what he terms 'kernels' and 'satellites'. The former refers to the events of a story that make it recognisable (Aarseth offers the example of when the wolf eats the grandmother in Little Red Riding Hood) while the latter refers to story events that can be removed or replaced without losing the essence of a tale. Approaches to these elements determine whether a work contains: 'a) fully plotted (pure story); b) dynamic satellites (playable story); c) dynamic kernels (multipath/quest games); and d) no kernels (pure game)' (p. 132).

Aarseth puts these four dimensions together into a single model that can be used to determine the extent of a game's narrative and ludic elements. Those works at the most narrative-based end of the spectrum might feature an inaccessible world, non-interactive objects, deep characters and a fully plotted sequence of events. Conversely, a game that heavily favours ludic elements, might feature an open landscape, inventible objects, bots as characters and no kernels (pure game) (p. 132). As Aarseth suggests, this model can be used to analyse an interactive work's design decisions, these having ramifications for player agency and authorial control.

Somewhat similarly to Aarseth, Ryan explores the spectrum of narrativity and interactivity that a game might feature, observing an oscillation between two forms: 'the narrative game, in which narrative meaning is subordinated to the player's actions, and the playable story, in which the player's actions are subordinated to narrative meaning' (2009, p. 54). The former, she suggests, involves enhanced game play (perhaps featuring elements associated with ludic pole of Aarseth's variable model) while the latter sees game play produce a distinct narrative.

With these models in mind, one might question the common narrative patterns or structures that appear in games. Ryan later suggests that computer games most often subordinate narrative to game play, or in other words, narrative exists primarily to motivate play (2018, p. 96). For this reason, she observes a limited variety of game narratives, the most common being an adaptation of the above-mentioned hero's journey: 'a solitary hero accepts a mission, goes on an adventure, passes a number of tests, and returns home victorious (or sometimes defeated, as may be the case in computer games)' (p. 96). Thus, 'standard game narratives follow predefined scripts that force players to pass though the same sequence of checkpoints, but every player creates variations on the fixed pattern, since no two players will perform the exact same actions' (p. 96). Koenitz et al. make a similar observation, noting that criticism of these structures and exploration of non-Western approaches has so far had 'only a limited impact on the design of interactive digital narratives and has not yet reached the status of "credible alternative" to the dominant models' (2018, p. 108). Questions arise as to whether the player immersion and presence associated with VR games creates an opportunity for the development of more diverse interactive narrative experiences.

Interactive Digital Narrative (IDN)

While games can be considered a form of IDN, this subcategory of digital media is much broader, encompassing interactive drama or documentaries, hyperfiction literature, interactive cinema, VR and other formats/media that foreground interactivity. Simply put, IDN can be defined as 'narrative expressions in the digital medium that change due to input from an audience' (Koenitz, 2023, p. 1). These formats leverage new technologies, specifically computers and the internet, as vehicles for artistic expression. In doing so, they challenge established concepts in narrative theory, including the traditional notions of authorship and a singular, unified plot (Koenitz, 2010, p. 176). Although the concept of IDN can be traced back to experiments undertaken in the 1960s (Koenitz, 2023; Ryan, 2017), this interdisciplinary field has gathered steam in the twenty-first century, building on concepts explored in seminal texts such as Janet Murray's *Hamlet on the Holodeck: The Future of Narrative in Cyberspace* (1997) and Ryan's *Narrative as Virtual Reality* (2001), which discuss immersive and interactive digital spaces. The field's recent advancement has been heavily influenced by the scholarship of Hartmut Koenitz, whose latest monograph (2023) interrogates a range of theories and arguments about IDN that have developed over the last 30 years. Such theories are useful for the further exploration of VR's narrative possibilities, considering works that react to audience input.

IDN scholarship examines the design and development of interactive 'systems' (encompassing computer applications and related hardware) that interact with participants. This systems view contends that an IDN is not a static narrative object that is interpreted by readers or viewers but a dynamic system that can be both interpreted and directly affected by the interactor (Koenitz, 2023, p. 3). In the case of an IDN, the 'system' might generate a number of possible narrative 'products' based on the participants' interaction with narrative elements. This involves a process of 'instantiation', which Koentiz describes as 'the relationship between the artefact (computer/software system) and the output' (2023, p. 67). This foregrounding of interactivity calls for a reconception of narrative as 'a function of our brain and no longer of any particular artifact' (p. 4). In other words, in a move away from traditional literary or cinematic definitions, one can conceive of narrative as an act of cognition in which narrative is conjured by an interactor.

Ryan considers the distinction between the interactivity that is fostered by a medium and the interactivity that can be a feature of a narrative delivered using that medium (2001). The former relates to the technological affordances of a medium, while the latter is concerned with the narrative structures or elements that capitalise upon these affordances. In the context of extended reality (XR), Bruni et al. cite haptic devices, tracking technologies, programmable features and artificial intelligence (AI) as an examples of interactive technologies, which can 'empower the user to influence the linear representation of the narrative in such a medium' (2022, p. 38). A VR IDN might allow a user to interact with and/or affect story outcomes through the use of these technologies, which calls for a corporeal engagement with narrative.

Koentiz's System–Process–Production (SPP) model provides one means of analysis of IDN works (2010, 2015, 2023). Adopting a viewpoint that is informed by cybernetics and computation, this model accounts for the participatory nature of an IDN. It contends that, as digital artefacts, IDN systems comprise a set of 'potential' narratives that unfold through user interaction (a process), culminating in the creation of an instantiated narrative (a product). In the case of a VR IDN, this might mean a 'system' consisting of a HMD, hand controllers and associated software, that offers an interactive experience to a user (a process), resulting in a narrative experience (a product). As Koenitz outlines, 'the actions of the user as interactor, and the opportunities provided by the system, define and shape the process' (2023, p. 75). I adopt this theory in Chap. 6 of this book as a means to explore user customisation of a VR narrative.

While IDN discussions and theories might usefully be applied to an analysis of some entertainment-based VR projects, it must be noted that not all narrative-based VR is interactive in the sense outlined by Koenitz. A VR work offering 3DoF, for example, might allow users to choose their field of view in 360-degree space but be constructed entirely of pre-rendered video. As such, there is no opportunity for the user to affect the narrative, although their experience of the narrative will depend on their choice of viewing direction throughout. Bruni et al. note that there may be certain issues of IDN that are specific to VR narratives and therefore deserve further scrutiny (2022, p. 27). A teasing out of these issues is one goal of this text and will be explored further below.

Theatre Narratives

Dramatic narratives contained within plays and other forms of theatre performance share many similarities with those of film and games. As for the two latter, dramatic theatrical performances typically feature characters (on a stage or elsewhere), situated in a particular time and space, who may react to a series of consequential events. In the case of genres such as immersive theatre, audience participation is encouraged. Regardless of the audience's active or passive role, similarly to games (but unlike film) a theatre narrative is constructed 'live', meaning that variables such as actor performance, logistical factors or audience participation have the potential to alter the narrative experience that is offered. As Lehmann notes 'in contrast to other arts, which produce an object and/or are communicated through media, here the aesthetic act itself (the performing) as well as the act of reception (the theatre going) take place as a real doing in the here and now' (2006, p. 17). This simultaneous act of realisation and reception creates 'a sense of immediacy in the action on stage' a site where performance and real life intersect (Pfister, 1988, p. 5).

Considering the long history of this storytelling form, it is surprising that only in semi-recent times have narratologists devoted significant attention to drama as a narrative genre (Fludernick, 2008, p. 355). The late start to this scholarship results from modern narratology's preoccupation with (a) the novel, and (b) the presence of oral or written narration as a defining feature of narrative. As is the case for film, traditionally, dramatic theatre has been based on the performance of a written text, in which plot is delivered by human figures through speech (primarily) and gest. As Hogan observes, 'a common view is that drama is "mimetic" rather than "diegetic," or narrated' (2014, p. 50). Fludernick cites Bal (1997) as the first narratologist to offer a definition of narrative that foregrounded plot, therefore including 'drama alongside film, ballet, cartoons and other forms of narrative outside the prototypical scenario of a narrator's telling a story' (Fludernick, p. 356). Other more recent scholarship has explored drama as not only involving a storyworld and plot, but a discourse (how that storyworld and plot is represented). In the remainder of this section I'll refer to scholars such as Pfister (1988), Richardson (2001) and Lehmann to further explore aspects of theatre as a narrative medium.

Perhaps one of the most specific features of dramatic narratives relates to the staging of plot in a particular time and space dimension that is shared between actors and audience. As Lehmann observes

> While the text gives the reader the choice to read faster or slower, to repeat or to pause, in theatre the specific time of the performance with its particular rhythm and its individual dramaturgy (tempo of action and speech duration, pauses and silences, etc.) belongs to the 'work'. It is a matter of the time no longer of one (reading) subject, but of the shared time of many subjects (collectively spending time). (2006, p. 153)

Within dramatic narratives, this dimension might be referred to as 'real-time', in that the time of the story presented on stage passes at the same rate as for the spectators of the story (excepting ellipses that take place between acts). In contrast to film narratives, which typically involve a series of perspectives and moments in time edited into sequences, for the plot of a dramatic text 'a single closed scenic unit is presented within a time space continuum' (Pfister, p. 24). Further to the notion of a dramatic space, one can observe that a dramatic narrative is constrained by the stage on which it is performed, which is shared with the audience. Pfister suggests that 'a dramatic text is conceived with a particular type of stage in mind, and this becomes clear when a text is performed on a stage whose dimensions and technical sophistication are different' (p. 19). This specificity of time and space that unites performances and audience creates an emotional bond that can foster an experience of catharsis. Like Lehmann, one might therefore consider a dramatic theatre performance to turn 'the behaviour onstage and in the auditorium into a *joint text*, a "text" even if there is no spoken dialogue or between actors and audience' (2006, p. 17 original emphasis). This joint text is constructed through a range of communication techniques and devices.

A further specificity of dramatic narratives relates to the use of sound. Whereas film narratives draw upon a range of sound elements to communicate a story, such as dialogue and location sounds (diegetic) or voiceover narration and music (non-diegetic), dramatic theatre performances generally feature less of the latter, this relating the aim of creation of a diegetic world in which the audience is present. The intrusion of non-diegetic elements in dramatic theatre could be seen to disrupt the audience's suspension of disbelief, breaking an emotional or mental bond with performers. Such practices have been utilised by theatre directors in the context of postmodern theatre to achieve this effect. One might also note that the increased influence of film techniques on the staging of theatre in contemporary times complicates distinctions between the two mediums' use of sound (Fludernick, p. 362).

Returning to the subject of narration, I note some theorists' broad consideration of this in relation to the theatre of the last century. For Richardson, 'narration has long been a basic feature of the twentieth-century stage, and one that ought to be more fully appreciated and extensively theorized' (2001, p. 691). On this front he and other theorists observe a number of strategies of narration that are employed in theatre contexts. Fludernick usefully distinguishes between five categories of narrative elements in drama:

> (a) elements that relate to drama's narrativity, i.e. the existence of a fictional world, of characters, of plot; (b) elements in the fictional world of the play that relate to narration—messenger reports, characters telling one another stories; (c) elements in plays that introduce a narrator figure or narratorial frame into the play; (d) elements of plays that display a mediational function, such as prologues and epilogues or, if one looks at the dramatic text, stage directions; as well as (e) metadramatic features (which can be located on different levels). (2018, p. 367)

Considering Genette's terminology, the first two of these elements might be further analysed in relation to the placement of a narrating character within the story (homodiegetic) or external to the story (heterodiegetic) (Richardson, 2001, p. 682). As for film, a character appearing within a play could appear as either a homodiegetic or heterodiegetic narrator figure.

The features noted above are most relatable to the tropes of dramatic theatre (a term used by Bertolt Brecht to describe a traditional theatre practice); however, it must be noted that epic theatre and other postmodern approaches draw upon a wide range of narrative and narratorial techniques. Lehmann uses the term 'postdramatic theatre' to describe a practice that emerged in the 1970s that involves reflection on notions associated with a centuries-old European theatre paradigm (2006). This style of theatre explores new aesthetic logics and possibilities for the representation of the human subject, reflecting a 'profoundly changed mode of theatrical sign usage' (Lehmann, p. 17). While acknowledging older aesthetics, it seeks to reflectively explore notions of time, space, body and media in the context of theatrical performance, sometimes involving the 'emancipation of the performance from the literary text' (Carlson, 2015, p. 578). This movement finds parallels with narrative experimentation in other media contexts, which could be seen to inform contemporary practitioners' use of virtual reality media.

Virtual Reality Narratives

As a narrative medium, VR draws heavily upon the conventions of film, games and theatre, and can be considered to be a form of IDN. The narrative theories and analyses outlined above offer several useful lenses through which to begin exploring the specificity of storytelling in VR; however, one must also acknowledge the fundamental aspect of the medium that defines it against these antecedents and as a specific form of IDN: the positing of the viewer or user, as a virtual body, *within* (rather than adjacent to) an all-encompassing, and potentially reactive, 360-degree storyworld.[8] I use the term 'storyworld' here to describe a world in which a story takes place, involving 'a spatial dimension, the setting, and a temporal dimension, the narrative events' (Ryan, 2015, p. 12). The VR narratives that I explore in this book insert the user in synthetic worlds that may contain a singular story, or multiple story threads. In either case, the user functions as the axis around which action takes place. As Aylett and Louchart rightly suggest, 'characteristic of VR is that the role of the

[8] I use the terms 'viewer' and 'user' in this book to refer to persons interacting with a VR experience. The term 'viewer' is used when referring to more 'passive' forms of VR, such as pre-rendered 360-degree videos. For these works, interaction is limited to the viewer's contemplation of the virtual environment. By contrast, room scale works may allow the interactor to touch objects and affect the environment. In these instances I use the term 'user'. This wording aligns with Aylett and Louchart's argument that a 'user' is 'a person who experiences a Virtual Environment through interaction and actively participates in the building of the resulting experience; a user does not contemplate or watch a narrative display as a spectator does' (2003 p. 3). One can note the use of a range of terms to refer to the VR interactor in contemporary scholarship, from 'viewer' and 'user' to 'viewser' (a combination of viewer and user) (Daly, 2010) and 'navigator' (Remedios et al., 2022). These terms point to the varying contributions of the interactor towards the shaping of a VR narrative experience.

subject (i.e. the user) to whom the narrative is communicated is, in terms of interaction, "active" in the unfolding of the narrative as opposed to its "passive" role in most of other classical narrative media (i.e. the spectator)' (2003, p. 3). Moreover, the active user experiences a sense of presence within the virtual environment, as a witness to, or participant in an unfolding story. While previous waves of VR moving image as artwork and/or entertainment have sought to harness these affordances of the medium, it is only thanks to recent advances in computer graphics and other technologies, which have fostered the creation of photo-realistic settings and/or sophisticated imagined worlds that VR storytelling has truly flourished. This more refined manner through which contemporary works create believable worlds, foster interaction and engage the human sensorium calls for a renewed examination of VR's specific narrative properties.

Further to the specificity of VR narratives, I note a specific form of immersion that involves 'the world as a living space and sustaining environment for the embodied subject' (Ryan, 2001, p. 68), which is fostered by VR technologies. Bruni et al. usefully point out that the term 'immersion' has a wider range of connotations than might be considered in the field of VR alone, and in the context of IDN, the term is more generally used to refer to 'narrative immersion' (2022, p. 40). Such narrative immersion relates to 'an engagement of the imagination in the construction and contemplation of a story world' (Ryan, 2009, p. 54). This understanding of immersion 'brings the construct into close relation with a series of other terms such as engagement, imaginative involvement, emotional response, suspension of disbelief and suspense' (Bruni et al., p. 40), and can be a feature of narratives across a range of media. By contrast, immersion in the context of VR technology is system-fostered and related to the feeling of presence in a virtual environment, which generates unique narrative possibilities. It is therefore necessary to consider both system-generated immersion and 'narrative immersion', as well as their intersection, when exploring the specificity of VR stories.

Useful ground on an examination of this subject has been laid by several scholars writing prior to the current wave. Notably, Aylett and Louchart offer an analysis of VR's form and means of communication, arguing that it should be considered a specific narrative medium (2003). They come to this conclusion following an interrogation of VR and its antecedents based on four comparative dimensions: Contingency, Presence, Interactivity and Narrative Representation (p. 3). The first dimension relates to how closely the time and space of a narrative is contingent on 'real' time and space. In accordance with my discussion of theatre above, they observe that 'literature and cinema are able to manipulate the time and space of the narrative very flexibly, while VR generally displays in real time, tying it very strongly to a specific space and time' (p. 3). This constraint, which is linked to the creation of immersion, aligns VR with dramatic theatre, although Aylett and Louchart consider the latter to be less contingent on time and space than VR, seeing as 'an episodic structure and the concept of "off-stage" activity are used to produce some sense of temporal and spatial richness' (p. 3). By contrast, VR experiences that offer the user access to a 360-degree world have no equivalent 'off-stage' area. In terms of Presence, Aylett and Louchart, question 'how far the spectator/user physically shares the time and space of the narrative', concluding that only theatre and VR enable physical presence (the latter doing so through virtual means) (p. 4). On Interactivity, they survey the extent to which users can interact with story processes, finding this is not possible in cinema or literature, but is assumed for VR and possible in the case of interactive theatre. Regarding the final dimension of Narrative Representation, they observe that like cinema and theatre, for VR, this involves a visual representation of story, rather than the mental representation that takes place for literature (scenes constructed in a reader's head) (p. 4). While VR narratives have become considerably more sophisticated in the 20 years since Aylett and Louchart authored this text, (and the same can be said of other media narratives) I would argue that, broadly speaking, these assertions hold true.

Further to this analysis, which aligns VR with theatre more so than cinema or literature, they note that 'theatre and cinema clearly work largely from a mimetic perspective, sharing a particular awareness of the spectator's visual engagement' (p. 5). In the case of cinema, this process is mediated through the camera—a device that is 'under authorial control' (p. 5). This means that the director can control the spectator's ingestion of story information through the adoption of particular camera angles and/or framing (likewise, a dramatic theatre narrative is presented with the same notion of authorial control, seeing as the spectator's position has been designed in relation to the stage). By contrast, the VR 'camera' is identified with the user, with their freedom to move this and/or choose a viewing direction being a defining characteristic of the medium. This means 'VR moves beyond mimesis – "showing" – with its implication of direction, to "experiencing"' (p. 5). Thus, Aylett and Louchart look towards process-based or emergent narrative theories for VR, which consider user participation in the creation of story. They conclude that 'contrary to other narrative media already mentioned, users in a 3D virtual environment play a central part in the building of the story and the constructing of their own overall experience since this depends upon their actions, reactions and behaviour within the world itself' (p. 6). This observation rightly stresses interactivity and user experience as core to VR narratives.

Considering the range of contemporary approaches to VR as an interactive medium, it is useful to consider Ryan's 2009 study of interactive narrative forms, which she divides into two broad categories: 'bottom-up, emergent systems that create stories during the run of (a) program' and 'and top-down systems that rely on prescripted content' (p. 51). As an example of the former, she refers to the Holodeck, the fictional VR experience that appeared in *Star Trek: The Next Generation*, and that was proposed as the future of storytelling in the aforementioned text by Murray (1997). Famously, the Holodeck allowed Starfleet Captain Kathryn Janeway to escape from her responsibilities into a virtual world that allowed free interaction with objects and characters. Murray described it as 'an illusory world that can be stopped, started, or turned off at will but that looks and behaves like the actual world. [...] The Star Trek Holodeck is a universal fantasy machine' (1997, p. 15). While it would be premature to claim that the latest wave of VR gives rise to an experience on par with that of the fictional Holodeck, currently available technologies bring us considerably closer to seeing such an experience as a reality than was ever possible in the past. Projects built with game engines and offering 6DoF, for example, allow users to navigate vast virtual worlds, encountering other characters and objects that may react to their presence. These VR projects can be experienced multiple times, each time featuring different narrative configurations or strands.

At the other end of Ryan's spectrum, top-down systems 'are meant for a single traversal, since the story does not renew itself' (Ryan, 2009, p. 51). This type of experience is typical of cinematic virtual reality experiences offering 3DoF, which offers a fixed, pre-authored narrative, giving the user few opportunities for interaction, beyond choosing a direction in which to look. Ryan also equates the top-down approach with narrative games in which there are no emergent elements: 'The player's progression is a journey along a path that is already traced and that leads to a fixed destination, or to several destinations when the system offers branching points' (p. 52). This categorisation (bottom-up or top-down) is a useful means to consider degrees of interactivity in contemporary VR narratives and will be referred to in the chapters that follow.

Beyond discussions of interactivity and authorial control, one might ask what else matters for a study of VR storytelling? Most important, I would argue, is an interrogation of the way VR entertainment incorporates or draws upon the user's body as part of a narrative experience. Generally speaking, Murray and Sixsmith observe that bodies are located in time and space and are 'bounded within the sensations they receive' (1999, p. 319). These sensations, I would argue, drive user participation in VR narratives, determining the paths that are taken or created. Surrounded by a frameless 360-degree image, the user might play the role of a silent observer or conversely, become a character in a story, perhaps even contributing to the outcome of unfolding events. This activity places them within a virtual space (real or imagined) at a specific time, as a physical (viewable) or invisible virtual being who must navigate a series of narrative cues. Depending on whether the VR work is pre-rendered or driven by a game engine, the user experiences events that are either predetermined or algorithmically driven, or which may involve live actors, making a series of choices (even if only to choose their viewing direction) to customise their experience. As such, the psychological experience of events, and resulting narrative, is conjured through the user's embodied experience, a phenomenon that is explored in this book's chapters from a multitude of angles.

Going forward, I consider the ways that VR can manipulate the user's experience of their own body. On this subject Ryan notes the medium's ability to create 'new experiences of embodiment':

> [VR] can create an out of body experience by projecting to the user an image of its own body; it can allow users to see themselves from the back; and it can place them in entirely different bodies: for instance into a black body if you are white, a disabled body if you are healthy, and a healthy body if you are disabled. (2018, p. 105)

This comment reveals the way that viewers might experience their own body from an unusual perspective, or inhabit a completely different human body, but moreover, as my opening quote from Lanier points out, one can observe that VR has the power to distort the scale of the body in relation to the corresponding environment, or to place the user in a non-human body. In this sense the affordances of VR offer a remarkably different experience to that of live or immersive theatre, not only because of its specific immersive properties, but because the user's bodily experience is not bound by real-world constraints. Within a VR narrative, a user might become a tiger, fly through the air or have any number of other experiences that would not be possible in the real world.

Furthermore, I consider the ways that users as bodies bring their inbuilt assumptions and prejudices to a narrative experience. In addition to the notion of VR as an embodied experience, Murray and Sixsmith stress 'that it is simultaneously and inescapably a social, racial, ethnic, gendered, and cultural one' (1999, p. 322). On a similar note, Flynn notes that the 'navigation of space does not exist outside of cultural forces but is socially constructed and historically and politically constituted' (2004, p. 57). These observations remind us that, as bodies, we are shaped by our histories in various geographical, social and cultural contexts, and we bring this history to bear when experiencing VR narratives. One might thus question the extent to which our reactions and behaviour within a virtual world mirror our real-world tendencies, and what capacity VR narratives have to foster changes of behaviour. While it is beyond the scope of this introduction to explore VR's capabilities as an 'empathy machine' (Milk, 2015), I acknowledge the many VR works that have been created to date with the goal of challenging assumptions and/or changing user attitudes. Some of these experiences will be explored in subsequent chapters of this book.

Key Research Questions and Methodology

This book examines works that blur media boundaries, drawing upon the conventions of cinema, theatre, games and digital media more broadly, and giving rise to unique and transformative narrative experiences.

The following questions guide my analysis of several case studies across chapters:

- How do the experiential and immersive qualities of contemporary VR experiences support or reject traditional narrative structures?
- How do contemporary VR narratives incorporate the user's body as a storytelling tool?
- How do interactive devices and user interfaces grant the user agency and assist in the delivery of narrative?

These questions call for an examination of VR projects as dynamic texts that affect and are affected by the user.

In response to the nascent status of the current wave of VR, as well as the embodied nature of immersive experiences, this study takes an interdisciplinary approach that draws upon the perspectives of the aforementioned disciplinary areas. As a scholar with a background in screen studies and screen production, I approach VR as a form of moving image production but also acknowledge the ways in which its 'frameless' screen sets it apart from cinema, which necessitates a consideration of the medium's interactive and immersive qualities. With the goal of producing a focused understanding of VR narratives, I adopt formal analysis, phenomenological analysis and production studies methodologies. My formal analysis seeks to identify and explore the narrative and stylistic features of a variety of VR experiences, as well as the relationships between these features. When conducting this formal analysis I refer to the theoretical tools of Aarseth, Ryan, Koenitz and others, as a means of further interrogating identified narrative elements. My discussion involves an investigation of each project's narrative structures at story and discourse level (what Ryan terms 'textual architecture') (2006, p. 100). Such an approach emphasises the interactive nature of contemporary VR experiences, considering how narrative elements, modes and models are affected by immersive technologies.

This formal analysis will be complemented by a phenomenological reading of each experience, based on my own visceral and emotional response to VR content. This methodological approach is taken noting that 'phenomenology has proved to be a method well-suited to exploring the experience of embodiment because it is fundamentally concerned with perception and bodily activity [...] enabling the exploration of phenomena as they are lived and experienced' (Murray & Sixsmith, 1999, p. 322). While it is beyond the scope of this introduction to outline the history of phenomenology and its use in various disciplinary contexts, I note that it is well established as a methodology for film analysis (see for example Shaviro, 2010 or Sobchack, 1992, 2004), and has also been productively used as a means to illuminate the nature of VR experiences by several researchers (Bender & Broderick, 2021; Cox & Yetter, 2022; Haj-Bolouri, 2023; Kelly, 2023; Murray & Sixsmith, 1999). Such approaches present analyses based on personal and subjective encounters with VR texts, highlighting the sensuous nature of the medium. Moreover, as Kelly observes, a phenomenological approach to the study of VR allows for qualitative understanding of presence, which due to the personal nature of engagement with the medium, can be viewed 'in terms of its experiential individuality' (2023, p. 1173). While virtual presence research has a history of exploration via quantitative methods, a phenomenological approach allows for insights to be collected via reflection on personal experience and construction of narrative events. By examining my own response to VR works as a body suspended in virtual space (with or without a visual physical representation, such as an avatar), I gather data about the way that narratives shape and are shaped by user interaction. My reading of works will acknowledge that 'the sensorial body is located within a sociocultural, gendered, and technological context', and seek to account for my own background, history, and preferences within this analysis (Murray and Sixsmith, p. 315).

The book's various chapters explore core aspects of contemporary VR narratives, and do so through detailed analysis of one or more narrative-based VR projects. The included works are examples of VR entertainment genres that have been observable in recent years but by no means represent all genres. It is noted that other forms of VR entertainment exist and that new types of experiences will most certainly have emerged by the time this book is published. This is inevitable given the rapid advancement of artificial intelligence and VR technologies more broadly.

Accessing VR projects can be difficult, particularly when they are location-based or feature live actors operating in a specific timezone. Moreover, it can be difficult for the interactor to take notes on a VR experience once they are fitted up with a HMD and hand controllers, meaning that aspects of a work can be missed. For this reason, my central case study analyses are generally based upon my repeated viewing or engagement with works in either my own home or a public setting (i.e. film or arts festival). Adopting production studies methods, I refer to secondary material such as reviews published in academic and non-academic forums, to complement my own reading of projects. Lastly, I draw upon creator interviews as an additional means of understanding case studies. These interviews expose how technological, logistical and creative opportunities and constraints have shaped practitioner approaches to VR narratives.

Breslin and Buchanan suggest that case studies, as a method, 'have a rich history for exploring the space between the world of theory and the experience of practice' (2008, p. 36). In the context of this book, they allow for a series of key concepts associated with the affordances of interactive and/or immersive media, such as: perspective; agency; liveness; and user customisation; to be investigated. By foregrounding these concepts in the case studies that follow, I attempt to isolate the unique aspects of VR narratives, as well as to highlight continuities with older media. Care has been taken to select VR projects from diverse geographical locations for study. The analysed works are varied in their content, production approaches and delivery platforms, providing the reader with insights into a range of VR experiences that are currently being produced and consumed.

As Ryan observes, a study of narrative offers a means to understand the 'strengths and limitations in the representational power of individual media' (2006, p. 4). By taking an interdisciplinary approach to the examination of VR narratives, which provides an expansion of vocabulary that can benefit further research in this area, this book highlights the representative power of VR media. Given the fast-moving creative and technological landscape for VR development, and the continued take up of VR headsets by consumers, I would argue that such an undertaking can provide considerable insights into this evolving medium as well as the broader and expanding category of immersive entertainment.

Chapter Breakdown

Chapters 2, 3 and 4 of this book take documentary or docu-drama case studies as their focus and analyse these with reference to a number of theoretical frameworks and concepts. Although centred on non-fiction work, the analysis featured in these chapters holds relevance for narrative-based VR more broadly and informs the chapters that follow.

Chapter 2, *A Body in the Story*, seeks to explore the narrative impacts of presence and embodiment in contemporary narrative-based virtual reality (VR) projects. With reference to three case studies, I question how interactive devices and stylistic choices, including representations of virtual bodies and user positioning within a scene, give rise to feelings of presence and embodiment. The chapter explores the varying body representations that are a feature of the case studies, drawing out how these have consequences for the user's sense of identification with a predetermined character.

Chapter 3, *Virtual Reality Narration,* interrogates the affective communication of first-person testimony in VR experiences by examining the inclusion of voiceover narration and game devices in three documentary-based works. This is undertaken with reference to the notions of 'voice' and 'focalisation' (Genette, 1980), which are reconsidered for the 360-degree medium. Additionally, user positioning in relation to story agents is further explored through this theoretical lens. Building on existing scholarship, I present a taxonomy of user positioning within VR narratives that foregrounds the centrality of the user to the VR narrative—as observer or explorer at the centre of the storyworld—and reinforces the first-person perspective of the medium.

Chapter 4, *Exploring Environmental Storytelling Techniques in Expressive, Virtual Reality Documentary*, considers the notion of environmental storytelling for VR through a close reading of three room-scale, non-fiction projects. In recent years, considerable academic criticism has been directed at 360-degree VR documentaries that have adopted the conventions of realist filmmaking, using lens-based technologies to capture live-action, or other tools to create photo-realistic environments based on the real world. Less academic work has considered abstract or expressive approaches that VR practitioners might adopt as a means to communicate a subjective narrative experience of space and time, a gap that this chapter addresses. The concept of environmental storytelling as discussed in video games and theme park contexts (Carson, 2000; Jenkins, 2004), is adopted as a framework to assist with this quest. The way that narrative might be enacted by the VR user, and/or how meaning might be embedded in objects in a 360-degree VR environment is interrogated.

Following this exploration of non-fiction case studies, Chaps. 5, 6 and 7 give time to dramatic, fictional narratives that offer an array of interactive devices. Chapter 5, *Time, Space and the Body in The Under Presents* (2019), turns its attention to a multiplayer VR game featuring immersive theatre elements to further explore the affective nature of narrative structures in VR. With reference to narrative theory for games, the chapter first interrogates the experience that *The Under Presents* (Tender Claws 2019) offers, noting the project's combination of linear story, improvised 'live' moments, and open-world narrative elements. It then argues that the player's manipulation of time and space within the game world is an embodied activity mediated by the VR HMD and hand controllers. Further to identifying overlapping emotional or strategic spaces within the game world, the term 'corporeal' space is proposed to address this constituting role of the player's body in the represented 360-degree VR environment. This concept reinforces the notion of a narrative journey that is literally in the hands of the player and results from their bodily interaction with spatial and temporal components.

Chapter 6, *Between Storytelling and Storyliving*, explores the user customisation of VR narratives through the analysis of two fictional, scripted VR projects: *Lustration* (New Canvas 2022) and *Fire Escape* (iINK Stories

2019). The notion of 'storyliving' gained traction as a means of describing the experience of VR narratives in 2017. I unpack this term with reference to the two case studies that feature a range of interactive devices, such as branching narratives and selectable vantage points of plot action. These devices allow the user to tailor their narrative experience through processes of personalisation and customisation so as to actively participate in the process of storytelling. With reference to the System, Process, Product (SPP) model of narrative production theorised by Koenitz (2010, 2015), the chapter argues that the two projects' interactive devices encourage some measure of 'storyliving', but that this occurs alongside the delivery of a fully scripted narrative.

Chapter 7, *Virtual Reality Narratives Live Online*, explores immersive VR theatre in the context of the social platform, VRChat, posing further questions about narrative experiences that involve real-time interaction with virtual actors. It discusses several recent productions, and takes *The Severance Theory: Welcome to Respite* by the US-based Co-Act Productions and Ferryman Collective (2021) as its central case study. This project features complex game mechanics and visual effects to encourage user interaction with live actors and other story agents. The chapter examines the way that *Welcome to Respite*'s narrative is constructed, considering onboarding and offboarding sequences (the methods by which performers prepare participants to enter and exit the virtual VR world) as well as the story itself. It argues that immersive VR theatre offers the user a 'personal' experience of a pre-authored narrative delivered through live performance, where one-on-one engagement with actors fosters high levels of engagement and feelings of immersion.

The book's concluding chapter returns to the central questions outlined in this introduction, bringing together insights gathered from the chapters as a whole. It explores the challenges for VR narratives in relation to diversity and inclusion and looks to the future of VR storytelling.

References

Aarseth, E. (2012, May). A narrative theory of games. In *Proceedings of the international conference on the foundations of digital Games* (pp. 129–133).

Arcagni, S., & D'Aloia, A. (2021). VR storytelling: Potentials and limitations of virtual reality narratives. *Cinergie–Il Cinema e le altre Arti, 10*(19), 1–7.

Aylett, R., & Louchart, S. (2003). Towards a narrative theory of virtual reality. *Virtual Reality, 7*(1), 2–9.

Bal, M. (1997). *Narratology: Introduction to the theory of narrative* (2nd.). University of Toronto Press.

Bender, S. M., & Broderick, M. (2021). *Virtual realities: Case studies in immersion and phenomenology*. Springer Nature.

Bordwell, D. (2012). Three dimensions of film narrative. In *Poetics of cinema* (pp. 97–146). Routledge.

Bordwell, D., Thompson, K., & Smith, J. (2016). *Film Art: An Introduction* (11th ed.). McGraw-Hill Higher Education.

Breslin, M., & Buchanan, R. (2008). On the case study method of research and teaching in design. *Design Issues, 24*(1), 36–40.

Bruni, L. E., Kadastik, N., Pedersen, T. A., & Dini, H. (2022). Digital narratives in extended realities. *Roadmapping extended reality: Fundamentals and applications*, 35–62.

Bye, K. (2022). Voices of VR (podcast) #1119: Venice Immersive Preview with Co-Curators + Expanded VRChat World Gallery Exhibition. https://voicesofvr.com/1119-venice-immersive-preview-with-co-curators-expanded-vrchat-world-gallery-exhibition/

Campbell, J. (1949). *The hero with a thousand faces*. Pantheon Books.

Carlson, M. (2015). Postdramatic theatre and postdramatic performance. *Revista Brasileira de Estudos da Presença, 5*, 577–595.

Carson, D. (2000). *Environmental storytelling: Creating immersive 3D worlds using lessons learned from the theme park industry* (vol. 1). Gamasutra. com.

Cox, M., & Yetter, C. (2022). "This Is So Cool": A phenomenological study on virtual reality novelty. *Journal of Communication Technology, 5*(1), 84–103.

Daly, K. (2010). Cinema 3.0: The Interactive-Image. *Cinema Journal, 50*(1), 81–98.

Dixon, S. (2006). A history of virtual reality in performance. *International Journal of Performance Arts & Digital Media, 2*(1).

Dooley, K. (2018). Virtual reality: Moving beyond a cinema of attractions. *Screen Education, 88*, 97–103.

Dooley, K. (2021). *Cinematic virtual reality: A critical study of 21st century approaches and practices*. Springer Nature.

Fire Escape. (2019). Writers Sam Butin, Navid Khonsari, Vassiliki Khonsari, Andres Perez-Duarte. Director Navid Khonsari. USA. Three episodes.

Fludernik, M. (2008). Narrative and drama. *Theorizing Narrativity, 12*, 355–383.

Fludernik, M. (2010). Narratology in the twenty-first century: The cognitive approach to narrative. *Pmla, 125*(4), 924–930.

Flynn, B. (2004). Games as inhabited spaces. *Media International Australia, 110*(1), 52–61.

Flynn, J. (2019). The History of VR: When was it created and who invented it? *3D Insider*. Retrieved October 2, 2022, from https://3dinsider.com/vr-history/

Frasca, G. (1999). Ludology meets narratology: Similitude and differences between (video) games and narrative. https://ludology.typepad.com/weblog/articles/ludology.htm

Frasca, G. (2003, November). Ludologists love stories, too: Notes from a debate that never took place. In *DiGRA conference* (Vol. 8). https://ludology.typepad.com/weblog/articles/frasca_levelUP2003.pdf

Genette, G. (1980). *Narrative discourse*. Cornell University Press..

Gumball Dreams. (2022). Dirs. Deirdre V Lyons & Christopher Lane Davis. Ferryman Collective: Los Angeles.

Haj-Bolouri, A. (2023). The experience of immersive virtual reality: A phenomenology inspired inquiry. *Communications of the Association for Information Systems, 52*(1), 32.

Hambly, G. (2021). The not so universal hero's journey. *Journal of Screenwriting, 12*(2), 135–150.

Heim, M. R. (2017). Virtual reality wave 3. In J. Gackenbach & J. Bown (Eds.), *Boundaries of self and reality online* (pp. 261–277). Academic Press.

Hogan, P. C. (2014). Emplotting a storyworld in drama: Selection, time, and construal in the discourse of hamlet. *Storyworlds across media: Toward a media-conscious narratology*, 50–66.

Jenkins, H. (2004). Game design as narrative architecture. *Computer, 44*(3), 11.

Jerald, J. (2015). *The VR Book: Human-centered design for virtual reality*. Morgan & Claypool.

Johnson, D. (2020). The Oculus Quest is sold out pretty much everywhere right now. Retrieved September 5, 2022, from https://www.cnet.com/deals/where-you-can-buy-hard-to-find-oculus-quest-right-now/

Kelly, N. J. (2023). Using interpretative phenomenological analysis to gain a qualitative understanding of presence in virtual reality. *Virtual Reality, 27*(2), 1173–1185.

Koenitz, H. (2010). Towards a theoretical framework for interactive digital narrative. In R. Aylett, M. Y. Lim, & S. Louchart (Eds.), *Interactive storytelling: Third joint conference on interactive digital storytelling* (pp. 176–185). Springer.

Koenitz, H. (2015). Towards a specific theory of interactive digital narrative. In H. Koenitz, G. Ferri, M. Haahr, D. Sezen, & T. I. Sezen (Eds.), *Interactive digital narrative* (pp. 91–105). Routledge.

Koenitz, H. (2023). *Understanding interactive digital narrative: Immersive expressions for a complex time*. Taylor & Francis.

Koenitz, H., Pastena, A. D., Jansen, D., Lint, B. D., & Moss, A. (2018, December). The myth of 'universal' narrative models. In *International conference on interactive digital storytelling* (pp. 107–120). Springer.

Kohn, E. (2020). VR can be the film industry's future, but the barriers to entry are surreal. Retrieved August 30, 2020, from https://www.indiewire.com/2020/06/virtual-reality-could-save-film-industry-1202234384/

Landa, J. A. G. (2005). Narrative theory. *University of Zaragoza. On Line Edition.* https://hcommons.org/deposits/objects/hc:18948/datastreams/CONTENT/content

Lanier, J. (2017). *Dawn of the new everything: A journey through virtual reality.* Random House.

Laurel, B. (2013). *Computers as theatre: A dramatic theory of interactive experience.* Addison-Wesley.

Lehmann, H. T. (2006). *Postdramatic theatre.* Routledge.

Lustration VR. (2022). Dir. Ryan Griffen. New Canvas, Australia

Mateer, J. (2017). Directing for cinematic virtual reality: How the traditional film director's craft applies to immersive environments and notions of presence. *Journal of Media Practice, 18*(1), 14–25.

Matney, L. (2019). Verizon picks up the assets of Disney-backed VR startup Jaunt. https://techcrunch.com/2019/09/30/verizon-picks-up-the-assets-of-disney-backed-vr-startup-jaunt/

Matney, L. (2022). Meta's Quest Store hits $1.5 billion in total revenue to date. https://au.finance.yahoo.com/news/metas-quest-store-hits-1-171520210.html

Milk, C. (2015). Empathy machine.

Mowbray, T. (2022). Evolution of the VR Headset- Part 1. https://aubika.store/blogs/news/evolution-of-the-vr-headset-part-1

Murray, C. D., & Sixsmith, J. (1999). The corporeal body in virtual reality. *Ethos, 27*(3), 315–343.

Murray, J. (2005). The Last Word on Ludology v Narratology in Game Studies. (Delivered as a preface to keynote talk at DiGRA 2005, Vancouver, Canada, June 17, 2005). https://inventingthemedium.com/2013/06/28/the-last-word-on-ludology-v-narratology-2005/

Murray, J. H. (1997). *Hamlet on the holodeck: The future of narrative in cyberspace.* MIT Press.

Ng, J. (2021). *The post-screen through virtual reality, holograms and light projections: Where screen boundaries lie.* Amsterdam University Press.

Nielsen, L. T., Møller, M. B., Hartmeyer, S. D., Ljung, T. C., Nilsson, N. C., Nordahl, R., & Serafin, S. (2016, November). Missing the point: An exploration of how to guide users' attention during cinematic virtual reality. In *Proceedings of the 22nd ACM Conference on Virtual Reality Software and Technology* (pp. 229–232).

Pfister, M. (1988). *The theory and analysis of drama.* Cambridge University Press.

Remedios, D. J., Mathew, D., & Schleser, M. (2022). Table for two—A parallel interactive narrative in VR (PIN VR). In J. Frith & M. Saker (Eds.), *The changing face of VR: Pushing the boundaries of experience across multiple industries.* Vernon Press.

Reyes, M. C. (2018, December). Measuring user experience on interactive fiction in cinematic virtual reality. In *International Conference on Interactive Digital Storytelling* (pp. 295–307). Springer.

Richardson, B. (2000). Recent concepts of narrative and the narratives of narrative theory. *Style, 34*(2), 168–175.

Richardson, B. (2001). Voice and narration in postmodern drama. *New Literary History, 32*(3), 681–694.

Riva, G., Mantovani, F., Capideville, C., Preziosa, A., Morganti, F., Villani, D., Gaggioli, A., Botella, C., & Alcañiz Raya, M. (2007). Affective interactions using virtual reality: The link between presence and emotions. In Cyberpsychology & Behavior: The impact of the internet, multimedia and virtual reality on behavior and society (Vol. 10, pp. 45–56). https://doi.org/10.1089/cpb.2006.9993

Ross, M., & Munt, A. (2018). Cinematic virtual reality: Towards the spatialized screenplay. *Journal of Screenwriting, 9*(2), 191–209. https://doi.org/10.1386/jocs.9.2.191_1

Ryan, J. (2017). Grimes' fairy tales: A 1960s story generator. In *Interactive storytelling: 10th international conference on Interactive Digital Storytelling, ICIDS 2017 Funchal, Madeira, Portugal, November 14–17, 2017, Proceedings 10* (pp. 89–103). Springer International Publishing.

Ryan, M. L. (2001). Beyond myth and metaphor: The case of narrative in digital media. *Game Studies, 1*(1) http://www.gamestudies.org/0101/ryan/

Ryan, M. L. (2002). Beyond myth and metaphor: Narrative in digital media. *Poetics Today, 23*(4), 581–609.

Ryan, M. L. (2006). *Avatars of story* (Vol. 17). University of Minnesota Press.

Ryan, M. L. (2009). From narrative games to playable stories: Toward a poetics of interactive narrative. *Storyworlds: A Journal of Narrative Studies, 1*, 43–59.

Ryan, M. L. (2015). Texts, worlds, stories: Narrative worlds as cognitive and ontological concept. In *Narrative theory, literature, and new media* (pp. 11–28). Routledge.

Ryan, M. L. (2018). Narrative in virtual reality? Anatomy of a dream reborn. *Facta Ficta. Journal of Theory, Narrative & Media, 2*(2), 91–111.

Ryan, M.-L. (2001). *Narrative as virtual reality: Immersion and interactivity in literature and electronic media.* Johns Hopkins University Press.

Sagot-Duvauroux, R., Garnier, F., & Ronfard, R. (2022, April). (Re-) Framing Virtual Reality. In *WICED 2022-10th Workshop on intelligent cinematography and editing.*

Shaviro, S. (2010). *Post cinematic affect.* John Hunt Publishing.

Shin, D. (2018). Empathy and embodied experience in virtual environment: To what extent can virtual reality stimulate empathy and embodied experience? *Computers in Human Behavior, 78*, 64–73.

Slater, M. (2003). A note on presence terminology. *Presence connect, 3*(3), 1–5.

Sobchack, V. (1992). *The address of the eye: A phenomenology of film experience*. Princeton University Press.

Sobchack, V. (2004). *Carnal thoughts: Embodiment and moving image culture*. University of California Press.

The Severance Theory: Welcome to Respite. (2021). CoAct Productions and Ferryman Collective.

The Under Presents. (2020). Dirs. Danny Cannizzaro & Samantha Gorman USA: Tender Claws.

Todorov, T., & Weinstein, A. (1969, October). Structural analysis of narrative. In *NOVEL: A forum on fiction* (Vol. 3, No. 1, pp. 70–76). Duke University Press.

Tricart, C. (2018). *Virtual reality filmmaking: Techniques & best practices for VR Filmmakers*. Taylor & Francis.

Vogler, C. (1992). *The writer's journey: Mythic structure for storytellers and screenwriters*. Michael Wiese Productions.

Zhang, Y., & Weber, I. (2023). Adapting, modifying and applying cinematography and editing concepts and techniques to cinematic virtual reality film production. *Media International Australia, 186*(1), 115–135.

CHAPTER 2

A Body in the Story: Exploring Body Representation, Presence and Embodiment in Virtual Reality Narratives

Introduction

In August 2023 I experienced several narrative-based virtual reality (VR) experiences at the Melbourne International Film Festival in Victoria, Australia. Among these was *Stay Alive, My Son* (dir. Victoria Bousis, United States, 2022), a work featuring vivid imagery and game mechanics that explores one man's story of survival in Cambodia during the time of the Khmer Rouge. Based on Pin Yathay's autobiographical novel of the same name,[1] *Stay Alive, My Son* presents a personal account of the author's experience from the arrival of the Khmer Rouge in Phnom Penh when he was 33 to his escape into Thailand more than two years later. During this time Yathay lost all members of his family, and heartbreakingly, was forced to abandon his six-year-old son in order to survive.

The harrowing narrative of *Stay Alive, My Son* begins in modern-day France where the now 80-year-old Yathay lives. As an experiencer of the VR project equipped with head mounted display (HMD) goggles and donning hand controllers, I found myself transported to a realistically rendered suburban neighbourhood. I moved towards the front door of a house, where a digital version of the elderly Yathay appeared behind glass. He motioned to a newspaper on the landing, which I retrieved and passed

[1] *Say Alive, My Son* was first published in 1987 under the French Title *Tu Vivrais, Mon Fils*.

K. Dooley, *Virtual Reality Narratives*,
https://doi.org/10.1007/978-3-031-64965-3_2

to him before entering. Moments later I followed Yathay up a set of stairs to the second level of his home. At this point he offered me a bracelet, suggesting that I take it 'to protect you on our journey'. My acceptance of the gift triggered a bodily transfer. When I looked down at my hands and arms I found that they resembled those of Yathay and I now embodied his perspective as a character within the storyworld. For the remainder of the VR experience I occupied his virtual body and relived his devastating experience of leaving his son in Cambodia.

For contemporary VR narratives like *Stay Alive, My Son*, high-end graphics and head tracking technologies foster a sense of presence and immersion within a realistically or imaginatively rendered storyworld. When experiencing the project I felt a range of emotions—sadness, dread and disgust at the historical realities that underpin the story—and also felt a deep empathy for Yathay as a father trying to keep his family intact under extreme conditions. Reflecting on the work, I pondered the relationship between my feeling of being present in the storyworld as a character and the emotions that I experienced. My sense of embodiment throughout the work, fostered by stylistic properties, interactive devices and the affordances of VR technology, seemed key to my feelings of empathy but I questioned the impact of this embodiment on my wider experience of the narrative.

This chapter seeks to explore the experience offered by contemporary narrative-based VR projects and specifically, the narrative impacts of presence and embodiment. When using the term 'embodiment' I refer to the feeling of having or experiencing a body (Palma Stade et al., 2023), which gives rise to affective experience. With reference to philosopher Baruch Spinoza (2001), Hickey-Moody defines affect as 'what moves us. It's a hunch. A visceral prompt' (2013, p. 79). This phenomenon, she suggests, comes 'in between feelings and changes to what you can do' (p. 79). I adopt this understanding of affect in my exploration of VR as a communication medium that fosters affective experience through engagement with an immersive environment. This engagement might see the user placed within a virtual body that is partially or wholly visible and attuned to their real-life bodily responses, or conversely, positioned as a present but invisible spectator within a storyworld. In either case the VR experience acts upon the user, creating emotional and bodily reactions. By this I mean that the content offered within a virtual environment has consequences for our actual body, perhaps making us recoil, flinch or reorient ourselves in 360-degree space. Twenty-first century explorations of affect theory by scholars such as Steven Shaviro (2010) and Vivian Sobchack (2004) have highlighted the ways in which screen media can involve 'a moment by moment manipulation of the spectator's affective state' (Shaviro, 2010, p. 118), and certainly, other media such as literature or games are also capable of delivering powerful embodied experiences; however, VR might be considered the supreme media in this respect, given the audience's feeling of physical presence and immersion within a virtual storyworld. This phenomenon, I would contend, has received insufficient analysis in the context of contemporary narrative-based VR considering the impact of body representation, stylistic properties and interactive devices on narrative understanding.

VR can be defined as a 'computer-generated experience that can simulate physical presence in real or imagined environments' (Shin, 2018, p. 65). Following the advancement of VR technology in the late 1980s and 1990s, many notable scholars have pondered its immersive qualities in foundational research. For Steuer et al. (1995), the perceiver of virtual reality experiences 'telepresence', which they define as 'the experience of presence in an environment by means of a communication medium' (p. 6). Sheridan (1992) uses the term 'virtual presence' to describe this phenomenon within the context of VR specifically, while Lee (2004) productively argues for use of the more general term 'presence' to encourage discussion of the phenomenon by scholars working across disciplines. I use this more general term in this chapter to refer to the feeling of 'being present' in a virtual environment. Scholars from a number of different fields, such as psychology, narratology and computer science have offered overlapping accounts of presence and immersion (see, for example, Lombard & Ditton, 1997; Popat, 2016; Riva et al., 2007; Ryan, 2001; Slater, 2009), generally agreeing that these terms relate to a medium's ability to position the user within a vibrant spatial and potentially social environment that exists as an alternative to the 'real' world. As Riva et al. observe, 'there is consensus that the experience of presence is a complex, multidimensional perception, formed through an interplay of raw (multi-) sensory data and various cognitive processes' (2007, p. 46).

A relationship between audiovisual elements, interactive possibilities and increased feelings of presence is suggested by Lombard and Ditton (1997) who conducted an extensive review of literature, finding that researchers conceptualised presence as resulting from a combination of factors. In their summary they suggest that an enhanced feeling of presence can stem from a combination of one or more elements including: the realism of the environment, including graphics and sound, contributing to the phenomenon of 'transportation'; the level of immersion created by the interface; and the user's capacity to perform meaningful and consequential actions within the environment (1997). Similarly, Steuer et al. suggest that two major determinants of telepresence are vividness, which they define as 'the ability of a technology to produce a sensorially rich mediated environment', and interactivity (p. 11). While contemporary VR researchers have established a correlation between a user's experience of presence, immersion and affective experience (Marcolin et al., 2021; Riva et al., 2007) the impact of narrative and stylistic elements on user embodiment is less clear. Tham et al. suggest the need for further study of 'embodied interaction in terms of the new forms of presence and interaction brought about by VR technologies', so as to understand the links between bodily experience, perception and presence (2018, p. 191). On a related note, Shin stresses the need for further investigation of immersion's impacts upon 'how (user's) empathies are formed (and) how value perceptions influence action' within the context of VR storytelling (2018, p. 64).

With these suggested gaps in knowledge in mind, the following questions to guide this chapter's study: How might interactive devices and stylistic elements, including representations of virtual bodies, give rise to feelings of presence and embodiment? Moreover, how might the VR user's sense of embodiment and agency in a virtual environment shape their experience of a narrative? This last question presupposes a feedback loop—that the participant is affected by the material that they encounter, and that this leads to choices in terms of their interaction with story agents, which then shapes their overall narrative experience. In other words, a user's embodied experience of a VR story has consequences for their overall narrative understanding of a work.

To explore these questions and presuppositions, I examine the interactive devices and stylistic features of three projects that offer various body representations and expressions of agency for the VR user. Firstly, I analyse *The Man Who Couldn't Leave* (Singing Chen, Taiwan, 2022), a 360-degree video that explores stories of imprisonment and persecution in Taiwan's Green Island Prison in the 1950s. I then present a more detailed examination of *Stay Alive, My Son*, exploring the narrative impacts of the user's placement in Yathay's virtual body. Lastly, I explore *Please, Believe Me* (dir. Nonny de la Peña 2022), a documentary work that explores one woman's journey through the diagnosis and treatment of Lyme Disease. This third work engages the user through a number of interactive devices while presenting the testimonies of the infected patient and her doctors. It must be acknowledged that all three projects explore non-fiction stories, approaching these with documentary and docu-drama methods.[2] While other genres of VR storytelling certainly exist, the three case studies have been chosen because of their common aims to communicate subjective experience, and because of their varying interactive and narrative devices. The different body representations and perspectives that these works offer will be compared and contrasted. Further to presenting a close analysis of narrative structures and stylistic approaches in these projects, I draw upon my own phenomenological experience as an interactor with each work, noting my emotional and embodied experience of story elements. My analysis is based on repeated viewing or interaction with the three works using a Meta Quest 2 headset in either a festival setting or my own home.

To guide this analysis, I consider Kilteri et al.'s definition of sense of embodiment (SoE) in virtual reality (2012). Considering the user's placement in virtual bodies and avatars in VR environments, this definition contends that a SoE can consist of three subcomponents: sense of self-location, sense of agency and sense of body ownership (pp. 375–377). I offer a more detailed summary of this definition in the following section of this chapter, noting differences between these authors' notions of self-location and presence. In my analysis of the three case studies, I note my SoE when inhabiting virtual bodies or conversely, appearing as an invisible entity, within the three storyworlds. This approach takes my lived experience of each narrative as a form of data. I note, however, the subjective nature of my experience as a VR participant and therefore stress the exploratory nature of this research. My study aims to highlight the links between presence, embodiment and narrative understanding in order to broaden a discussion that is of value to VR researchers and designers alike.

Presence and Embodiment in Virtual Reality

While existing research has noted links between the concepts of presence and embodiment in virtual reality environments (Biocca, 1997; Lee, 2004), one must note that these are distinct though related notions. I use the former to refer to the feeling of being present in a virtual environment, and the latter to describe the feeling of being present in a virtual

[2] For an overview of VR documentary practice, see Chap. 4.

environment as a body. Following definitions by Steuer et al. (1995) and Lombard and Ditton (1997) one might define presence as a psychological state that gives rise to immersivity. Slater suggests two important dimensions of presence in VR: the compelling sense of 'being there' that he calls place illusion (PI) (2009, p. 3551) and the perception that 'what is apparently happening is really happening' that he called the 'plausibility illusion' (Psi) (2009, p. 3553). The latter dimension, Slater suggests, might be evoked by direct eye contact between character and participant in a virtual environment (p. 3553). Such a suggestion highlights the way that VR content can be manipulated to affect the participant on a bodily level.

Lombard and Ditton suggest that VR creates a 'perceptual illusion of non-mediation' (1997). Such an illusion occurs when 'a person fails to perceive or acknowledge the existence of a medium in his/her communication environment and responds as he/she would if the medium were not there' (1997). While contemporary experiences of presence in a virtual environment can be powerful, Bolter et al. remind us that 'even the best VR technology cannot deceive users into believing that they are having an unmediated experience' (2021, p. 72). These authors consider presence as an experience that is 'both mediated and immediate at the same time' (p. 72). This means that while we may become immersed in a VR story, we never quite forget that we are wearing a headset or holding other pieces of technology. The illusion of reality that VR storytelling presents is strong, however, and encourages the engagement of our whole body in a 'suspension of disbelief' (Coleridge, 1960) as can also be experienced when consuming media such as film or television.

Further to the psychological state of presence, the concept of embodiment captures the corporeal experience of feeling present in a virtual environment, which may involve the physical manifestation of a virtual body. Tham et al. suggest that '[b]oth presence and embodiment have a phenomenological sense, which can refer to the things we consciously notice about the role of our bodies in shaping our self-perception and identities through conscious introspection and deliberate reflection on our experience' (p. 183). This phenomenological sense of both terms is foregrounded in this chapter's study.

One must note, however, that the term 'embodiment' has been used differently in a range of disciplinary contexts, and its conceptualisation depends on the lens through which it is considered (Kilteri et al., p. 374). A phenomenological standpoint defines it as 'an existential condition in which the body is the subjective source or inter-subjective ground of experience' (Csordas, 1999, p. 143). This phenomenon is explored by philosopher Maurice Merleau-Ponty in his seminal text *Phenomenology of Perception* (originally published in 1945), which suggests that

> Sensation, such as it is presented to us by experience, is no longer an indifferent matter and an abstract moment, but rather one of our surfaces of contact with being, or a structure of consciousness. Rather than presenting us with a unique space or universal condition of all qualities, each sensation gives us a particular manner of being in space and, in a certain sense, of creating space. (Maurice Merleau-Ponty, 2012, p. 267)

As Matthews summarises, Merleau-Ponty's work suggests that 'to be-in-the-world is necessarily to be embodied: it is our bodies that give us our place within the world, the place that defines our point of view' (2014, p. 183). This description of embodiment stresses the body as the vessel that mediates our sense of self and experience of space. In this way we respond to stimuli on a visceral as well as cognitive level. Hummels and van Dijk describe this as 'embodied sensemaking', considering cognition from the perspective of a 'body-in-action' (2015, p. 21).

In the context of virtual reality research, embodiment has been discussed in relation to the generation of presence in virtual environments (Biocca, 1997; Gall et al., 2021; Kilteni et al., 2012; Lee, 2004). Biocca (1997) suggests that embodiment gives rise to 'self-presence', involving mental models of the self made salient within a virtual environment. He also discusses the concept of 'social presence' within the VR context, describing this as the perception of being present alongside a perceived intelligence (human or non-human, such as animal, alien or AI). Lee (2004) takes up these notions alongside that of 'physical presence', this referring to the experience of virtual objects as real. As Lee suggests, the three domains of 'physical', 'social' and 'self' provide a productive means of categorising virtual experience (p. 38) and will be returned to later in this chapter.

As a solution to the existence of multiple and potentially confusing definitions of embodiment, Kilteni et al. adopt the term 'Sense of Embodiment (SoE)' to refer to the 'ensemble of sensations that arise in conjunction with being inside, having, and controlling a body, especially in relation to virtual reality applications' (2012, pp. 374–375). This notion of SoE relates to the occupation of a virtual body and as mentioned above, consists of three subcomponents: sense of self-location, sense of agency and sense of body ownership (pp. 374–375). Sense of self-location refers to the spatial experience of being in a body (as opposed to the spatial experience of a world), which might be fostered through vestibular signals or tactile input (p. 376). On a related note, sense of agency relates to having control of one's body to perform actions as one intends (p. 376), while sense of body ownership refers to 'one's self-attribution of a body' or in other words, the sense that the virtual body is the source of experienced sensations (p. 377). On this latter subcomponent, Kilteni et al. refer to a body of research that has demonstrated the ways that artificial body parts or even whole bodies can be experienced as real as a result of 'bottom up information' (e.g. sensory information delivered via visual, tactile, and proprioceptive input) or 'top down information' (cognitive processes that modulate the processing of this sensory input) (p. 377). A SoE results from a synthesis of these three subcomponents, they argue, and may be experienced to varying degrees. This definition is productive for the analysis featured later in this chapter, as the various subcomponents provide a framework through which to consider the affective experience offered by contemporary VR projects. I therefore refer to the definition's components when examining the case study works.

One must note however, that this definition of SoE is concerned with physical body representations or the occupation of avatars in virtual worlds, which may not necessarily be a feature of a VR narrative. In fact, a study of VR experiences produced at the beginning of the latest wave found that the vast majority of works featured no visible avatar (Murphy, 2017).[3]

An example of such a work is this chapter's first case study, *The Man Who Couldn't Leave*, which does not offer a virtual body for the user to occupy. Rather, the viewer embodies the camera that was used to film the experience, adopting a narrative perspective described by Palma Stade et al. as the 'trinomial user-camera-subject/object' (2023). Despite the absence of a represented body, I would argue that a SoE is nonetheless present for the user of such a work. On this subject Kilteni et al. suggest

[3] In his survey of the top 200 HTC Vive applications available via the Steam store in August 2016, Murphy found that 86.5% of the sampled items featured fully invisible avatars, 9% depicted hands only, and 4.5% featured a head, torso or legs (2017, p. 1). His findings suggest that 'users may experience a sense of ownership and/or agency over their virtual actions even in the absence of visible avatar body parts' (p. 1).

consideration of 'a dichotomy of space' between the space occupied by a virtual body or avatar (in which the user perceives themselves to be located) and 'the external/environmental space (the space-environment world where the self is perceived as situated even if this does not include a body)' (p. 375). The former aligns with the aforementioned sense of self-location while the latter is an example of the presence or 'the relationship between one's self and the environment' (p. 375). While Kilteni et al.'s definition of SoE focuses on the relationship between self and virtual body, a more extended approach to embodiment, they argue, 'could potentially include the presence subcomponent' (p. 376). Going forward, I take up this suggestion based on my belief that a VR user can have an embodied experience of a work without occupying an avatar or operating virtual limbs. I would argue that with or without a body representation, the user is present in a virtual environment as a body surrounded by space. As such they may feel a sense of self or social presence, as posited by Biocca and Lee.

Further to Hummel and van Dijk's notion of embodied sensemaking (2015), the suggestion that one's level of embodiment might influence an understanding of narrative in VR is supported by results of a study conducted by Gall et al. (2021), which found that virtual embodiment amplifies emotional reactions to virtual stimuli. Noting that virtual body ownership can affect social perception and responses to perceived physical threat stimuli, these researchers posit that 'virtual embodiment might have a general effect on information processing' (p. 2). Their conclusion that 'virtual embodiment might play an active role in organizing emotional responses to virtual stimuli' (p. 2) has ramifications for VR applications beyond the realm of entertainment and emphasises the corporeal nature of human lived experience. This chapter contributes to this growing area scholarship through the examination of three innovative contemporary VR projects. In the case study analysis below I will explore the stylistic features and interactive devices that each work presents, considering how these give rise to an embodied experience of narrative.

Case Study Analysis

The Man Who Couldn't Leave *(2022)*

This 35-minute experience tells the story of inmates at the Taiwan Lyudao Prison on Green Island during the 'White Terror' era. Following a declaration of martial law in Taiwan on 19 May 1949, civilians and political dissenters (including leftists and intellectuals) were repressed by the Chinese Nationalist Party (KMT) government leading to occurrences of mass murder and imprisonment. This continued until martial law was lifted in 1987, after which time the facility was renamed Green Island Prison. Drawing upon real documents recounting the experiences of dissidents imprisoned during the 1950s, director Singing Chen presents the fictionalised story of two symbolic characters: A-Kuen, an inmate who survived his stay in the prison, and his friend A-Ching, who was executed. The VR experience also portrays A-Ching's wife and daughter, the latter of whom seeks to keep her father's story alive in the present day. This tale of persecution, hope and friendship, which was commissioned by the country's National Human Rights Museum, fosters an understanding of the White Terror era for a new generation of Taiwanese citizens, and audiences more broadly.

The Man Who Couldn't Leave is a stereoscopic work offering three degrees of freedom (3DoF) meaning that the viewer can rotate their head to look around the various 360-degree environments portrayed in the work but has no further opportunity to interact with the content. Following discussions of digital media user agency by Aylett and Louchart (2003) I use the term 'viewer' rather than 'user' when describing the experience of spectatorship that this work offers in acknowledgement of the limited agency granted to its audience.[4] Whereas a more interactive VR experience (such as the second or third case study in this chapter, for which I adopt the term 'user') might offer a storyworld that reacts to audience input, or allow a user the opportunity to contribute to the creation of the story, this work does not. It is nonetheless a captivating project featuring cinematic live action imagery and complex visual effects sequences, which was awarded the 'Best Experience Award' at the 2022 Venice Immersive competition (a sidebar of the prestigious Venice International Film Festival).

The experience begins with a 360-degree exterior landscape of Green Island Prison captured by a camera placed on a wooden path that stretches

[4] In their discussion of a narrative theory for Virtual Reality, Aylett and Louchart (2003) contend that a user is defined as 'a person who experiences a Virtual Environment through interaction and actively participates in the building of the resulting experience; a user does not contemplate or watch a narrative display as a spectator does' (p. 3). *The Man Who Couldn't Leave* could be considered to sit at a more passive end of the spectrum of VR's interactive capabilities, therefore rendering use of the term 'viewer' rather than 'user' appropriate in a discussion of its experience.

out into the ocean. As a viewer of the work, I look down from my fixed vantage point, noticing waves crashing over a path in the area below me. I turn and look at the island in the distance. The work offers no body representation for me as a viewer; however, the camera is positioned at a human vantage point (around 1.5 metres above the watery path), which helps to foster a sense of physical presence in the photographically real environment. By this I mean that although I am unable to touch the prerendered image that surrounds me, I have a sense that I am seeing the world as I would if I were physically present in the environment. As I swivel to look around I hear an unseen male voice singing that 'everything will pass' and 'a new dawn is coming'.

A moment later the scene transitions to a large wooden cell inside the prison that contains several male inmates dressed in white. Bright light streams in through lines of small windows, illuminating the various figures resting on or among wooden bunk beds. I am once again positioned to occupy a human vantage point within the scene, as though I am standing in the aisle between the bunks. My initial impression is that the scene is a still image, as none of the figures move although their poses suggest action. A moment later; however, an elderly man wearing a dark blue shirt (A-Kuen) enters the cell and walks towards me while the various inmates remain static. It is as though the scene is filled with wax figures designed to recreate life inside the prison. As A-Kuen comes closer towards me, he makes eye contact and addresses me directly (see Fig. 2.1). 'I've been

Fig. 2.1 A screenshot from the trailer for *The Man Who Couldn't Leave* (2022). (Courtesy of The Walkers Films Ltd.)

waiting, almost too long', he says. 'For a moment I forgot that you weren't really here'.

This eye contact and direct address fosters the sense of social presence that is theorised by Biocca and Lee. Although on the one hand I am aware that I am experiencing a pre-rendered stereoscopic video, the direct address presents a form of social experience that is artificially created by technology. This results in 'a psychological state in which virtual (para-authentic or artificial) social actors are experienced as actual social actors in either sensory or nonsensory ways' (Lee, 2004, p. 45). Further to the camera being positioned at a height that corresponds with an experience of being physically present within the scene, I am offered a first-person engagement with A-Kuen that feels somewhat personal, akin to a guided tour of the real location. Lee suggests that the experience of social actors in a virtual setting is a subcategory of experiencing physical objects but points out the special mechanisms that humans have developed to recognise and respond to humans as an evolutionary necessity (2004). In this respect, as would be the case in real life, I find myself compelled to return A-Kuen's gaze and to carefully consider his speech and gestures.

While this social experience fostered by A-Kuen's eye contact and direct address is very much a one-way communication, I would argue that it is nonetheless an embodied experience, seeing it requires a bodily engagement with the social actor. Despite my lack of body representation, I find myself relating to the aged and fragile figure of A-Kuen as an invisible body in the virtual environment, meaning that my virtual self is psychologically assumed rather than physically manifest. A-Kuen's direct address makes me feel self-conscious, and I reflect on our differing social and cultural circumstances as the scene unfolds. In this way the VR experience fosters an experience of self-presence, which Lee defines as 'a psychological state in which virtual (para-authentic or artificial) self/selves are experienced as the actual self in either sensory or nonsensory ways' (p. 46). This self-presence is not generated through any physical representation but rather through A-Kuen's reaction to me as a 'virtual visitor' of the prison. In other words, A-Kuen reacts to me as if I were actually there, making me feel as though I am there.

I watch and listen as A-Kuen moves around the cell, recalling details of his life in the prison and the characteristics of his various cellmates, some of whom were artists or musicians. He talks about their harsh and boring daily routines, and the sense of comradeship that enabled him to survive. Two inmate figures are given particular attention, one of whom is posed writing a letter. A-Kuen explains that these are representations of himself and his friend, A-Ching, who was a political prisoner. 'I am here today because of A-Ching', A-Kuen explains. 'I hope after you finish watching this you can spread the word'.

At around this point in the experience the scene transitions to a moving image where the static figures are replaced by living actors portraying the young A-Kuen and A-Ching. As a viewer, I am positioned in close proximity to the two actors, as though I could be a fellow inmate listening in to their quiet conversation; however, I am not acknowledged as being present by either party.[5] As such I feel somewhat like a voyeur who is eavesdropping on their conversation. A-Ching tells A-Kuen of his wife and young daughter, to whom he is writing a letter. A-Kuen studies a small photo of the young girl before lying down to sleep. Tactile details attract my attention as the scene passes, from the hard wood on which A-Kuen attempts to slumber to footprint impressions on the sandy floor, which again, fosters an embodied viewing experience. By this I mean that I relate to the two men's experience of the uncomfortable living conditions on a bodily level, imagining what it must have been like to spend years in such an environment.

After a moment of darkness, a new and more theatrical sequence begins. The sound of a marching band precedes the spectacular vision of a convoy of citizens singing revolutionary songs and proudly playing various instruments. This band emerges from the darkness to my left, filling an otherwise empty landscape, and passes by me. A-Ching walks at the rear of the group. As the band members file away, he stops some metres away from me and turns to his right. I follow his gaze, finding that another scene is being staged in the quadrant that was initially behind me. This dream-like scene portrays A-Ching's wife and toddler daughter in their dimly lit home, struggling to survive whilst under the surveillance of authorities. Their simple living room, in which the young woman toils at a sewing machine, is framed by darkness that separates them from A-Ching as onlooker. The staging and lighting of these parallel scenes draws on the conventions of theatre to create a mental link between characters occupying separate physical spaces, creating a sense of loneliness and heartache. As an invisible witness to the event I feel as though I occupy a third space

[5] For a discussion of proximity as a staging tool in virtual reality experiences see: Dooley, K. (2020). A question of proximity: Exploring a new screen grammar for 360-degree cinematic virtual reality. *Media Practice and Education*, *21*(2), 81–96.

in the drama, watching the imprisoned A-Ching imagine the life of his family in his absence.

A moment later, an even more theatrically lit scene emerges from the darkness. I see a barefoot A-Ching suspended by a rope that ties his hands behind his back. Other prisoners are suspended in the space behind him (see Fig. 2.2). Hearing sounds behind me, I turn to see his persecutor located in the opposite quadrant of 360-degree space. An interrogation takes place, which calls for me to swivel my attention to the left and right between the two parties. As with the previously described scenes, my positioning within the space as camera/viewer approximates a human vantage point, fostering a sense of physical presence within the virtual environment. But further to the SoE fostered by this vantage point, my need to swivel my body to take in the various actions that unfold around me gives rise to an active viewing experience that engages my whole body. This experience is the result of strategic staging of action across all quadrants of the 360-degree space, which is described by Williams, Love and Love as a 'Copernican' approach (2021). This is one of two trends that these authors observe within contemporary VR narratives, the other consisting of a 'Newtonian' approach that sees action largely unfold in front of the viewer, requiring little movement of the head or body. In either case the viewer/camera is the axis of 360-degree space; however, I would argue that the former approach encourages a greater SoE, seeing as it calls for a higher

Fig. 2.2 A screenshot from the trailer for *The Man Who Couldn't Leave* (2022). (Courtesy of The Walkers Films Ltd.)

degree of participation by the viewer as a body. This strategic staging technique is featured throughout *The Man Who Couldn't Leave* and gives rise to a dynamic viewing experience.

In the scenes that follow we witness intimate conversation between A-Kuen and A-Ching in the moments before the latter's execution, as well as his wife's discovery of his death. The story then returns to the wax museum where the older A-Kuen meets A-Ching's middle-aged daughter and passes on the letter that was written decades earlier. Throughout the work a SoE results from the viewer's human vantage point of the various scenes, as well as the vivid, photographically real imagery that fosters a sense of physical presence. Moreover, as described above, a sense of self-presence and social presence is generated through A-Kuen's direct address to the viewer. I would argue that the emotional impact of the work results from the strategic positioning of the camera and approaches to staging and lighting featured throughout the VR experience, which implicates the viewer as a virtual body that is present alongside the protagonists in 360-degree space.

Returning to Kilteni et al.'s three subcomponents of a SoE (self-location, sense of agency, and sense of body ownership), one can observe that the viewer of *The Man Who Couldn't Leave* is granted no physical body representation and limited agency to interact with the work. While they therefore lack a sense of self-location, agency or body ownership in regard to a physically manifest body, I would contend that the sense of physical, self and social presence that the work fosters through its various stylistic approaches produces something akin to a sense of self-location for the viewer as an invisible witness to the unfolding narrative events. Even though the viewer lacks a body representation they are positioned within the narrative as an invisible bystander, which demands reflection on their own social and cultural status in relation to the unfolding events. Moreover, their positioning within the work affects their real body (e.g. causing them to bend over or turn to witness events). In this way the viewer's SoE is highly implicated in their processing of narrative events and emotional response to the suffering and hopes of the protagonists.

Stay Alive, My Son *(2022)*

This VR interpretation of Pin Yathay's novel offers six degrees of freedom (6DoF) to its audience, meaning that in addition to being able to rotate their head to choose a field of view within the 360-degree environment, the user can move around the diegetic space of the work and also use hand controllers to touch or operate objects. Such action is required to progress through the work's narrative, although the speed at which the user does so is unfixed.[6] This increased level of interactivity and unfixed duration is the result of real-time rendering enabled via the work's game engine (Unreal Engine) and sits in contrast with *The Man Who Couldn't Leave* as a pre-rendered video. *Stay Alive, My Son* is thus responsive to user input within individual scenes although the overall narrative conclusion is predetermined. Given the complexity of the project, which involves multiple scenes and environments set in past and present, my analysis will focus on key early moments within the VR experience.

As mentioned above, the VR experience begins in modern-day France, and specifically, a realistically rendered, middle-class suburban neighbourhood. Wearing a head mounted display (HMD), I find myself located in the front garden of Yathay's house. I study this vivid environment, noting falling rain and the sounds of passersby on the street behind me—elements that engage me on a sensory level. I use the term 'vivid' here to describe 'the representational richness of a mediated environment as defined by its formal features, that is, the way in which an environment presents information to the senses' (Steuer et al., p. 11). A window within the front door of Yathay's house reveals a warm glow within the building, which alongside my natural tendency to seek shelter from rain, compels me to approach. This is perhaps evidence of Hummel and van Dijk's notion of embodied sensemaking (2015), seeing as my embodied response to the virtual stimuli influences my decision to move towards the house rather than linger in the rain or turn back towards the street.

As is the case with the previous case study, my vantage point of the scene corresponds with a human viewpoint of the environment, fostering a feeling of physical presence in the virtual environment. Using the thumbsticks on my hand controllers, I glide towards the front door of a house, up a small set of stairs and then press a doorbell. As I take this action I note the somewhat generic representation of my virtual hands, which I manoeuvre using the controllers. While generic, this representation of my hands is sufficient to grant a SoE as posited by Kilteni et al. (2012) seeing as they create some degree of self-location, agency and body ownership. By this I

[6]The director of *Stay Alive, My Son* has been quoted as saying that the experience is 55 minutes long, although this duration does not fully account for user input. See AWE (2023): https://www.youtube.com/watch?v=awIcs2iBodU

mean that the movement of my virtual hands is attuned to that of my real hands, which allows me to take actions such as pressing the doorbell, fostering a sense that the virtual body is my own. Although I cannot physically 'feel' the doorbell within the scene, the visual representation of my hands taking the action of pressing, and the reactiveness of the environment (the sound of a doorbell chiming) creates this illusion. As Popat observes in regard to the nature of action in virtual worlds, my body is 'both present and absent, experiencing agency and aspects of sensation even though there is no direct contact between flesh and world' (2016, p. 359). Moreover, the reorienting of my physical body (e.g. swiveling or taking steps to the left or right) results in a change of my vantage point within the scene, just as it would in real life. This creates a sense of what Saker and Frith label as 'coextensive space', meaning 'a symbiotic relationship between physical and digital that is increasingly proximate, extensive and transformative' (2020, p. 1429).

After some moments, a digitally constructed version of the elderly Yathay appears in the doorway and acknowledges my presence. His representation has been created using Unreal Engine's 'Metahuman' technology and is extremely detailed and realistic. 'Bonsoir', Yathay exclaims before ushering me inside the house. Once in the door he comments on the headlines of his newspaper, which concern the war in Ukraine. This becomes a one-sided conversation as I follow him towards a sideboard adorned with burning candles and other objects. 'Join me in a buddhist ritual', he requests. At this point in the experience I note that Yathay's eyes follow me as I move around the room in exploration. He seems to be waiting for me to come closer to him. I do this and his ritual begins. As is the case with *The Man Who Couldn't Leave*, this first-person engagement with Yathay fosters a sense of self-presence and social presence within this scene. His direct address and eye contact make me feel as though I inhabit the space of the house alongside him but moreover, my virtual presence and reactions to his instructions are required to initiate the various beats of action of the scene. In other words, my response to his prompts (to enter the house or to join him at the sideboard, for example) drives the scene forward. In this way my embodied reactions to Yathay impact upon the unfolding of the project's narrative.

The bodily transfer that occurs in the stairwell after Yathay passes me his bracelet is punctuated by a heightened soundtrack and the appearance of golden light orbs. I initially notice a slight change in my vantage point of the scene as well as the disappearance of the protagonist. Suspecting that something significant has occurred, I look down at my virtual hands, finding that they now resemble those of the elderly Yathay—his distinct blue checked shirt now adorns the visible parts of my arms and my hands are wrinkled. I take a moment to study my new limbs before continuing on my journey up the stairs of the house. Seeing as I have had some minutes to become acquainted with Yathay before the bodily transfer, I avoid a situation of narrative uncertainty that William, Love and Love label the 'persona gap' (2021), where a VR user becomes aware that they have adopted the viewpoint of a specific character but have little or no information about who that character is. For the remainder of the VR experience I embody Yathay's point of view, which allows me to access his memories as a first-person experience.

In the scenes that follow I am transported back in time to engage with Yathay's experience as a 33-year-old engineer inhabiting an SS-21 concentration camp under the Khmer Rouge regime. I initially find myself in a dark and cavernous outdoor space filled with burnt objects—old furniture, clothes, children's toys and twisted metal—and puddles of water under foot. Guided by buzzing haptic feedback in my hand controllers and highlighted icons that are displayed in the 360-degree space I am encouraged to pick up a small torch and shine it on the various objects: however, the torch light is dim, meaning that I must move close to items of interest in order to illuminate them. As such, I find myself up close to stacks of human bones, examining the blood stains that mark them. For director Victoria Bousis, this torch provides a means for audience immersion and education, as she explains:

> The viewer uses it to find artefacts and objects, but it is also an essential element of their narrative progression and education about Cambodian history and culture. In fact, the flashlight also invoked a feeling of exploration of the world and details based on actual places (i.e. the concentration camp of S-21). (Bousis quoted in Gayet, 2022, n.p)

I would contend that this interaction with the environment via the torch fosters an increased SoE, seeing as the activity furthers my sense of body ownership, agency and self-location. But moreover, it gives rise to strong feelings of unease and dread. I note that my interaction with the torch in the somewhat repellent space determines what I can actually see in front of me, which not only encourages a strong emotional response to the abhorrent subject matter, but also contributes to my sense of presence.

A study of VR user experience in both 'neutral' and 'emotional' environments that was conducted by Riva et al. (2007) sheds some more light on my embodied experience of this scene. They suggest that a 'sense of presence will be greater in [...] "emotional" environments: It is more likely that an environment that is able to elicit anxiety, relaxation, etc. could make users feel more present in that environment' (2007, p. 46). On a related note Gall et al. find that 'virtual embodiment increases the intensity of emotional responses to general virtual stimuli' (2021, p. 2). With this in mind I observe a clear link between my embodied experience, emotional response and sense of presence, which is fostered through the work's interactive device of the torch. As I explore the scene and illuminate its horrors, I do so from both my own and Yathay's point of view as a participant with the agency to explore, which fosters a sense of identification and feelings of empathy for the protagonist.

Gall et al. suggest that virtual body ownership influences social perception and specifically, the way that we identify with social groups (p. 2). With this in mind one might ponder the degree to which my ownership of Yathay's virtual body in *Stay Alive, My Son* (and adoption of his point of view of events) affects my understanding of the narrative and feelings of empathy for those affected by the terror of the Khmer's Rouge regime. By placing me within a virtual body and granting me 6DoF, this second work offers a more active narrative experience than that of *The Man Who Couldn't Leave*, seeing as I must directly interact with objects so as to drive the story forward. My virtual embodiment is therefore directly implicated in the conjuring of the narrative as well as my emotional response to the virtual stimuli.

Please, Believe Me *(2022)*

Please, Believe Me follows the story of American pediatric nurse and mother of one, Vicky Logan, who was diagnosed with Lyme disease in the 1990s. Logan was offered the standard treatment of a course of antibiotics, but failed to recover. One doctor stood by her while others in the medical field dismissed her ongoing symptoms and those of Lyme disease patients more broadly. The approximately 28-minute VR experience, which is available as a free download via the Oculus App Lab, seeks to explore why Lyme disease patients were not listened to as well as to highlight Logan's tragic case.

As with the second case study, *Please, Believe Me* offers 6DoF to the user and allows them to pick up objects within the virtual environment. *Whereas Stay Alive, My Son* uses controller-based locomotion to allow the user to glide through various 360-degree scenes (users can move around by manipulating the thumbsticks on their hand controllers), *Please, Believe Me* features a teleportation system of locomotion that is likewise controlled via the hand controllers. This eliminates the need for lengthy walking within a scene and rather, allows the user to quickly jump from one position to another within the virtual environment. This movement is limited to particular zones within the 360 space, however, which means that completely free exploration of virtual environments is not possible. While limiting, this design approach ensures that users are adequately positioned to receive narrative information and to engage with the interactive devices that move the narrative forward. My analysis will focus on key scenes that encourage a SoE for the user in the first half of the experience.

For the work's opening scene, I find myself in a darkened space that resembles a home office. I am positioned next to a large wooden desk upon which a 1990s era computer, keyboard and mouse rests alongside a box of files, framed photographs and other personal items (see Fig. 2.3). As with the previous case studies, my viewpoint of the scene is aligned with a natural human viewpoint of the environment, as though I am sitting at the desk. Noting a black office chair that sits empty beside me, I look down and see generic white hands as representations of my real hands. I use one of these to reach forward and retrieve a copy of Newsweek magazine from the desk, which features a cover story on Lyme disease. This story, titled 'Tiny Tick, Big Worry', is also displayed in an enlarged format in the space above the desk. As I study this, I see that one of the two framed photographs on the desk (of a young Nonny de la Peña, the director of the VR experience) has come to life. De la Peña makes eye contact with me as she explains that she was one of the writers of the 1990s Newsweek article. In this role of journalist she initially became aware of Vicky Logan. 'Soon after we published, something happened' de la Peña recalls. 'The medical community became dismissive of (Lyme disease) patients if they complained of symptoms after treatment with antibiotics'. After she outlines further information about the disease, the photo returns to its static form and the second framed photo, of Doctor Kenneth Liegner, then becomes animated. Liegner also makes eye contact with me as he explains his role as Logan's doctor and supporter. 'You only get a case like this once or twice in a career', he suggests. 'It was extremely well

Fig. 2.3 Screen capture from *Please, Believe Me*, directed and produced by Emblematic Group founder Nonny de la Peña and made in collaboration with Paper Crane games

documented. All (Vicky) wanted was to get well'. The scene ends with a return to de la Peña who recalls her determination to figure out the 'puzzle' of why Lyme disease patients like Vicky were dismissed by the medical establishment. An animated yellow puzzle piece then appears in the space above my head with an instruction to 'grab'. I reach up to do so, transferring the piece to an empty slot in a small puzzle board that floats nearby. This causes the scene to fade to black and a title sequence begins.

As with the previous two case studies, my positioning at a human vantage point within the scene would seem central in fostering a sense of presence in the virtual environment. The virtual hands, while generic, foster a degree of self-location, body ownership and agency, seeing as they allow me to engage with the magazine and puzzle piece in the virtual space. The testimony offered by de la Peña and Liegner might be viewed as a form of first-person address but I would contend that this does not foster an experience of social presence within the scene, seeing as their representation is contained within the photo frames, which locates them in a different diegetic space to that of the office. In other words, while I feel a sense of presence within the office space, I do not feel that the two speakers occupy this space alongside me as they deliver their testimony. Rather the experience is akin to watching interviews on a television screen, although I do so from within the virtual environment. In this way the photo frame device, as well as the enlarged display of the magazine article on the wall, delivers backstory in a fashion that is not dissimilar to a standard documentary. I complete the scene with the feeling that my perspective at the desk, as well as the puzzle mechanic, positions me as an investigator of Logan's case—someone who, like de la Peña, must (literally) assemble the pieces of a puzzle so as to understand the story.

Later I find myself in a darkened environment that combines indoors and outdoor elements. The space initially resembles that of a public library, with large bookshelves, filing cabinets and a collection of vintage televisions resting on a linoleum floor. Within seconds, however, tall trees and patches of undergrowth burst through the flooring, creating a type of forest around the shelves. Three abstracted deers wander within this environment, grazing on foliage somewhat indifferently as I teleport about the space to explore its qualities. After a few moments the various televisions come to life in turn, each displaying documentary footage that further illuminates Lyme disease, and specifically, how it is contracted from ticks that also infect animals. A voice instructs me to look at my hands. I do so, finding a black tick stuck to the back of the right one. I attempt repeatedly to brush this off with my left hand, but the system allows me no ability to do so. Instead I can only watch as a red ring that indicates infection appears around the tick (see Fig. 2.4).

This is a powerful moment in the VR experience, in which the experience of contracting Lyme disease is made personal for me as user. Although I am cognisant of the virtual nature of the experience and therefore know that I am not in any danger, my inability to remove the tick from the back of my hand nonetheless gives rise to a feeling of unease. I would argue that

Fig. 2.4 Screen capture from *Please, Believe Me*, directed and produced by Emblematic Group founder Nonny de la Peña and made in collaboration with Paper Crane games

my sense of ownership of the generic white hands, and subsequent embodied experience of the scene is key here.

The powerful effects of body ownership illusions (described by Kilteni et al. as 'the illusory perception of non-bodily objects (e.g., artificial limbs) as being parts of one's own body and as being the source of the associated bodily sensations, such as touch' (2015, p. 2)] have been evidenced in studies conducted over several decades (e.g. Armel & Ramachandran, 2003; Botvinick & Cohen, 1998; Ehrsson et al., 2007; Giummarra et al.,

2010; Tastevin, 1937).[7] In their well-known experiment, Botvinick and Cohen orchestrated a rubber hand illusion, whereby healthy adults had one hand hidden from view whilst viewing a 'replacement' rubber hand that was positioned in a similar posture in close proximity to the hidden hand. When both rubber and real hands were stroked simultaneously for some time, the majority of participants in the study reported a perception that the touch was coming from the rubber hand, as though it was a part of their own body (1998). Following this experiment Ehrsson et al., conducted a study in which participants were encouraged to experience a rubber hand as their own and then registered anxious responses to seeing it stabbed with a needle (2007). More recently, Pilacinski et al. (2023) suggest that virtual reality users might experience a 'phantom touch illusion' which involves the sensation of touch without physical contact. This discovery is based on a study of 36 users who experienced a tingling sensation when virtually self-touching their own bodies. Like the earlier studies, this VR experiment evidences the complex links between the brain's multisensory processing and bodily representations (illusionary or real).

These studies of body ownership illusions (virtual or otherwise) shed light on my feeling of unease when noticing the tick stuck to the back of my virtual hand in *Please, Believe Me.* Returning to Hickey-Moody's definition of affect as a visceral phenomenon that comes 'in between feelings and changes to what you can do' (p. 79), I would suggest that my impulse to try to brush the tick away is an affective response that stems from my prior life experience and a real fear of contracting disease. According to this logic, my unease as I am unable to remove the tick results from a feeling of danger, even though I'm aware on a cognitive level that the virtual hand is not my own.

This anxiety returns moments later in the VR experience when I am presented with the task of passing three objects (a sphere, cube and a triangular prism) through corresponding-shaped holes in a wooden board. This activity emerges at the tail end of a scene in Doctor Liegner's office, where he speaks of Lyme disease patients' range of symptoms and the dismissal of these by medical practitioners. The realistically rendered Liegner makes direct eye contact as he speaks to me from behind a large wooden desk, an action that gives rise to a sense of social presence. This physical positioning in the room aligns me with the role of 'patient', a

[7] For a comprehensive overview of studies of body ownership illusions, see Kilteni et al. (2015).

notion that I digest based on my lived experience of medical appointments in which I have found myself seated opposite a doctor. The sense that I am a patient is reinforced when the wooden puzzle appears on Liegner's desk as a 'test' for me to complete. He watches as I attempt to line up each object with its corresponding hole (i.e. the cube with the square hole or the sphere with the circular hole), but I find that the objects randomly change shape as I move them, so that a match is impossible. I change my approach to try to anticipate the changes to the objects but this action also fails. Regardless of my efforts, I am not able to succeed with the task. In other words, while my hand controllers grant me some degree of agency to pick up objects, the system ultimately controls my ability to manipulate these objects. This physical activity, and the negative emotions that it generates, are no doubt intended to provide an embodied understanding of Logan's experience as a patient caught up in an antagonistic medical system. In this way the VR experience acts upon me, generating emotional and physiological responses to the virtual stimuli.

Please, Believe Me thus positions the user in dual roles: as investigator of Lyme disease treatment but also a sufferer of the disease who gains insight into Logan's experience. Interactive devices (such as the tick on the hand) encourage the user to identify with Logan's journey of infection, diagnosis and treatment on a bodily level. These moments of affective storytelling are important to communicate the sense of frustration, helplessness and despair that Logan must have felt as a sufferer. In contrast, other scenes offer a more objective delivery of information related to the disease. Similarly to *Stay Alive, My Son*, the project's user cannot change the outcome of the story; however, their interaction with story agents is required to propel the narrative forward.

Conclusion

The three case studies that are analysed in this chapter display contrasting approaches to the representation of the interactor as a virtual body. One can observe an invisible avatar (*The Man Who Couldn't Leave*); a partially represented body with generic hands (*Please, Believe Me*); or the appearance of a specific character's body that is likewise only partially represented (*Stay Alive, My Son*). These varying approaches to body representation have consequences for the user's ability to interact with the storyworld using hand controllers, which is not possible in the case of the 360-degree video work. Moreover, the varying approaches have consequences for the user's sense of presence and embodiment, as well as for their identification with a predetermined character, although one must note the contribution of other factors in this regard. The user's placement within Yathay's physically represented body (or arms, to be specific) in *Stay Alive, My Son* most obviously aligns them with this defined character's point of view and bodily experience; however, a user identification with the character of Vicky Logan is achieved in *Please, Believe Me* through the physical positioning and treatment of the generic body within scenes (e.g. experiencing a tick on the hand or being spoken to by a doctor, as described above). A user's sense of embodiment then seems to be the result of a complex interplay between bodily representation (or absence of representation), user positioning and the staging of action in the 360-degree space in these narrative-based VR works.

Regardless of the varying body representations that are featured in the case studies, I would contend that the user experiences a sense of self-presence within each virtual environment, viewing events with their own eyes and responding to stimuli based on their lived experience. One can observe that across all three projects, the user is positioned at a human vantage point within the virtual environment, which fosters a sense of physical presence. Moreover, the user's acknowledgement as 'present' by characters who make eye contact or engage them through direct address in the early scenes of all three projects generates powerful feelings of social presence in the realistically rendered environments, and further encourages an embodied understanding of the narrative material. This chapter's analysis of the three projects thus suggests that a virtual body representation is not a prerequisite for powerful corporeal engagement with a VR work.

One can observe that the three projects seek to engage their users in bodily movement through the staging of action across multiple quadrants of 360-degree space, through their play with interactive devices and/or by offering somewhat free exploration of virtual environments. The interactive devices described above might be viewed as tools for the generation of emotional and embodied experience, which impact upon the user's overall narrative understanding; however, these devices do not allow the user to affect the narrative itself. It is notable that all three projects involve somewhat linear narratives that play out to a fixed conclusion. With this in mind one might consider the staging of action within each work (as well as the interactive devices featured in the second and third case study) as a series of visceral prompts designed to engage their audience in embodied sensemaking.

While varied, the three case study projects that are given time in this chapter demonstrate but a few of the many possible approaches to body representation in VR storytelling. Further research might explore the narrative impact of works featuring full body representations, or the representations of other body parts in a broader range of projects. The implications of specific stylistic choices (such as camera positioning and the staging of actors) on user embodiment are also worthy of further investigation through empirical inquiry. Such work can highlight the powerful ways that VR stories affect us, and offer intelligence for practitioners seeking to create enhanced experiences of embodiment.

References

Armel, K. C., & Ramachandran, V. S. (2003). Projecting sensations to external objects: Evidence from skin conductance response. *Proceedings of the Royal Society of London. Series B: Biological Sciences, 270*(1523), 1499–1506.

Aylett, R., & Louchart, S. (2003). Towards a narrative theory of virtual reality. *Virtual Reality, 7*(1), 2–9.

Biocca, F. (1997). The cyborg's dilemma: Progressive embodiment in virtual environments. *Journal of Computer-Mediated Communication, 3*(2), JCMC324.

Bolter, J. D., Engberg, M., & MacIntyre, B. (2021). *Reality media: Augmented and virtual reality*. MIT Press.

Botvinick, M., & Cohen, J. (1998). Rubber hands 'feel' touch that eyes see. *Nature, 391*(6669), 756–756.

Coleridge, S. T. (1960). *Biographia literaria or biographical sketches of my literary life and opinions*. J. M. Dent. (Original work published 1817).

Csordas, T. J. (1999). Embodiment and cultural phenomenology. In G. Wiess & H. F. Haber (Eds.), *Perspectives on embodiment: The intersections of nature and culture* (pp. 143–164). Routledge.

Dooley, K. (2020). A question of proximity: Exploring a new screen grammar for 360-degree cinematic virtual reality. *Media Practice and Education, 21*(2), 81–96.

Ehrsson, H. H., Wiech, K., Weiskopf, N., Dolan, R. J., & Passingham, R. E. (2007). Threatening a rubber hand that you feel is yours elicits a cortical anxiety response. *Proceedings of the National Academy of Sciences, 104*(23), 9828–9833.

Gall, D., Roth, D., Stauffert, J. P., Zarges, J., & Latoschik, M. E. (2021). Embodiment in virtual reality intensifies emotional responses to virtual stimuli. *Frontiers in Psychology, 12*, 674179.

Gayet, M. (2022, October 6). Changing the world: the challenges of STAY ALIVE MY SON. *XR Must.* Retrieved November 21, 2023, from https://www.xrmust.com/xrmagazine/victoria-bousis-stay-alive-my-son/

Giummarra, M. J., Georgiou-Karistianis, N., Nicholls, M. E., Gibson, S. J., & Bradshaw, J. L. (2010). The phantom in the mirror: A modified rubber-hand illusion in amputees and normals. *Perception, 39*(1), 103–118.

Hickey-Moody, A. (2013). Affect as method: Feelings, aesthetics and affective pedagogy. *Deleuze and research methodologies*, 79–95.

Hummels, C., & Van Dijk, J. (2015, January). Seven principles to design for embodied sensemaking. In *Proceedings of the ninth international conference on tangible, embedded, and embodied interaction* (pp. 21–28).

Kilteni, K., Groten, R., & Slater, M. (2012). The sense of embodiment in virtual reality. *Presence: Teleoperators and Virtual Environments, 21*(4), 373–387.

Kilteni, K., Maselli, A., Kording, K. P., & Slater, M. (2015). Over my fake body: Body ownership illusions for studying the multisensory basis of own-body perception. *Frontiers in Human Neuroscience, 9*, 141.

Lee, K. M. (2004). Presence, explicated. *Communication Theory, 14*(1), 27–50.

Lombard, M., & Ditton, T. (1997). At the heart of it all: The concept of presence. *Journal of Computer-Mediated Communication, 3*(2), JCMC321. https://academic.oup.com/jcmc/article/3/2/JCMC321/4080403

Marcolin, F., Wally Scurati, G., Ulrich, L., Nonis, F., Vezzetti, E., Dozio, N., Ferrise, F., Stork, A., & Basole, R. C. (2021). Affective virtual reality: How to design artificial experiences. *IEEE Computer Graphics and Applications, 41*(6), 171–178. https://pubmed.ncbi.nlm.nih.gov/34890316/

Matthews, E. (2014). Maurice Merleau-Ponty: Phenomenology of perception. In J. Shand (Ed.), *Central works of philosophy* (Vol. 4, pp. 177–194). Routledge New York.

Merleau-Ponty, M. (2012). *The phenomenology of perception* (D. Landes, Trans.). Routledge.

Murphy, D. (2017). Bodiless embodiment: A descriptive survey of avatar bodily coherence in first-wave consumer vr applications. In *2017 IEEE virtual reality (VR)* (pp. 265–266). IEEE.

Palma Stade, T., Schofield, G., & Moore, G. (2023). Narrative perspectives and embodiment in cinematic virtual reality. In *International conference on extended reality* (pp. 232–252). Springer Nature.

Pilacinski, A., Metzler, M., & Klaes, C. (2023). Phantom touch illusion: Unexpected phenomenological effects of tactile gating in the absence of tactile stimulation. *bioRxiv*, 2023–02.

Please, Believe Me. (2022). Dir. Nonny de la Peña. United States.

Popat, S. (2016). Missing in action: Embodied experience and virtual reality. *Theatre Journal, 68*(3), 357–378. https://doi.org/10.1353/tj.2016.0071

Riva, G., Mantovani, F., Capideville, C., Preziosa, A., Morganti, F., Villani, D., Gaggioli, A., Botella, C., & Alcañiz Raya, M. (2007). Affective interactions using virtual reality: The link between presence and emotions. In *Cyberpsychology & Behavior: The impact of the internet, multimedia and virtual reality on behavior and society* (Vol. 10, pp. 45–56). https://doi.org/10.1089/cpb.2006.9993

Ryan, M.-L. (2001). *Narrative as virtual reality. Immersion and interactivity in literature and electronic media.* The Johns Hopkins University Press.

Saker, M., & Frith, J. (2020). Coextensive space: Virtual reality and the developing relationship between the body, the digital and physical space. *Media, Culture & Society, 42*(7–8), 1427–1442.

Shaviro, S. (2010). *Post cinematic affect.* John Hunt Publishing.

Sheridan, T. B. (1992). Musings on telepresence and virtual presence. *Presence: Teleoperators and Virtual Environments, 1*, 120–126.

Shin, D. (2018). Empathy and embodied experience in virtual environment: To what extent can virtual reality stimulate empathy and embodied experience? *Computers in Human Behavior, 78*, 64–73.

Slater, M. (2009). Place illusion and plausibility can lead to realistic behaviour in immersive virtual environments. *Philosophical Transactions of the Royal Society B: Biological Sciences, 364*(1535), 3549–3557.

Sobchack, V. (2004). *Carnal thoughts: Embodiment and moving image culture.* Univ of California Press.

Spinoza, B. (2001). *Ethics.* Wadsworth.

Stay Alive, My Son. (2022). Dir. Victoria Bousis. United States.

Steuer, J., Biocca, F., & Levy, M. R. (1995). Defining virtual reality: Dimensions determining telepresence. *Communication in the age of virtual reality, 33*, 37–39.

Tastevin, J. (1937). En partant de l'expérience d'Aristote les déplacements artificiels des parties du corps ne sont pas suivis par le sentiment de ces parties ni par les sensations qu'on peut y produire. *L'Encéphale: Revue de psychiatrie clinique biologique et thérapeutique.*

Tham, J., Duin, A. H., Gee, L., Ernst, N., Abdelqader, B., & McGrath, M. (2018). Understanding virtual reality: Presence, embodiment, and professional practice. *IEEE Trans. Profession. Commun., 61*(2), 178–195. https://doi.org/10.1109/TPC.2018.2804238

The Man Who Couldn't Leave. (2022). Dir. Singing Chen. Taiwan.

The Man Who Couldn't Leave (Trailer). (2022, August 30). Published on YouTube by Kaohsiung Film Festival. https://www.youtube.com/watch?v=JK5MLoJpAK4&t=40s

Williams, E., Love, C., & Love, M. (2021). *Virtual reality cinema: Narrative tips and techniques.* Routledge.

CHAPTER 3

Virtual Reality Narration: Listening to and Reliving Stories Through First-Person Testimony

Introduction

In 2021, the Grand Jury Prize for Best VR Immersive Work at the Venice VR-Expanded competition (a sidebar of the Venice International Film Festival) was awarded to *Goliath: Playing with Reality* (dirs. Barry Gene Murphy and May Abdalla 2021). This approximately 25-minute game engine-driven VR work explores the experience of a young man with schizophrenia (named Jon but known online as Goliath) who was committed to a psychiatric facility for several years, but eventually left and found solace in the playing of online multiplayer games. Based on a true story, *Goliath* allows the user to share the narrator's troubled headspace, and to relive his memories through observation and simulated game play. Additional interactive devices encourage the user to question their own understanding of reality within the virtual and 'real' world. Throughout the work, a non-visualised female narrator (Tilda Swinton) addresses the interactor directly, encouraging them to use their voice and visually represented hands, and to question their everyday reality. Speaking about this aspect of the work in a *Voices of VR* podcast, co-director May Abdalla comments that

> We just wanted there to be moments where it wasn't merely a story about Jon and his life. It's also a story about you and the things that you notice,

The original version of the chapter has been revised. A correction to this chapter can be found at https://doi.org/10.1007/978-3-031-64965-3_9

K. Dooley, *Virtual Reality Narratives*,
https://doi.org/10.1007/978-3-031-64965-3_3

> the things that you don't notice [...]. Those moments where the narrator kind of cuts through that story [...], it's a bit risky because it effectively is breaking immersion [...]. (Quoted in Bye, 2021)

Such an approach, Abdalla suggests, might reflect a maturing of VR storytelling: 'I feel like we don't need to be protective of VR, convincing you that it's real, which I feel like a lot of projects in the early days, [...] didn't want to break the fourth wall because you wanted to allow people to "fall for it"' (quoted in Bye, 2021). This observation on the changing nature of narration for VR, defined here as the process or style of telling a story, points to the range of approaches that practitioners might take to foster an embodied experience for the user. I use the term 'embodied' here to describe the corporeal experience of feeling present in a virtual environment as a physically manifested or invisible avatar. In the case of *Goliath*, the insertion of a non-diegetic narrator who directly addresses the user, alongside narration from a diegetic protagonist, is a complex style of narration that draws attention to the user's dual existence in virtual and non-virtual worlds.

This third chapter explores narration in contemporary VR storytelling through an analysis of three documentary-based works, including *Goliath: Playing with Reality*. Specifically, the chapter interrogates the affective communication of first-person testimony in VR experiences by examining the inclusion of voice over narration and game devices to engage the user. Additionally, user positioning in relation to story agents will be explored. My interrogation of these areas seeks to uncover the specificity of narration for VR media, considering the role of the user as a body placed in the storyworld.

In terms of classical narratology, 'narration' denotes the individual or entity that we perceive as the origin of the information being conveyed. While narration for cinema, defined by Bordwell et al. as 'the moment-by-moment process that guides viewers in building the story out of the plot' (Bordwell et al., 2016, p. 87) has received significant analysis, few studies to date have explored techniques in the context of VR storytelling, considering narrative point of view and the user as participant. To investigate these areas, I present a close reading and narrative analysis of the three recent VR works with reference to prior explorations of narration for VR (Dolan & Parets, 2016; Mateer, 2017; Nicolae, 2018; Weaving, 2021) and its antecedent media. Regarding the latter, I discuss 'voice' and 'focalisation', two key concepts explored by literary theorist Gerard Genette

(1980). On 'voice' he poses the question who narrates and from where and suggests the options of the 'intra-diegetic' (narration from inside the storyworld) and the 'extra-diegetic' (narration from outside of the storyworld). Using the term 'focalisation', he asks 'who sees?' or in other words, whose point of view and understanding of events orders the narrative perspective (1980, p. 186). This seminal work on approaches to narration in literary or cinema contexts presents a useful means through which to draw out the key aspects of VR narration, considering the modes of interaction offered to the user, and moreover, to isolate the specificity of VR as an embodied medium.

The chapters' three case studies have been chosen for their diverse approaches to VR narration and VR storytelling in general. Two of the case studies appear in the Meta 'VR for Good' program, a collection of works commissioned with the intention of advancing social movements and expanding understanding of people and cultures around the world (Meta 2022). The first is the aforementioned *Goliath: Playing with Reality*, which offers a number of game-like interactive devices within an environment that enables six degrees of freedom (6DoF), meaning that the user has the ability to rotate their view and physically move around space. The second case study, *We Live Here* (dir. Rose Troche 2020), explores the testimony of Rockey, a middle-aged woman experiencing homelessness in Los Angeles. This game engine-driven VR experience takes the user into Rockey's tent, where they can activate objects that tell her life story. This also offers 6DoF as defined above. Both *Goliath* and *We Live Here* foster reflection on the individual protagonists' daily struggles. In contrast, the third case study, *Sorella's Story* (dir. Peter Hegedus, 2022), is a 15-minute live-action VR experience that recreates the final moments of a group of Jewish women killed in the Latvian Holocaust in 1941. This is an experience offering three degrees of freedom (3DoF), meaning that the viewer can rotate their head to choose a field of vision from a fixed position in space. This work that premiered at the 2022 Venice Immersive festival, is based on a found photograph of ten-year-old Sorella Epstein, who becomes the narrator of the story. All three of the case studies feature a narrative that plays out to a fixed and predetermined ending, meaning that while they offer differing levels of interactivity, it is not possible to alter the narrative outcome. I experienced all three works using a Meta Quest 2 headset at a film festival and/or in my home.

The chapter will interrogate the way that voiceover narration is used to relay experience and/or to encourage user interaction and reflection in these works. In the case of *Goliath and We Live Here*, character narration sits alongside that of a non-diegetic narrator, so that the user receives multiple forms of address, the ramifications of which will be discussed. The chapter will also interrogate the positioning of the user's body in each work, and how this shapes interaction with the story agents.

User Positioning in VR

Regardless of whether a VR work offers 3DoF or 6DoF to user, when viewed through a head mounted display unit (HMD), the user is positioned at the centre of the 360-degree storyworld. Perhaps with this in mind, Laurel argues that 'VR is utterly a first-person point-of-view medium' (2014, p. 184). Nash agrees and suggests that 'in locating the spectator imaginatively "within" a simulated space, albeit with varying degrees of intensity, VR creates an experience of physical "navigation" fostered via the turn of their head or the movement of a mouse' (2018a, p. 97). Furthermore, with reference to Gunkel (2000) and Manovich (2001), Nash notes that this means that contemporary VR stories involve a shift from representation to simulation, which is 'fundamental to VR's moral force' (2018b, p. 123). On this subject Manovich describes spatial simulation in VR as occurring whenever 'the scale of a representation is the same as the scale of our human world so that the two spaces are continuous' (2001, p. 112). This means that the spectator explores a physical space that has no rectangular framed boundary, as is the case for traditional screen media (p. 112). In doing so, they can occupy a number of viewing positions, including the point of view of a character.

As I've explored elsewhere (Dooley, 2021), several scholars (Dolan & Parets, 2016; Mateer, 2017; Nicolae, 2018; Vosmeer & Schouten, 2017) have explored this viewer positioning within VR experiences, with some corresponding findings. Mateer refers to two viewer perspectives: the first-person role that might involve direct address from story characters, and the third-person role that might see more objective observation of narrative events (2017). Nicolae considers the former to be a 'hero' perspective, which 'puts the spectator at the heart not only of the filmic space, but also at the heart of the story, much like it would happen in a video game of sorts – regardless of the level of interactivity' (2018, p. 174). On this point, Weaving aptly notes that this perspective known as 'first-person' in gaming and cinema contexts actually corresponds with the literary category of second person: '"you" or the reader's perspective' (p. 154). This is a useful observation in the sense that within a VR story, agents might speak directly to 'you', the user. Conversely, for Nicolae, the third-person perspective is akin to being a 'witness', where 'the spectator takes part in the film events as a digital specter / silent avatar – at the heart of the filmic space but not at the heart of the events –, where no character is aware of their "presence"' (2018, p. 174). Vosmeer and Schouten similarly describe a third-person 'fly on the wall-perspective' (2017, p. 4).

Moreover, Nicolae identifies an additional perspective that she describes as the 'impersonator', this being the 'spectator's perspective *within* the body of a character – literally, the body of the character is visible in the film and sometimes so is the gender – and in some cases even the face is visible if there are shots that show the character in a reflective surface' (2018, p. 175). One could argue that the 'impersonator' is a variation of the 'hero' perspective, seeing as both involve direct interaction with narrative content; however, the former requires the user to adopt the viewpoint of a defined character or 'other'. Taking a different stance, Weaving argues that the VR viewer is 'always a witness, and is either acknowledged or not, and can become partially visible due to rendering of body parts' (2021, p. 154). He thus offers a user positioning taxonomy of invisible witness, acknowledged witness and embodied witness, the last of which corresponds with Nicolae's 'impersonator' position. Weaving notes that the viewer as 'embodied witness' occupies an unusual position in 3DoF works of having a virtual body that they have no agency to control. The potential frustration of this position, and that of a viewer occupying the first-person perspective in 3DoF works more generally is also noted by Larsen (2018), who observes a problematic lack of agency. As remedy, he argues for a 'second-person sidekick' role for a viewer, which situates them at the side of a protagonist who drives the story as per a cinema narrative.

Much of the theorising above takes place in the context of discussions of cinematic virtual reality (CVR) (Mateer, Vosmeer & Schouten, Weaving) or 'narrative virtual reality' (Larsen), which generally involves experiences that offer 3DoF and/or limited interactive devices (Dooley, 2021). Taking a slightly different approach, Dolan and Parets (2016) present an analysis of user positioning that is applicable to more interactive forms of VR, as well as 360-degree video. They identify four positions that centre around differing levels of interaction and the user's ability to influence the story outcome—the observant active, observant passive, participant active and participant passive. Looking firstly at the two passive positions, I note that the 'observant passive' position accords with Nicolae's 'witness' role, where 'the viewer simply watches dramatic or comedic events unfold in a procedural manner' (2016). This would somewhat resemble the traditional cinema experience where 'the viewer does not exist in the story's universe and cannot impose any influence on its events' (2016). As for the 'hero' position described above, Dolan and Parets propose the 'participant passive' perspective as 'a relatively new form in which the viewer exists in the world as a character, or a story device, but the story does not ask anything of the viewer, or permit them to inform the course of events' (2016). These two positions are applicable to many CVR experiences. By contrast, the two 'active' positions described by Dolan and Parets involve additional interactive devices where 'the viewer is given a share of the storyteller's power to affect the outcome of the story's events' (2016). The 'observant active' position grants the viewer 'God-like decision-making power', to influence the direction of the narrative although this is 'limited by a predetermined set of choices (nodes) laid out by the storyteller, by which the storyteller has construed a variety of outcomes' (2016). This might, for example, take the form of a 'choose your own adventure' style story, the multiple ending of which have been predetermined by the work's creator. I would suggest that VR experiences adopting this approach to narrative exist across the spectrum of those offering 3DoF and 6DoF. Lastly, the 'participant active' position allows the viewer to exist in the world as a character or story device, and to influence the story in a more bespoke way. While 'the viewer interacts with the world and is bound by its laws and underlying story', they also have 'the ability to go off on a tangent, but the story will reset, adapt, or evolve based upon certain parameters' (2016). This model, Dolan and Parets propose, aligns with video games such as *Grand Theft Auto*, which present a universe for the user to explore. This last category might be best aligned with VR experiences that offer 6DoF to the user, enabling exploration and interaction using hand controllers within certain parameters.

My own taxonomy of user positioning for VR acknowledges Newton & Soukup's observation that 'having a body (in VR) means being somebody. There is no such thing as a neutral observer' (2016). In other words, the user's position *within* the storyworld casts them as a character of sorts in the unfolding narrative, even if they are not acknowledged as such, or have no ability to interact with narrative content. On this subject, Newton & Soukup refer to an experiment where VR users were dropped into a classroom scene as invisible, passive observers, finding that those positioned among students identified with this role, while those positioned at the front of the class identified with the lecturer role. This observation is not incongruous with Weaving's view that all VR viewers are witnesses but moreover, suggests that all viewers (as bodies) adopt an embodied role within the narrative world, despite whether they are positioned in the visually represented body of a defined character. Thus, there is no 'third-person' user position. Rather, the user participates by viewing through their own eyes (user as character) or by adopting a predefined character's point of view. Taking these points into consideration, my own taxonomy proposes the two positions of 'observer' and 'explorer' for the VR user (either of which may or may not be physically manifested and acknowledged by story agents) and considers other factors, such as degrees of agency and representation in relation to these roles (see Table 3.1). The key difference between the two positions is the user's ability to interact with story agents and move through space, which may or may not influence the outcome of the narrative. While these differing abilities are somewhat aligned with the affordances of 3DoF and 6DoF technologies (e.g. 360-video vs free roam VR), this is not always the case. Some 3DoF works may include branching narratives and/or other interactive devices (e.g. interaction based on head tracking) that allows the user to influence the outcome of the narrative. Considering the diversity of contemporary VR

Table 3.1 User roles within VR narratives

User role	*Observer*	*Explorer*
Representation within the narrative	Non-visualised, not acknowledged by story agents or Non-visualised, acknowledged or Visualised, acknowledged	Non-visualised, not acknowledged by story agents or Non-visualised, acknowledged or Visualised, acknowledged
Perspective	Own (user as character) Or An authored character	Own (user as character) Or An authored character
Agency within the narrative	Fixed position in space, no ability to interact with story agents	No ability to explore space (typically 3DoF) but can interact with story agents via other interactive devices or Ability to explore space (typically 6DoF) and to interact with story agents
Potential to impact upon the narrative	No	Yes

narratives, my taxonomy therefore presents general principles for consideration.

This taxonomy foregrounds the centrality of the user to the VR narrative—as observer or explorer at the centre of the storyworld—and reinforces the first-person perspective of the medium. With this in mind, I would propose that a user immersed in a VR narrative is commonly implicated in what Genette labels the 'internal focalisation' of the story as the one 'who sees' (1980). Genette proposes three distinct types of focalisation that have been used as tools for analysis of older media: Non-focalisation, internal focalisation and external focalisation (1980, p. 189). Non-focalisation relates to a narrative that is presented with '*zero focalization*' (1980, p, 189) or in other words, where events are presented from an omniscient point of view, thus granting the reader/viewer access to all narrative information. Internal focalisation occurs when events are seen and understood from the point of view of a specific character, hence restricting some story information (p. 189). This may involve access to a specific character's inner thoughts. By contrast, external focalisation sees an objective telling of story events through actions and speech only, and allows for little insight into a character's inner world (p. 191). As Allison notes, Genette's concept of focalisation is similar to that of perspective but also considers the selective presentation of narrative information in relation to the experience and understanding of characters within the diegesis (2015). In other words, 'whereas perspective describes the position from which a story is observed, focalization describes what can be observed as compared to a character' (Allison, p. 2).

On the one hand I would suggest that all three of Genette's categories of focalisation are possible within the context of VR narratives. One could understand a narrative from the perspective of a particular character whose inner thoughts are delivered by voice over (internal focalisation) or based on a character's behaviours and spoken dialogue only (external focalisation) or via an omniscient point of view of several characters (non-focalisation). However, I would argue that Genette's concept of focalisation, when applied to VR storytelling, is complicated by the positioning of the user within the storyworld as an observer or explorer character. In the sense that the user exists within the diegesis, and ingests material from their own unique perspective, their actions as a participant with agency are implicated in a form of internal focalisation. Narrative information is restricted to what the user (as active participant) sees and hears, and story information might be missed if, for example, the user is not looking in the right direction at the right time. There is thus a dual process of focalisation at work, concerning the user as character (internal focalisation) and the perspectives of other characters that the user interacts with (internal, external or non-focalisation).

Bal reinterprets Genette's theory and proposes the term 'focaliser' to describe the specific character who experiences and ingests narrative information (2009), suggesting that internal focalisation concerns a character who 'participates in the fabula as an actor' (2009, p. 152). This reinterpretation equates the concept of focalisation more squarely with that of perspective. In other words, for Bal, the focaliser is the character or agent whose point of view orders the narrative. This notion of 'focaliser' can be more closely aligned with the user of VR narratives who perceives and ingests narrative material from their position within the storyworld. I therefore adopt the term in my case study analysis later in this chapter. In doing so I do not wish to suggest that the user's experience as focaliser is not aligned with a particular story protagonist. Such a phenomenon is particularly the case when the user is privy to the thoughts and feelings of a story protagonist who might speak to them directly or through voice over. In a work with this structure, the narrator of a story informs the experience and perspective of the user as a focaliser but ultimately, the user sees from their own perspective as an entity positioned within the storyworld.

The Position of the Narrator

The question of who narrates a work, Genette suggests, is not to be confused with the question of 'who sees?' As stated above, he uses the term 'voice' to explore the location of the narrator, positing that narrators as characters might be 'homodiegetic' (visualised within the storyworld and recounting their own story) or 'heterodiegetic' (non-visualised and recounting a story in which they do not take part) (1980, p. 245). While the latter sits outside the story diegesis, it remains a part of the narrative experience. Genette suggests two varieties of homodiegetic narrators: 'one where the narrator is the hero of his narrative [...] and one where he plays only a secondary role, which almost always turns out to be a role as observer and witness' (1980, p. 245). In the context of VR, this is not to be confused with the viewer as observer or witness (the focaliser). Moreover, narration might occur in two different ways when considering the teller and the story being told, the first being 'extradiegetic' (narration is offered from outside of the storyworld) and the second being 'intradiegetic' (narration comes from within the storyworld) (1980, p. 248). In her exploration of this area in the context of screenplay writing, Igelstrom observes that 'a narrator that exists on the extradiegetic level must be heterodiegetic since a narrator on the extradiegetic level is outside the story' (2014, p. 55). I would argue that, as is the case for antecedent media such as film and television, VR experiences can contain any of these narrating voices suggested by Genette, and that multiple narrating voices can be present within a single work.

In the analysis that follows, I seek to isolate approaches to user and narrator positioning, adopting Bal and Genette's terms as points of reference. As the three case studies are reasonably lengthy (running between 15–30 minutes each) I will centre my analysis on key elements within each experience, while also attempting to convey a sense of the overall narratives.

Case Studies

Goliath: Playing with Reality

In the opening sequence of Goliath, I find myself in a dark, void-like, computer-generated environment that has a video game aesthetic. Purple and grey fragments swirl upwards at my sides as an unknown female narrator addresses me directly. 'The mind is a mysterious place. Everyone's works a little differently. 'Tell me your name', she says. I speak my name into my HMD and it is immediately repeated back to me. Happy with this recording, I press a green button to continue. The female voice returns, acknowledging the darkness and encouraging me to look at my hands. I do so and see that they are illuminated in the darkness. A thin line appears between them and a caterpillar-like creature shuffles across this. A moment later I can use buttons on my hand controllers to produce dull sounds. Then the representation of my hands changes, firstly to a sphere and a triangle, meaning that I lose the ability to activate sounds, and secondly, to show a bright pink balancing game that rests on top of my right hand. This game involves keeping a square platform horizontal so as to guide a small ball into the centre. I play this for some seconds, before it shatters and disappears. The female voice states that 'reality is just a story after all. It's what we tell ourselves to make sense of the world. Some stories are not true. This one is. This is the story of Goliath, told from inside his mind'.

This opening sequence presents a number of onboarding activities, allowing the user to acclimate to the VR storyworld and identifying key buttons for future use on the hand controllers. But moreover, it allows the user to settle into their virtual body, of which only the hands are visualised. Existing studies have revealed the power of VR to use first-person perspective to create the illusion of 'body swapping' or 'body transfer' (i.e. of inhabiting an other's 'virtual body') (Petkova & Ehrsson, 2008; Slater et al., 2010). Although the majority of my CGI body is not visible in *Goliath*, this illusion comes into play in this opening sequence. I look down and move my virtual hand to play the balancing game, even though I know it is an illusion. De la Peña et al. (2010) remind us that people 'tend to respond realistically to virtual situations and events even though they know that these are not real' and that this occurs even in situations where levels of fidelity and/or realism in regard to representations of physical reality are reduced (p. 293). But, as is noted in the introduction to this chapter, as I immerse myself in *Goliath*'s virtual world and respond to the stimuli that is offered, the female voice cuts through the diegesis to remind me that what I am seeing is an illusion. This reminder of the dual worlds that I occupy (real and virtual), reinforces the protagonist's journey through many worlds as he experiences mental illness and discovers online gaming.

The opening sequence introduces a heterodiegetic narrator (a nameless, non-visualised person who sits outside of the storyworld) who, as a guide, speaks directly to the user throughout the experience. In the following sequence, we meet Goliath, a homodiegetic narrator whose life experience is at the centre of the work and who is visualised in a variety of forms throughout. The dark environment of this sequence is illuminated by brightly coloured neon lines and flashes of light as Goliath's voice fades in: 'I don't tell anyone about this shit ... My fuckin head's just fucked'. Several streams of small cubes rise up around me. Using my hand controllers, I can put a blue neon loop around these, which tunes me into information streams (more voice over) of people talking about the symptoms and effects of Schizophrenia. I explore this for several seconds before Goliath's voice re-enters. He recalls his diagnosis of Schizophrenia, and his recovery via gaming. 'People call me Goliath and I'm a gamer. It's the gaming and streaming that saved me', he states. At this point a 1980s arcade-style video appears before me and I am encouraged to use my hand controller as a joy stick to navigate through a game illustrating his

Fig. 3.1 The user plays a retro arcade game that illustrates Goliath's early life experience in *Goliath: Playing with Reality* (2021). (Courtesy of Anagram)

pre-diagnosis life journey (see Fig. 3.1). Goliath recalls his childhood, being kicked out of school, self-destructive fighting and his entry into the DJ scene. In parallel, I navigate a 2D video game avatar of Goliath across several game screens, trying to avoid, respectively, school yard bullies, fight opponents on city streets and then pills and dancers in a nightclub. This is one of several 'gameplay' moments when I could be seen to occupy Goliath's point of view. I'm simultaneously offered a representation of his childhood (within the 2D game), and the experience of reliving his childhood as an arcade gamer, which is a highly immersive experience.

In his exploration of digital games, Calleja emphasises the medium's potential to affect players emotionally and that these 'compelling and mood affecting qualities are often associated with the concept of escapism' (2011, p. 135). This concept, which implies a mental shift from one space to another, holds relevance for my journey as a VR user immersed in a 'vivid spatial and social system that is alternative to the real world' (Arcagni & D'Aloia, 2021), as well as for Goliath's journey as a gamer. Further to notions of immersion and presence, Calleja proposes the term 'incorporation' to capture the experiential phenomena of game play, suggesting that 'the player incorporates (in the sense of internalizing or assimilating) the game environment into consciousness while simultaneously being incorporated through the avatar into that environment' (2011, p. 169). In the case of the *Goliath* VR experience, I would suggest that this process of incorporation occurs on several levels. As user, my participation in 2D arcade games (and later, in a first-person shooter game) creates emotions that might mirror Goliath's original experience, while on another level, my participation in the broader interactive elements of the VR experience, which brings together narrative elements with ludic components, fosters a different form of emotional engagement. As user, I give rise to the existence of multiple virtual environments (the 2D game world and the broader virtual environment) through my interaction and am simultaneously incorporated into these.

In the following sequence I'm positioned on the edge of an oversized DJ mixing desk, watching records spinning and seeing flashes of nightclub revellers in the background. Goliath recalls his descent into psychosis in this environment. 'I went mad but no one could hear me because of the music. It was some scary shit. You can't tell what's real and what's not real'. The female voice cuts through, asking 'How are you feeling? Are you not so sure?' The visuals that surround me shatter into pieces and I'm left, again, in darkness. 'The connections are fragile', the unseen narrator continues. 'When it all comes crashing down, what is left to hold onto?'

At this point my hands transform into faded spheres with no interactive abilities. This state of embodiment is reflective of Goliath's journey, as co-director Abdalla, suggests: 'you feel useless and it's depressing. And it's kind of like your hands don't function there' (quoted in Bye, 2021). In other words, the visualisation of my hands, as spheres, cubes or other in forms, affords me various levels of agency that parallels Goliath's experience of the world.

A new scene emerges from darkness—Goliath's prison cell-like room within a psychiatric hospital. We see his body represented as a fluorescent yellow and pink form that is huddled on a bed in the semi-transparent environment. In voice over Goliath recounts the terrible anxiety and confusion that he suffered in the hospital, and his inability to respond to people. A loud mess of sounds builds up around him. Within this, I am slightly alarmed to hear my own voice repeating my name over and over (the earlier recording). This perhaps is intended to create reflection around the female narrator's later statement that 'Lots of people slip between worlds. It can happen to anyone'.

Goliath's remaining scenes portray his recovery and discharge from the hospital. The experience ends with images of Goliath (as avatar) playing online video games with his gamer community. He describes how the game play takes his mind off his ongoing anxiety: 'If I didn't have online gaming, I don't know where I would be'. The female voice then returns with an offboarding message: 'There are many layers to the world. When you leave this place, the next place will appear real. But it is an illusion created by your brain. Your brain joins up the dots between what you see and what you feel'. This statement reinforces concepts that are emphasised throughout the work: that human experience of reality is illusionary and that emotions generated through interaction in game or virtual environments are no less valid than those experienced in the 'real' world. We're left with the suggestion that reaching out to others is most important in life: 'All realities are imagined but the ones we share, endure'.

Based on the analysis above, I would propose that the user, as 'focaliser', both observes and relives Goliath's journey in this VR experience, adopting an 'explorer' role within the diegesis. As such, they are partially visualised and directly acknowledged by the female narrator, although not by Goliath. In other words, while the female narrator addresses the user as 'you', Goliath narrates in a more objective manner, without breaking the fourth wall. The user views events from the perspective of their own body for most of the experience, although there are moments, such as in the gameplay sequences described above, where they arguably also occupy Goliath's perspective. While the user is not able to influence the outcome of Goliath's story, they can impact upon its telling, with their participation as game player and interactor shaping the unfolding of some sequences. Moreover, the direct address to the user from the non-visualised female narrator creates an additional narrative layer that revolves around the user as character (a narrative journey that is related to but separate to that of Goliath). As such, the user's embodied experience as an explorer of Goliath's reality fosters reflection on their own perceptions of reality.

We Live Here

Somewhat similarly to *Goliath*, *We Live Here* also features both heterodiegetic and homodiegetic narrators, in this case with the goal of creating insight into a contemporary experience of homelessness. The experience begins with a black and white, 360-degree animation of an unbridled horse galloping in a circular pen. Over the sounds of the outdoors, a visualised female voice over (the heterodiegetic narrator) instructs the user directly: 'Imagine that you had a dream job breaking in horses. Then your boss dies, and you've got no safety net. [...] Imagine being Rockey, who's 59'. The simply animated scene fades to black.

A moment later, 360-degree live-action footage appears, and we meet Rockey as she exits one of a series of tents that are erected in the corner of a park. Rockey is neatly dressed and has long, dark hair. She carries a saucepan, which she fills with water from a hose, before re-entering her tent. I watch with 3DoF, so I can shift my field of vision but have no other abilities to interact with the story. My viewpoint shifts to inside of the tent, a spare but somewhat homely environment that includes a single bed and makeshift kitchen with a gas burner. The bed is covered by a crocheted quilt and an assortment of other belongings such as a table, suitcase and trinkets are spread around the space. Suddenly a male neighbour appears in the doorway with news that the LAPD are about to raid the area. He suggests that Rockey leaves with some urgency as her lack of identification is a problem. After a moment's hesitation, Rockey retrieves some special belongings that are hidden in the bed and makes her exit. I hear a police siren ring out as she zips up the tent door, and I'm left alone inside. The female voice over returns:—'Imagine you've done nothing wrong. You lose your home and with it the right to exist, to be seen. Imagine having to become invisible'.

This opening sequence positions the user in a non-visualised observer role. Rather than occupying a defined virtual body, I follow events from the perspective of an invisible onlooker who is aligned with Rockey by nature of being inside her tent. While my presence is not acknowledged by Rockey, it is acknowledged by the heterodiegetic narrator who addresses me directly. While the use of heterodiegetic narration in *Goliath* facilitates the user's journey of questioning reality, in *We Live Here* it seems to serve a more didactic purpose. By this I mean that the use of voice over seemingly seeks to guide my interpretation of the 360-degree content, encouraging me to empathise with Rockey.

After a short title sequence, I find myself returned to Rockey's tent, but this time the environment is created through volumetric video capture and game engine technology, meaning that I am able to walk around the space and to touch objects using my hand controllers (a 6DoF experience). Thus, my role within the experience changes to that of explorer and the 360-degree space becomes a site for embodied experience, fostering reflection on Rockey's life story and identity. The heterodiegetic narrator encourages me to explore Rockey's things. At this stage it becomes clear that the VR experience will not progress unless I take this action, as the act of picking up objects triggers short stories to play in various formats. I start by retrieving a journal placed nearby. A poem called 'Smokers Under

Fire' is written on a page inside. As I watch, a colourful animation plays out on the journal pages, which illustrates Rockey's reading (as homodiegetic narrator) of the poem. This short narrative sequence recalls how, as a child, she saw a smiling 'hobo' pick up a cigarette butt off the pavement. Rockey expresses her surprise and displeasure to find herself doing the same thing some years later.

Subtle sound cues direct me to pick up several other items in the tent: a trinket box, a postcard, and Rockey's mobile phone, which is hidden in a canister. Doing so triggers narrative sequences that provide insight into Rockey's early years at school, her desire to leave Los Angeles to become a cowboy, and her marriage on the back of a motorcycle in 1978. This is interspersed with a news story about homelessness that plays on Rockey's small transition radio, and a phone message to suggest that she might have found temporary accommodation.

A final 360-degree animation is triggered when I retrieve a copy of the book, *Black Beauty,* from a table in the tent. Like several of the other short narrative sequences that explore Rockey's backstory, this offers 3DoF with no additional interactive devices, meaning that I am returned to the observer role. This animation is similar to the one that starts the VR work in that we see an animated version of Rockey taming a wild horse in a circular arena. I watch as Rockey lovingly interacts with the horse but then suddenly my perspective changes. Now I am in the body of Rockey, rendered using animation, as she cares for the horse. Reflecting on her life at this time, 'It was freedom', Rockey exclaims in voice over. This moment where I am offered Rockey's perspective provides insight into her connection with the horses that she tamed, and fosters reflection on the lack of connections and care that she now experiences as a homeless woman. As for several of the other stories that unfold in *We Live Here*, this is a powerful embodied experience of reliving Rockey's memories.

The sounds of a police raid drift into the animation and the experience transitions back to the live-action scene of Rockey's tent. As an invisible observer, I watch from a fixed position inside the tent as a police officer pries the door open, enters and rummages through Rockey's possessions. Rockey appears in the doorway for a moment and watches with sadness before the police officer shouts at her: 'Get outta here!' As a witness to this scene, I'm left with a feeling of injustice regarding the reality of homelessness.

It can be observed, therefore, that in *We Live Here*, the user switches between observer and explorer roles as they activate and view various narrative sequences that teach them about Rockey's life story and current reality. This is an engaging and educative VR work that overcomes the stigmas of homelessness by giving voice to Rockey, a relatable protagonist. The series of animations that are included in the work emphasise the different stages of Rockey's life, capturing her multidimensionality. In the observer role the user has no ability to impact upon the unfolding narratives (the pre-rendered 360-degree live action or animated sequences) and sometimes assumes Rockey's subjective point of view; however, as explorers of Rockey's tent, the user's interaction drives the experience forward. In this sense, while the narrative outcome is fixed, the user as explorer can determine the pace at which the story unfolds through the speed and breath of their exploration of objects.

Director Rose Troche's use of the VR medium to tell this story allows the audience to virtually inhabit the protagonist's environment and to relive her memories. This phenomenon evidences my earlier claim that focalisation might involve a dual process in the context of VR storytelling, seeing the user sees from both their own perspective and that of the story protagonist. On this approach, Troche comments that 'I want you to spend time with Rockey—with her life, her experiences. I want you to feel the loss of her home, her safety, her dignity and ask yourself, why do we allow this?' (quoted in Oculus, 2020). I pondered this question as I viewed the various sequences and explored Rockey's belongings from my position inside the tent. I would suggest that Troche's approach to user positioning and use of interactive devices fosters a pseudo 'first-hard' experience of homelessness, placing the viewer alongside Rockey, or even in her shoes, as memories and events unfold. In this sense, the 'we' of the title *We Live Here* could be seen to reflect this alignment between the protagonist and VR user in the work.

Sorella's Story

While *Goliath* and *We Live Here* explore the experience of protagonists inhabiting the twenty-first century, *Sorella's Story* looks back on a dark chapter of human history. Following the German occupation of Latvia, approximately 2700 Jews from the city of Liepaja were massacred on the nearby Skede Beach on 15–17 December in 1941, most of them being women and children. This followed the earlier execution of their male relatives. In *Sorella's Story,* Peter Hegedus, an Australian director with Hungarian heritage, recreates the final moments of a group of captured women. This is based around a found photo of ten-year-old Sorella Epstein and her family members, which was taken by a soldier moments before their deaths. In doing so, he offers a VR experience that is 'a visceral reminder and warning of how prejudice can escalate to devastating tragedy' (Hegedus, 2022). Such a work is important, Hegedus suggests, as memory of the Holocaust fades and extreme right-wing ideologies gather steam (Hegedus, 2022). Ceuterick and Ingraham suggest that 'one of the great benefits of VR as a storytelling medium is its ability to create access to scenes of encounter and experience to which viewers might not otherwise be privy' (Ceuterick & Ingraham, 2021, p. 9). While they make this comment in acknowledgement of the generally high cost and therefore low accessibility of VR technologies, noting the generally privileged lives of VR headset owners, the notion has resonance when considering VR's ability to offer users an embodied encounter with scenes from the past, as is the goal of Hegedus' project.

Sorella's Story is a live-action 360-degree video, meaning that the narrative plays out to a pre-authored and pre-rendered conclusion. The user has 3DoF, so they can choose their field of vision from a fixed central axis, but are offered no other interactive devices. This means that they take on an observer role, having no means to impact upon the unfolding story. The project has been filmed with a 360-degree camera, whose position the user adopts. While this work therefore offers a more passive viewing experience than *Goliath* and *We Live Here*, I would argue that it is no less powerful in terms of its emotional impact.

The experience begins with the sounds of waves crashing on a beach and a young female voice humming. I am surrounded by a black screen, from which an image of a stark winter landscape slowly emerges. As the darkness slowly recedes, the female voice narrates: 'Hi, can you hear me? You're probably wondering where you are. I wish I knew. I need to tell you. I have no memory of my past. No memory of me. I do not event know my name … Please stay with me!' The winter landscape, which is represented in black and white, now surrounds me. I see leafless trees, gritty snow on the ground when I look down beneath me, and buildings to my left and right. The sound of a brutally cold wind and then of children playing can be heard. 'I can feel the cold. I hear children', the narrator exclaims. I turn as two warmly dressed boys who are play-fighting with sticks emerge from behind the building to my left. A moment later, a truck reverses round the corner of the building opposite. There is a soldier with a gun standing on its back who yells at the boys. 'Why is he so angry with the boys? Maybe he is here to collect the animals, to feed to people in winter', the narrator suggests. From my position between these two parties, I watch as the boys quickly scurry away. Then suddenly a group of women dressed in coats and boots enter my field of vision from behind a building to my right. An armed solider, behind them, forces them onwards. 'These women, their faces, so familiar', says the narrator. The women come to a stop in close proximity to me. A guard orders them forward, onto the truck. As they move forward, a young girl at the back of the group becomes prominent in the scene. The image freeze-frames as she locks eyes with the camera/viewer and colour fades into the previously black and white scene (see Fig. 3.2). 'Ah, see this girl. It can't be. She is ... it is me. I am her', says our narrator, revealed at this moment to be the ten-year child.

This opening sequence establishes the stark world of *Sorella's Story* and allows the user time to explore this environment before the protagonist physically appears. Sorella's direct address via voice over creates an alignment between user (as focaliser) and protagonist (as narrator), in that both parties see and hear the visual and auditory elements at the same time, and both are unsure of their surroundings. It is initially unclear whether Sorella is a heterodiegetic or homodiegetic narrator, as her identity is unknown. Her physical appearance some minutes into the scene reveals her identity and connects her narration to the storyworld, making

Fig. 3.2 Sorella makes eye contact with the camera/viewer in *Sorella's Story* (2022). (Courtesy of Soul Vision Films)

it clear that she is telling her own story (and is thus a homodiegetic narrator). However, this narrator position is blurry, seeing as Sorella does not seem to recall all of the details of the story, and is in some sense experiencing them alongside the user. As an observer of the scene, the user's body is not visualised and is not unacknowledged by the characters, with the exception of this one freeze-frame moment when Sorella appears to look directly at the camera. Nash suggests that such looks to camera are a power form of direct address that can foster social presence, which she defines as 'the illusion of "being there" with another' (2018b, p. 127). In the context of *Sorella's Story* this glance at the camera works with the voiceover narration to generate a feeling of presence in Sorella's storyworld for the user. As such, they adopt a 'witness' role but a partial one, seeing as they are privy to Sorella's thoughts and feelings.

In the following three sequences, I watch as the women are forced onto the back of the truck. Three of them attempt to run away, but one is immediately captured. A guard scrambles after the two others, and they all disappear from sight. A moment later we hear a distant gunshot. 'I feel I know these women. Are they my family', Sorella exclaims in voice over. In the following scene I find myself in the middle of a dirt road covered in snow and ice, surrounded by barren trees on both sides. The truck containing the women approaches and passes but then comes prematurely to a halt, the result of a mechanical failure. A soldier orders the women to descend at gunpoint. A moment later, I am moved closer to the women as they step down from the truck on my right. At this point Sorella (as narrator) recognises her mother and other family members among the group. My attention shifts as the two escapees reappear in the distance on my left. The two women stagger forward, one supporting the other who has been shot. When the pursuing guard reappears from the opposite direction, the women turn to flee again, but the guard catches up. He pulls them into a back-to-back position and shoots them in the head, the one bullet killing both women. As their bodies fall to the ground, I turn my attention back to Sorella and the group of women who cower against the truck on my right. They shriek, scream, and then quietly sing a prayer. Over this, we hear the shocked and heavy breathing of Sorella as narrator. This scene ends as the guards march the women down a sideways track. Sorella as narrator then fully recalls her identity: 'My name is Sorella. [...] I am Jewish. I was born in Latvia ....' As darkness eclipses the scene she exclaims, 'I wish I could stop time'.

The following sequence begins with a freeze-frame of an icy clearing occupied by multiple groups of women and soldiers. Discarded clothing and suitcases are placed in mounds on the ground. Near to me, one group of freezing, half-naked women attempt to cover themselves as a photographer takes their picture. Guards watch with rifles drawn. 'Can you hear me? Move, Run, Get away!' Sorella exclaims in voice over. This moment reminds me of her dual presence in the narrative, as both child victim and omniscient spirit who relives the moments before her death alongside the user. The scene transforms from freeze-frame to moving image as Sorella and her family are marched forward and ordered to strip off their clothes at gunpoint. This happens to my right, while to my left, several idle guards watch while passing cigarettes among themselves. As an observer I am positioned between these two parties, closer in proximity to the guards than the women. My lack of agency in the VR work mirrors that of Sorella who states, 'I want to say something, but I cannot speak.'… 'I wish you didn't have to see me like this. I wish that you didn't have to remember me like this'. A fade to black transitions me to a position closer to the women who have now stripped down to their underwear. As a soldier behind me snaps a photo of the women, the image freezes. Sorella's narration restarts: 'I remember now what happens next …'. As she recalls the grim details of the group's execution on nearby sand dunes, the recreated image is replaced by the real-life photograph that inspired the work. I study the women's haunting stares.

In the final sequence of the work, a series of names appear on a black screen around the user, each one representing a victim of the Skede Beach massacre. This fades out and is replaced with vision of Skede Beach in the present day. I hear echoes of the past—the laughter of children, the sounds of ball games and waves crashing—as I study this deserted and seemingly peaceful environment. Such sounds provide insight the protagonist's happy childhood at the beach in the years prior to World War Two. The VR experience ends as Sorella's voice over returns with a final line of dialogue: 'Please, never forget us'.

Key to the engaging nature of this work is the alignment between the user as observer and Sorella (as narrator), which is fostered through direct address. Like Sorella, the user can only observe the unfolding narrative and wait for its devastating conclusion. They are therefore offered a first-person experience of the event, with no opportunity to interact with story agents beyond choosing the direction in which they look. I would argue that this lack of agency fosters feelings of powerlessness that heighten the emotional impact of the work. But moreover, the lack of agency allows for a respectful retelling of events that many viewers will finds triggering. The decision to position the user as a non-visualised entity, rather than as a predefined character with a virtual body, prevents the work from adopting what Nash terms as an 'improper distance', where the body of the other becomes 'indistinguishable from ourselves' (2018b, p. 120). On this subject she suggests that 'if empathy points to an affective response grounded in an imaginative engagement with the experience of the other, analysis calls for a more distanced relationship that recognises the distinctiveness of self and other' (p. 124). The recognition of distant others as persons involves 'both proximity and distance' (p. 124), meaning that the user is positioned alongside characters or participants in a shared storyworld but does not confuse or conflate their own experience (which is based on their specific identity) with that of the characters. Such positioning can be observed for the user of *Sorella's Story* in as much as the user witnesses events through their own eyes in close proximity to Sorella and the other characters.

Conclusion

In this chapter's exploration of narration for VR storytelling, I have suggested that users might adopt either an 'observer' or 'explorer' role within the storyworld, and that these roles involve a number of variables in terms of the user's representation, perspective, levels of agency and ability to shape the narrative. My analysis of these roles within the three case studies demonstrates that user positioning within VR narratives is varied and dynamic, meaning that multiple positions might be adopted within a single work. I observe that the moment-by-moment process by which VR stories unfold is complex, involving devices that foster immersion and/or self-reflection in an embodied manner. My analysis has sought to highlight and critically explore these approaches of contemporary VR creators, an undertaking that, as suggested by Abdalla in my introduction, evidences a maturation of the medium.

The three VR experiences that receive analysis in this chapter powerfully document past or present-day realities through their depiction of three individuals' experience. But more than just represent this experience, they provide a simulation of experience that users can interact with in a corporeal sense. In the case of *Sorella's Story*, this interaction is restricted to a choice of viewing direction in 360-degree space, a lack of agency that I have argued fosters feelings of powerlessness for the user, and parallels that of the protagonist. By contrast *Goliath* and *We Live Here* offer the user additional interactive possibilities that are afforded by game engine technologies. For the former, this interaction involves participation in game play, an activity that puts the user in the shoes of the protagonist, Goliath, while the latter involves the physical exploration of the homeless protagonist's tent to trigger story threads. All three experiences engage the user through the use of direct address, this taking the form of voiceover narration (in all three works) or looks to camera (in *Sorella's Story*). As I've explored above, the inclusion of heterodiegetic and/or homodiegetic narration in the works produces a number of effects, but commonly serves as a means to engage the user on an emotional level.

Moreover, one can observe that all three of the projects feature internal focalisation as defined by Genette, seeing as the various narratives are informed by the perspectives of protagonists whose inner worlds can be accessed through voiceover narration. In the analysis above I have isolated what I have termed a 'dual process' of focalisation that concerns (1) what the user sees as an active agent located in the storyworld; and (2) the perspectives of other characters that the user interacts with. In the case of *Goliath* and *We Live Here* the perspectives of the user and story protagonist align when the user is encouraged to directly relive the protagonist's experience. *Sorella's Story* offers more separation between user and protagonist, but nonetheless a complex approach to focalisation is at play. This complexity points towards the specificity of VR storytelling, which I have argued positions the user within a storyworld as 'focaliser' (Bal, 2009). Further work might explore this area with reference to additional case studies, including those that do not feature voiceover narration.

Ceuterick and Ingraham rightly suggest that non-fiction VR storytelling documents the 'inevitably incomplete experience of exposure to others', but nonetheless, its power as a medium for simulation is significant (2021, p. 10). This power, they suggest, might derive from 'the felt intensity of being made present to unspeakable and ineffable things' (p. 10), an observation that resonates with my experience of *Sorella's Story*. Moreover, as Ceuterick and Ingraham also observe, it involves the location of the viewer in a world that they may not otherwise be able to access, 'whether because it is nonlocal, imaginary, forbidden, or because it involves people whose different identities and communities—and hence whose stories, histories, and ways of being—are ordinarily beyond the purview of a viewer's personal experience' (p. 10). This observation holds relevance for all the case studies explored above considering the insights they offer into the realities of marginalised individuals or groups in the past or present.

References

Allison, F. (2015, May). Whose mind is the signal? Focalization in video game narratives. In *DiGRA Conference*.

Arcagni, S., & D'Aloia, A. (2021). VR storytelling: Potentials and limitations of virtual reality narratives. *Cinergie–Il Cinema e le altre Arti, 19*, 1–7.

Bal, M. (2009). *Narratology: Introduction to the theory of narrative*. University of Toronto Press.

Bordwell, D., Thompson, K., & Smith, J. (2016). *Film art: An introduction* (11th ed.). McGraw-Hill Higher Education.

Bye, K. (2021). Voices of VR: #1003: A powerful interactive story about schizophrenia in *Goliath: Playing with Reality*. (Podcast). Published September 7. https://voicesofvr.com/1003-a-power-interactive-story-about-schizophrenia-in-goliath-playing-with-reality/

Calleja, G. (2011). *In-game: From immersion to incorporation*. MIT Press.

Ceuterick, M., & Ingraham, C. (2021). Immersive storytelling and affective ethnography in virtual reality. *Review of Communication, 21*(1), 9–22.

De la Peña, N., Weil, P., Llobera, J., Spanlang, B., Friedman, D., Sanchez-Vives, M. V., & Slater, M. (2010). Immersive journalism: Immersive virtual reality for the first-person experience of news. *Presence, 19*(4), 291–301.

Dolan, D., & Parets, M. (2016). Redefining the axiom of story: The VR and 360 video complex. *Tech Crunch*. https://techcrunch.com/2016/01/14/redefining-the-axiom-of-story-the-vr-and-360-video-complex/

Dooley, K. (2021). *Cinematic virtual reality: A critical study of 21st century approaches and practices*. Springer.

Genette, G. (1980). *Narrative discourse*. Cornell University Press.

Goliath: Playing with Reality. (2021). Dirs. Barry Gene Murphy and May Abdalla. Anagram, UK.

Gunkel, D. (2000). Rethinking virtual reality: Simulation and the deconstruction of the image. *Critical Studies in Media Communication, 17*(1), 45–62.

Hegedus, P. (2022). *Sorella's Story* - 360° - Message from the Director. https://www.peterhegedus.com/

Igelström, A. (2014). *Narration in the screenplay text*. Doctoral Dissertation. Bangor University.

Larsen, M. (2018). Virtual sidekick: Second-person POV in narrative VR. *Journal of Screenwriting, 9*(1), 73–83.

Laurel, B. (2014). *Computers as theatre* (2nd ed.). Addison-Wesley.

Manovich, L. (2001). *The language of new media*. The MIT Press.

Mateer, J. (2017). Directing for cinematic virtual reality: How the traditional film director's craft applies to immersive environments and notions of presence. *Journal of Media Practice, 18*(1), 14–25.

Nash, K. (2018a). Virtually real: Exploring VR documentary. *Studies in Documentary Film, 12*(2), 97–100.

Nash, K. (2018b). Virtual reality witness: Exploring the ethics of mediated presence. *Studies in Documentary Film, 12*(2), 119–131.

Newton, K., & Soukup, K. (2016). The storyteller's guide to the virtual reality audience. *Medium*. Retrieved October 14, 2019, from https://medium.com/stanford-d-school/the-storyteller-s-guide-to-the-virtual-reality-audience-19e92da57497

Nicolae, D. F. (2018). Spectator perspectives in virtual reality cinematography. The witness, the hero and the impersonator. *Ekphrasis. Images, Cinema, Theory, Media, 20*(2), 168–180.

Oculus. (2020). VR for good: 'We live here' puts a face on homelessness. https://www.oculus.com/blog/vr-for-good-we-live-here-puts-a-face-on-whomelessness/

Petkova, V. I., & Ehrsson, H. H. (2008). If I were you: Perceptual illusion of body swapping. *PLoS One, 3*(12), e3832.

Slater, M., Spanlang, B., Sanchez-Vives, M. V., & Blanke, O. (2010). First person experience of body transfer in virtual reality. *PLoS One, 5*(5), e10564.

Sorella's Story. (2022). Dir. Peter Hegedus.

Vosmeer, M., & Schouten, B. (2017, June). Project Orpheus a research study into 360 cinematic VR. In *Proceedings of the 2017 ACM international conference on interactive experiences for TV and online video* (pp. 85–90).

We Live Here. (2020). Dir. Rose Troche. Afrobel/ Oculus VR for Good/ VR Playhouse: United States.

Weaving, S. (2021). Evoke, don't show: Narration in cinematic virtual reality and the making of entangled. *Virtual Creativity, 11*(1), 147–162.

CHAPTER 4

Exploring Environmental Storytelling Techniques in Expressive, Virtual Reality Documentary

Introduction

In recent years, virtual reality has been embraced by creators working in non-fiction contexts to enhance experiential elements of their work. The development of omnidirectional camera systems and other technologies in the early 2010s gave rise to a wave of immersive journalism, a trend spearheaded by Nonny de la Peña, with her 2012 work, *Hunger in Los Angeles*. This short VR work that debuted at the Sundance Film Festival portrayed the true story of a starving diabetic man's collapse whilst queuing for food at a Los Angeles food bank. A few years later, *The New York Times* was among the pioneers in adopting virtual reality technology by distributing 'Google Cardboard' viewers to its Sunday edition subscribers.[1] At the same time, the publication released its first journalistic VR piece, *The Displaced* (dirs. Imraan Ismail, Ben C. Solomon, and Dan Edge 2015),

[1] Google Cardboard viewers were first developed by a team of Google engineers in 2014. The device was created as an affordable and accessible way to experience virtual reality using a smartphone. The viewer itself is made of cardboard and uses lenses to create a stereoscopic 3D effect when paired with a smartphone running VR applications. The open-source design of Google Cardboard also allowed third-party developers and manufacturers to create their own versions of the viewer, which helped to popularise the use of VR technology. Since its launch, Google Cardboard has been used for various applications, including gaming, education and journalism. However, Google announced in 2019 that it would be discontinuing support for the Cardboard platform.

K. Dooley, *Virtual Reality Narratives*,
https://doi.org/10.1007/978-3-031-64965-3_4

which chronicled the experiences of three refugee children who had to leave their homes due to the ravages of war. Shortly afterwards, *The Guardian* launched a program of VR works, starting with *6x9: A Virtual Experience of Solitary Confinement* (dirs. Francesca Panetta and Lindsay Poulton 2016). This offered photo-realistic rendering of a segregation prison cell, so that viewers could explore the space first-hand while hearing stories of the psychological consequences of this method of punishment. Other VR works produced by the *New York Times* or The *Guardian* explored social or political topics and themes such as climate change, immigration and inequality.[2] Also around this time, one could observe the more widespread appearance of VR documentary works at festivals, conferences and other venues around the globe. For example, *Clouds Over Sidra* (Chris Milk 2016) and *My Mother's Wing* (Gabo Arora 2018), both of which were produced by the United Nations Virtual Reality (UNVR) program, offered viewers the experience of being in a Syrian refugee camp or the Gaza conflict. Created with the aim of having social impact, these and other early non-fiction VR works positioned the viewer at the centre of a narrative so that they could experience a sense of being in another time and space (Soler-Adillon & Sora, 2018). Reflecting on the practice of journalism, De la Peña et al. suggest that creating a connection between the news story and audience via different kinds of immersion 'has long been considered ideal' (p. 291).

The examples listed above adopt the conventions of realist filmmaking, using lens-based technologies to capture live-action, or other tools to create pre-rendered, photo-realistic environments based on the real world. This harnessing of new technologies has been much celebrated for its ability to 'almost fully embed the viewer into another reality to explore' (Kool, 2016, p. 3) or to allow the viewer to 'walk in the shoes' of their subjects (Jones & Dawkins, 2018). Considerable academic scholarship has explored this field, with particular attention and debate centring on the degree to

[2] The *New York Times* produced a *Daily 360* series (2016 to 2020) of 360-degree videos that allowed viewers to explore a variety of locations and experiences around the world. The videos were published daily on *The New York Times* website and YouTube channel and were compatible with VR headsets. These Daily 360 videos covered a wide range of topics and social issues. While the series ended in 2020, the *New York Times* has continued to produce VR content through its Op-Docs team and other departments.

The *Guardian*'s VR Lab (2016–2018) aimed to experiment with virtual reality (VR) and 360-degree video to tell immersive stories. The project was a collaboration between The *Guardian*'s in-house virtual reality team and the VR studio ScanLAB Projects.

which these VR narratives give rise to viewer empathy (Barbot & Kaufman, 2020; Bevan et al., 2019; Hassan, 2020).

Less academic attention, however, has been directed towards more abstract, expressive and/or interactive approaches that VR practitioners might adopt to depict and communicate a subjective narrative experience of space and time, a phenomenon that is linked to VR production trends and accessibility issues. Whereas the majority of the projects cited above adopt the 360-degree video format, which can be viewed using affordable headsets such as the aforementioned Google Cardboard model, one can note the increased production of room-scale documentaries that offer six degrees of freedom (abbreviated to 6DoF, meaning the ability to walk around a virtual environment and interact with objects via hand controllers) in the last five years. Driven by game engines such as Unity and Unreal Engine, these room-scale works offer a range of possibilities of interaction. The increased production of these works has paralleled the rise of more advanced consumer-facing HMDs, such as the Meta Quest (formally known as the Oculus Quest, currently in its third incarnation). This affordable headset allows the user to experience narratives that are potentially reactive to user input.

With this gap in scholarship in mind, this chapter presents an analysis of expressive documentary and docu-drama works that feature explorable and expressive 360-degree environments. Moving away from the aforementioned journalistic works, I focus on non-fiction VR that adopts animation and visual effects, to question how narrative is conveyed within these more stylised and interactive virtual environments. The studied projects may also draw upon or incorporate lens-based practices but do so with a suite of tools that are harnessed to emphasise subjective human experience. McRoberts suggests that the specificity of non-fiction VR is its aim to 'immerse users within real-world stories, offering opportunities for first-hand experience, of empathic engagement with others confronting challenging issues and thus opportunities for personal and/or social transformation' (p. 102). By focusing on expressive non-fiction VR works, I seek to explore an expanded toolkit for the capturing and communicating of first-hand experience, which is made possible by advancing technologies and a maturation of VR storytelling approaches.

The focus of this chapter (and of this book) is VR storytelling experiences that have been produced since 2020. In the book's introduction I have suggested that this year that was marked by Covid-19 lockdowns was a notable point in time for immersive storytelling. Not only was there considerable consumer uptake of virtual reality technologies in this year, as populations grappled with communication, entertainment and other facets of life whilst in pandemic-induced isolation, but it was a time that saw artists and exhibitors respond to the challenges of remote collaboration and creation in innovative ways. The three case studies that are explored in this chapter, which offer diverse and innovative representations of true stories that are illustrated through a range of expressive techniques, are produced during or after this time. I examine *The Changing Same: An American Pilgrimage (Episode 1: the Dilemma)* (dir. Michèle Stephenson 2020); *Child of Empire* (Project Datsaan 2022); and *On the Morning You Wake (to the End of the World)* (Archer's Mark 2022). *The Changing Same* combines direct address to camera, archival footage, and fictionalised re-enactments to create an immersive narrative that highlights the enduring legacy of racial violence and injustice in America. Meanwhile *Child of Empire*, an animated work, presents a sensory and psychological experience of the 1947 Partition of British India, as recalled through two narrators' childhood memories. *On the Morning You Wake (to the End of the World)* explores the first-person testimony of witnesses to the onset of a nuclear emergency in Hawai'i, based on the real-life ballistic missile warning that occurred on 13 January, 2018. In this work photo-realistic environments and character bodies are dissolved into animated particles, creating a visceral representation of the subjects' physiological and physical experience of potential annihilation.

I present a close analysis of each project's narrative and stylistic elements, which is complemented by a phenomenological reading that reflects upon my own visceral and emotional response to the VR content and interactive devices. As I've noted in this book's introduction, phenomenological methods are well-equipped to explore the embodied experiences offered by virtual reality storytelling as phenomenology 'is fundamentally concerned with perception and bodily activity [...] enabling the exploration of phenomena as they are lived and experienced' (Murray & Sixsmith, 1999, p. 322). I examine the three case studies as a body immersed in interactive, 360-degree storyworlds, noting my physical sensations as well as emotional responses. As Murray and Sixsmith rightly point out, 'the sensorial body is located within a sociocultural, gendered, and technological context' (p. 315). I therefore take account of my own background and life experience when responding to the VR narratives.

Additionally, I look to the concept of environmental storytelling, as discussed by Jenkins (2004) and others in relation to game narratives, as a framework that can usefully shed light on the three works' approaches to interactivity and spatial storytelling. This storytelling approach, which Carson earlier explores in relation to physical spaces in theme parks (2000), involves the embedding of narrative elements in the environment that a user explores. Questions remain as to the extent that expressive non-fiction projects draw upon the environmental storytelling techniques described by these authors. Through an analysis of the three case studies' narrative structures, aesthetic elements, interactive devices and production techniques, this chapter will argue that VR technologies (incorporating binaural audio and real-time rendering of live-action and/or animated elements) can be harnessed to create powerful documentary narratives that communicate subjective human experience. The creation of a synthetic environment that captures a subject's impressions of time and space is a key feature of this work.

Virtual Reality Documentary

Documentary works are created with a variety of aims, such as to record or interrogate an event, to express an idea or convey an argument.[3] Virtual reality as a storytelling media, allows creators to pursue any one of these aims by immersing the viewer in a 360-degree environment. VR can be defined as a 'computer-generated experience that can simulate physical presence in real or imagined environments' (Shin, 2018, p. 65). Whereas documentaries created with traditional screen media (film or television) deliver a narrative to a passive viewer, the VR documentary locates the viewer *within* an enclosed diegetic world that reflects, represents or simulates real places or events.[4] Wearing a VR headset, they find their body positioned at the centre of a storyworld, and have the ability to choose their viewing direction or perhaps even interact with reactive story content. As McRoberts observes, VR documentary 'offers people opportunities to enter alternate worlds, outside their normal perspectives and to experience how human beings act and interact in challenging circumstances' (2018, p. 104). I would add that this exploration of alternate worlds can involve different times as well as different spaces. Simulations

[3] Renov (1993, p. 21) usefully outlines four fundamental tendencies of documentary: (1) to record, reveal, or preserve, (2) to persuade or promote (3) to analyse or interrogate and (4) to express.

[4] My use of the term 'passive' in this instance refers to the traditional (film or television) documentary viewer's inability to interact with narrative content. I acknowledge that the practice of viewing a documentary involves the cognitive processing of narrative material, which requires active engagement with a text.

of past events in 360-degree virtual environments can offer viewers a chance to relive historical moments as a fly on the wall or story participant, gaining a sense of what it might have felt like to be in that past moment.[5]

Live-action VR documentaries, such as those touched upon briefly above, have been noted for their ability to bring the viewer 'closer' to the documentary subject, enabling understanding of contemporary conflicts and crises such as war and displacement. Central to this work is VR's ability to foster a sense of presence for the viewer—of being in a real-life setting where action is unfolding—and as McRoberts notes, creating 'a sense that one exists with others within that space' (2018, p. 103).

VR Documentaries constructed in non-realist virtual environments also seek to generate a sense of presence for the viewer but may offer more scope to portray complex ideas or emotions, which are accentuated using visual or sound elements. As is the case for traditional documentary, expressive techniques are particularly powerful when applied to a recreation or dramatisation of an event or experience. Approaches to visual imagery (e.g. the use of light, shadow or plays with scale) and sound (use of music or effects) can help to foster a sense of place and time, which gives rise to an immersive experience. One can observe this when looking at seminal VR works such as *Notes on Blindness* (2016, dirs. Arnaud Colinart, Amaury La Burthe, Peter Middleton, and James Spinney), which explores the real-life audio diaries of theologian and writer John Hull who recorded his experience of going blind in the 1980s. The graphics in the experience—composed of simple shapes and colours—are abstract and impressionistic, so as to evoke Hull's own subjective experience of blindness. To take another example, working in an Australian context, director Michael Beets' *The Unknown Patient* (2018) explores the intersection of memory, trauma, and identity by dramatising the true story of a soldier who, after losing his memory, spent 12 years in Sydney's Callan Park Mental Asylum. In this work, stylised environments that emphasise the soldier's confused mental state and gameplay elements encourage the viewer to piece together his identity, fostering a powerful and engaging narrative world. These and countless other projects have demonstrated the capacity of virtual reality storytelling to not just transport the viewer to another world, but to provide them with insight into a portrayed subject's mental state and emotions. Questions remain as to how the virtual environments featured in

[5] *Sorella's Story* (dir. Peter Hedegus 2022) is a powerful live-action VR docu-drama that recreates past events. See Chap. 3 for an analysis of this work.

these expressive projects foster an experience of space and time so as to engage the VR viewer in the documentary subject's view of the world.

Environmental Storytelling in Virtual Reality

One might draw upon the notion of 'environmental storytelling' as a means to investigate relationships between a virtual environment, user interaction and the construction of narrative. This concept can be traced back to the work of US video game pioneer Roberta Williams, in her design of adventure games in the 1980s and 90s, which 'privileged efforts of visual and auditory immersion and world building' (Nooney, 2013, p. 12). Several years later the term was used by Disneyland theme park designer Don Carson in his article 'Environmental Storytelling: Creating Immersive 3D Worlds Using Lessons Learned from the Theme Park Industry' (2000), to describe the infusion of story elements in physical spaces. This storytelling approach 'relies heavily on the users exploring and discovering the narrative by interpretation of nonverbal elements placed in (or built into) the environment', which can allude that 'something has occurred' (Bruni et al., 2022, p. 43).

Game theorist Henry Jenkins expands on environmental storytelling in his 2004 article addressing the so-called academic ludology vs narratology debate.[6] Erupting in the late 1990s, this debate was concerned with the status and study of video games as a narrative medium. In his contribution, Jenkins argued that discussions around narrative in the context of video games were conducted with a limited conception of narrative elements. Moving away from rules and conventions associated with classical storytelling, he argued for a consideration of 'spatial exploration over causal event chains or which seek to balance the competing demands of narrative and spectacle', which he labels as environmental storytelling (2004, p. 121). The concept is also taken up by Michael Nitsche in his book *Video Game Spaces* (2008).

[6] The ludology vs narratology debate developed between so-called ludologists who wished to shift discussions about narrative to foreground mechanics of game play and 'narratologists' who wanted to study games in the wider context of storytelling media. Jenkins offered what he termed as a 'middle-ground position' (p. 119). As well as arguing that the discussion needed to be conducted with a wider model of narrative, Jenkins argued for a wider understanding of narration and of how narrative elements 'might enter games at a more localized level' (p. 121).

Seminal works by Janet Murray (1997) and Brenda Laurel (1993) have emphasised the links between digital spatiality and interactive narrative experience, foreshadowing Jenkins' central argument that 'Game designers don't simply tell stories; they design worlds and sculpt spaces' (p. 121). Given the interactive nature of VR narratives, which draw upon user agency and participation as a means towards immersion in a storyworld, the concept of environment storytelling provides a useful lens through which to consider the impact of design and spatiality on user experience of a narrative in this context. While virtual reality experiences are not the same as games, one can observe some overlap between the two as storytelling media. When examining the 3D worlds of narrative-based VR experiences, one might therefore question the way that environmental elements, such as objects and settings, (1) provide narrative information, and (2) allow the user to engage with the storyworld to piece together this information.

For Jenkins, environmental storytelling fosters the creation of immersive narrative experiences that can manifest in at least one of four ways:

> spatial stories can evoke pre-existing narrative associations; they can provide a staging ground where narrative events are enacted; they may embed narrative information within their mise-en scene; or they provide resources for emergent narratives. (Jenkins, 2004, p. 123)

He expands on these approaches to define four types of environment storytelling approaches that he labels (1) Evocative Spaces, (2) Enacting Stories, (3) Embedded Narrative and (4) Emergent Narratives (p. 123). The first of these approaches is concerned with amusement park attractions that draw upon pre-existing stories or genre traditions (Jenkins gives the example of the Hollywood *Back to the Future* franchise or the haunted house genre), which allow audiences to 'enter physically into spaces they have visited many times before in their fantasies' (p. 123). The second category (Enacting Stories) relates to games that similarly draw upon pre-existing stories but also allow the player to enact the role of character (e.g. they can assume the role of a character from Star Wars, which may involve play with a light saber) (p. 124). It is here that we see the idea of a 'staging ground' within a virtual environment take focus. For this type of storytelling, narrative elements relate to 'broadly defined goals or conflicts and on the level of localized incidents' (p. 124). The third category of 'Embedded Narrative' involves control of the narrational process and the distribution of narrative information across the game space. Jenkins suggests that 'within an open-ended and exploratory narrative structure like a game, essential narrative information must be presented redundantly across a range of spaces and artifacts, because one cannot assume the player will necessarily locate or recognize the significance of any given element' (p. 126). This means that narrative information drawn from props, settings and other visual elements (what is in film studies termed 'mise en scène'), is sighted or uncovered, processed and interpreted by the user. This approach would seem adaptable to explorable VR environments although questions arise as to how an embedded narrative approach might work within the context of linear rather than open-ended narrative structures. One can note that the former is standard within the documentary genre. The final approach (Emergent Narratives) conceives of narrative as an unfixed structure that takes shape in response to game play. In other words, a narrative is generated through user interaction with stimuli in the game space. Jenkins stresses that in all of these cases 'choices about the design and organization of game spaces have narratological consequences' (p. 129). He thus considers game designers as 'narrative architects' who use spatial design as a storytelling tool.

More recently, Habgood et al. add to this discussion in their exploration of an educational environmental narrative framework for a Playstation VR game (2018). Their definition of environmental storytelling is taken from game designers Smith and Worch who describe it as 'staging player-space with environmental properties that can be interpreted as a meaningful whole, furthering the narrative of the game' (2010, p. 15). As Habgood et al. aptly summarise, this definition 'emphasises the holistic nature of designing Environmental Narrative games, where the environment and story are inextricably linked' (2018, p. 3). As with Jenkins' description of embedded narratives, Habgood et al. describe a mode of storytelling that 'invites interpretation of situations and meaning according to players' views and experience' and that 'creates games spaces in which the player is fundamentally invested and immersed in' (p. 3). One can observe here an emphasis on environmental design as a means to engage the user in the active construction of narrative. Transposing Smith and Worch's concept into the space of virtual reality, one might question the way that the user's body, which is placed at the literal centre of a 360-degree storyworld, is implicated in the task of making sense of environmental storytelling. In this context, the participant is making sense of stimuli on not just a cognitive but also a corporeal level, as they make choices relating to their orientation and interaction with story agents.

The need to consider user orientation and interaction within a discussion of environmental storytelling is stressed by Shibolet (2019) who observes that 'game designers do not just design space, but also the dynamics of moving through it' (p. 97). Further to environmental design, Shibolet also calls for consideration of movement dynamics as an additional element of design, 'which determines, alongside the design of spatial landscape or geography, how interactions within the digital environment instantiate narrative experiences' (p. 98). Adapted to the context of VR, this position foregrounds the notion of spatial storytelling, where a virtual world is perceived by an interactor based on their bodily interaction and movement within an environment.

The case studies analysed below feature narrative elements that align with traditional storytelling structures—characters that narrate stories and causal chains of plot events—however, they also offer the user the opportunity to explore the space of the story with six degrees of freedom (6DoF). My interrogation of these projects will consider the orchestrated delivery of narrative information in space via objects, settings and other stimuli within the storyworld.

Case Study Analysis

The Changing Same: An American Pilgrimage (Episode 1: The Dilemma)

The Changing Same: An American Pilgrimage is a magic realist project available in both 6DoF and 3DoF formats that explores the critical role of American history in shaping current social and cultural conditions in the United States.[7] This episodic, immersive experience simulates time-travel to explore 400 years of racial inequality, making links between mistreatments of the past and present. It is inspired by the true story of Claude Neal, a man who was falsely accused of a rape and murder and then lynched in Marianna, Florida in 1934 (Fisher, 2022). The VR work features human

[7] A VR work offering 3DoF allows the interactor to rotate their head so as to choose a field of view within a 360-degree scene. This occurs from a fixed central axis, meaning that interaction with content is limited. The interactor cannot move around as they would within a 6DoF experience.

figures that have been captured using volumetric video and inserted into computer-generated environments. As with the two case studies to follow, I experienced Episode 1 of this project in the 6DoF format at home using a Meta Quest 2 headset.

The experience opens in a magical forest setting that is a representation of Marianna. I find myself surrounded by large, multicoloured trees and shrubs that are clouded in mist and illuminated by an eerie soft light. Co-director Michèle Sephenson describes this environment as a beautiful but anxiety-producing space: 'History is there, you feel it, and you feel the ghosts around you' (quoted in Pietroben, 2021). Created in part using photogrammetry imagery drawn from the real Marianna environment, this beautiful but unsettling forest is inhabited by glowing fireflies that buzz in various directions. A rectangular wooden ranch is positioned in a clearing in front of me. My guide through the experience, Lamar Wheaton, sits upon the front porch of this ranch, swaying in time to a music track that seems both diegetic and extra-diegetic. This rhythmic music continues across various scenes of the VR experience, but can be heard by Wheaton in this scene, a stylistic decision that foreshadows his ability, as narrator, to travel through space and time.[8] As I take a few steps towards Wheaton, he makes eye contact with me and introduces himself. 'Here in Marianna, you can experience the past and the future', he suggests. I watch as Wheaton's body dissolves into sparkles of yellow light, like the fireflies, and then materialises in a position closer to me. He encourages me to journey with him, to walk in his shoes so as to understand my own place in the world.

In this first scene I experience a sense of timelessness drawn from the mystical forest setting. I am positioned at a human vantage point of the action, although I do not have a physically represented body. As I look up and down, and take steps around the represented space to acclimate myself in the environment, I find that laws of physics and gravity apply as per the real world. My perception of this world and tangible interactions with the environment are in this way implicated in my narrative understanding of the experience as an act of 'embodied cognition' (Shapiro, 2010). This concept rejects the notion of a mind-body divide and suggests that the body is a fundamental part of our cognitive system. Writing on this phenomenon in the context of video games Shibolet uses the phrase

[8]Wheaton stands in for real-life Marianna resident and poet L. Lamar Wilson, who has sought to maintain public attention on Neal's lynching.

'embodied narrativity', suggesting that 'it is bound together with "higher order", more abstract and diachronic narrative structures of plot and identity [...] in a relationship of dynamic circularity [...] but already actualized in our active, immediate consciousness of environment' (2019, p. 72). Embodied narrativity, as a phenomenon, draws upon the notion of 'enactivism', which posits that 'embodied experience is never passive receptivity [...]. Rather, our living systems actively perceive and (make) sense through our immanent state of being in constant dynamic interaction with environment' (Shibolet, p. 60). This concept resonates considering my embodied experience of this scene, and the experience overall, which is understood based on my physical interactions with Wheaton and other story agents within the represented 360-degree VR environment.

As Wheaton dissolves into sparkles of yellow light at the end of the forest scene, distant rumbles signal a change to come. Suddenly the forest environment that surrounds me begins to shatter and tear, as though it was made of two-dimensional glass. Its pieces break apart and I find myself floating in space. The ranch house moves away from me, becoming one of many architectural structures that drift in space. Alongside upside down trees and shards of the previous scene, I see walls of historical venues such as The Cotton Club and The Apollo Theatre (venues that championed black musicians in the early to mid-twentieth century), sets of staircases, an upturned police car and a series of monuments recalling key moments in the history of the revolutionary black power movement (see Fig. 4.1). In this second scene I am literally passing through time, unanchored. At this moment my vantage point of the action is unaligned with any 'realistic' human experience. Rather, I exist in a vacuum on the time-space continuum, and must piece together a narrative from the objects and architectural structures that pass by.

After several moments the jagged shards of imagery that drift around the space suddenly snap together, revealing a second coherent 360-degree environment. I'm now standing on the side of the road in a middle-class US suburban neighbourhood at night. After a moment of acclimation a police car approaches on my left and pulls over at the side of the road. There is a flash of bright light as two police officers step out of the vehicle. They address me directly in turn: 'Excuse me... we got a call... Are you familiar with this area? Yes or no?.... This call describes you perfectly.... You'll have to come with us'.

Fig. 4.1 *The Changing Same: The Dilemma*, Directed by Joe Brewster, Yasmin Elayat, Michèle Stephenson. (Produced by Rada Studio and Scatter. © Changing Same Collaborative LLC)

A moment later I find myself positioned in the backseat of the police car, with Wheaton sitting in handcuffs beside me. He speaks of his anger of being arrested for no good reason. At this point I realise that I have been cast as a character in this VR simulation—as an offsider who is arrested alongside Wheaton—although, as previously noted, I have no physically manifested body. Suddenly the space in the car expands and the scene once again fragments. I'm floating in space once more, although this time the objects and structures that float past me point more clearly towards black oppression than black power. For example, I see images of slaves in chains and the walls of a prison.

After several seconds, a new 360-setting snaps together and I find myself in a large cell in a police station. Wheaton sits on a seat to my left, holding his head with one hand, while another black prisoner is located on my right. A police officer stands guard, while another calls through a list of names of arrestees. I can take a few steps towards or away from other characters as I might in real life. A female lawyer approaches and speaks to me directly. I look her in the eyes as she tells me that I have been arrested on a Class D Felony assault charge, which carries a three- to seven-year sentence. The lawyer suggests that I take a plea deal, advice that makes Wilson lower his head in despair.

The spatiality of this large holding cell and the movements of its inhabitants are grounded in a sense of realism. However, the mise en scene also has various magical realist elements, such as a large window on my right that provides a vast view of the space-like void that I've previously experienced. A series of thick metal chains float around wooden beams across the ceiling, rattling as they slowly twist and contort. These two elements—the window and the chains—work together to emphasise a continuum of black history, reminding me that present-day oppression builds upon past events. A sense of past/present collision is further fostered when the scene suddenly transitions to the past, portraying a time of black slavery. I observe several men in chains, while listening to one man unsuccessfully plead for his freedom. The scene transitions back to the present-day jail cell. The female lawyer again encourages me to take the plea deal. This will however mean testifying against Wheaton, who will surely be jailed as a result. Wheaton approaches us, angry once more. As he calls for justice, the sounds of chains rattling become prominent. The lawyer yells for assistance, and the lights in the cell dim.

In the final scene of Episode 1, I find myself in a large white space that contains little detail other than a set of stairs to my left. Within this somewhat blank canvas, a tall female figure in a multilayered white dress sings to herself (see Fig. 4.2). This is Harriet, who is described by co-director Yasmin Elayat as a '13 foot tall hybrid avatar' created through a merging of motion capture and volumetric capture (Pietroben, 2021). Harriet's direct address challenges me to contribute to a rewriting of black history. Stephenson refers to this final scene as a 'version of the Matrix red pill/blue pill dilemma. Are you going to be conscious and aware, and make the decision to stay and join the rewriting of our common narrative or do you prefer to bury it all and leave?' (quoted in Pietroben, 2021).

As the scene ends and I remove my VR headset, I am left with many questions about black history in the United States. As an Australian, this is a history that was not foregrounded in my formal education and of which my knowledge is limited. In this way my cultural and social specificity is implicated in my consciousness of the represented 360-degree environments and subsequent narrative understanding. Throughout the experience I feel aligned with Wheaton; however, my specific response to the work may not be shared by all. As Fisher points out in his analysis of

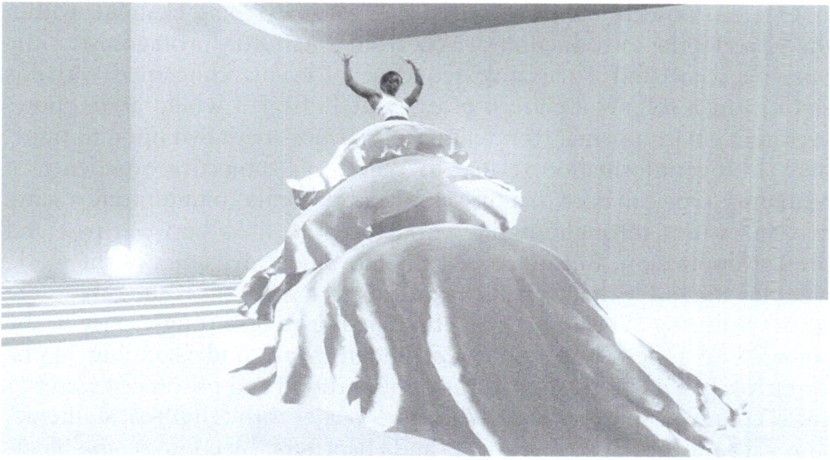

Fig. 4.2 *The Changing Same: The Dilemma*, Directed by Joe Brewster, Tasmin Elayat, Michèle Stephenson. (Produced by Rada Studio and Scatter. © Changing Same Collaborative LLC)

the work, persons of different identity may understand the scenes differently (2022).

This first episode of *The Changing Same*, which was scripted following considerable research into historical events and current realities, provides a visceral experience of current and past oppression, and a first-hand experience of prejudice. The dramatised events of the arrest and prison cell scene might be considered an example of 'speculative documentary' practice (Bellinck & van Dienderen, 2019). This recently defined practice is based on speculation and assumption rather than the recording of events that occurr in a specific time and place, and as such, offers a means 'to resist, to challenge, (and) to subvert dominant epistemologies that are still rooted in colonialism and global capitalism' (Bellinck & van Dienderen, p. 13). While throughout the experience, my agency as a user is limited (I can choose my viewing direction, take steps in space but have no ability to influence the unfolding narrative), my simulated arrest and jail cell experience alongside Wheaton gives rise to an understanding of the subject matter that is drawn from embodied experience.

One can observe the existence of classical storytelling elements within the episode: the introduction of Wheaton as narrator/protagonist in the opening scene and a narrative sequence of events concerned with his arrest, which follows a pattern of cause and effect. I would argue, however, that environmental storytelling approaches are drawn upon to transmit narrative information related to Wheaton's subjective experience of Marianna. One can note that mise en scene elements communicate a sense of timelessness throughout the work, fostering links between past and present oppression. But moreover, the movement dynamics of the work, whether aligned with a 'real-life' experience of space (as is the case in the scenes featuring Wheaton) or an abstracted drifting through space in the connecting 'time-travel' sequences, underpin my understanding of the narrative. In the forest, suburban neighbourhood and prison cell scenes, I am encouraged to experience Wheaton's reality through physical interaction with the virtual environments and characters. By contrast, the 'floating space' scenes explore black history in the United States more broadly. One could view these gravity-free scenes as offering what Jenkins' terms as 'embedded narrative', where story information is presented across a range of artefacts (p. 126). In other words, narrative is embedded in objects and architectural structures that must be decoded by the viewer and interpreted as a meaningful whole. To make sense of this scene, I consider not just the objects presented to me but my positioning as one more element floating in the void space.

The suburban neighbourhood and prison cell environments are spaces where narrative is offered as a simulation for the user, that is the user is cast in the role of felon, even though they cannot interact with story agents in a consequential manner. Once could consider the environments featured within these scenes as spaces where narrative is enacted, even though the user exists as a passive character within the drama. This approach 'invites interpretation of situations and meaning according to players' views and experience' (Habgood et al., p. 3). This returns us to the notion of embodied narrativity and 'enactivism' as posited by Shibolet (p. 60), involving meaning-making through constant and dynamic interplay with the environment. This results in a powerful exploration of the social and cultural realities of America, in the past and present.

Child of Empire

This chapter's second case study is an animated docu-drama experience that recalls the 1947 Partition of India and Pakistan. This historical event is explored via the personal stories of two men of the Partition generation told in a series of flash backs. An Indian Hindu, Ishar Das Arora (voiced by Adil Hussain), recalls his childhood experience of migration from Pakistan to India, while Iqbal-ud-din Ahmed (voiced by Salman Shahid), a Pakistani Muslim, tells of his similar childhood journey in the opposite direction. The style of animation that is employed draws upon digital techniques but has a handdrawn quality that somewhat links the aesthetic of the work to its historical subject matter. The user is positioned as witness to the portrayed events and as well as exploring each environment with six degrees of freedom (6DoF), has some additional abilities to interact with story elements. Given the complexity and overall length (17 minutes) of the experience, I will focus my close analysis on the first of the two stories that is presented.

For the opening scene of *Child of Empire* I find myself in an ornate and colourful hexagon-shaped room that is adorned with burning candles and hanging vines. I note my ability to move with 6DoF in this space and look down at my hands, which resemble those of a decaying wooden mannequin. While I can move these hands around, I am not granted any further ability to interact with the environment at this time. In a large window in front of me, a paper theatre production that presents an overview of historical events leading up to the Partition of India is staged (see Fig. 4.3). The paper theatre, as a storytelling object, offers a link to both colonialism and childhood experience. Also known as a 'toy theatre', the paper theatre was born in nineteenth-century England as a child's toy, and quickly became popular across Europe and further abroad (Farr, 2008, pp. 43–45). Its inclusion at the start of the VR experience sets the scene for a tale told through the eyes of two seven-year-old children who may even have played with such a toy in their childhood days. A female voice narrates as paper puppets and props illustrate multicultural life in precolonial India, the subsequent entry of the British and the 1909 divide of Muslim and Hindu peoples. As the events of this swiftly delivered backstory become darker in tone, colour drains out of the hexagon room. Suddenly the environment transitions and I find myself in an animated scene of a deserted street, surrounded by stone buildings. Fire burns at the end of the road, while black clouds overhead and paper pamphlets that float up into the sky—notice of

Fig. 4.3 *Child of Empire*. (© *Project Dastaan*)

the Partition—signal trouble to come. The ground begins to shake beneath my feet and a line appears in the middle of the street. A moment later the landscape breaks in two along this line, revealing a fiery red river below. I note that this line runs directly underneath two places of workshop (presumably Muslim and Hindu) that sit at opposite ends of the road. Although no human characters are featured in this street scene, this representation of geography powerfully conveys a sense of the desolation and tragedy that the Partition will bring about. As I reflect upon this representation of the physical effects of the forced divide, my vantage point of the scene rises up, so as to provide a bird's eye view of the landscape. This image morphs into a map of India and Pakistan that is marked by fiery red boundary lines.

Having established the events that led up to the Partition, the experience's second sequence introduces its two elderly protagonists who sit at a small, round table by candlelight, drinking chai tea (see Fig. 4.4). Their relationship is amicable with small talk focussing on their similarities rather than differences. A half-finished game of Snakes and Ladders sits on the table between them as they compare notes on their life experiences. One must note that although mainly known in its Westernised form, Snakes and Ladders originates from a traditional Indian dice and board game, which was adapted by the British. Topsfield suggests that the traditional

Fig. 4.4 *Child of Empire*. (© *Project Dastaan*)

version's theme is 'the spiritual quest for liberation from the vicissitudes of karma or the hindrances of passions' (1985, p. 143). The snakes and ladders of this game are layered upon a map of India and Pakistan and its playing thus becomes a metaphor for the journey across dangerous terrain in the aftermath of the Partition. As the board game sits idle, Iqbal-ud-din Ahmed recalls his family's forced migration to Pakistan on foot, while Ishar Das Arora tells of his journey into India by train.

As Arora reflects on his life before the Partition, we transition to a new street scene. In voice over, he recalls a day of celebration, where people of all faiths shared food in the street. Whereas the previous street scene was dark and deserted, this street is populated by people of various ages and faiths who are adorned in brightly coloured clothing. I note green, yellow and red foodstuffs piled into round pots, which suggests an abundance of resources. The animated human characters that surround me stand with their arms raised into the air, seemingly frozen, although the soundtrack suggests movement. Using my hand controllers, I find that I have the ability to shoot streams of colour into the environment, although this does not seem to impact upon the characters. It feels somewhat curious that, as an invisible witness to this scene, I can move but the characters cannot. This is a constraint that is perhaps driven by the technical aspects of production; however, it has the effect of emphasising the scene as Arora's subjective memory of a particular moment in time. Arora's memory seems only partial or incomplete—limited to a snapshot rather than a fully animated scene. My actions within the space of this scene are playful rather than consequential. In conversational voice over, Ahmed suggests that life wasn't quite as rosy prior to the Partition as Arora's memory suggests, further emphasising the subjective nature of his experience.

A moment later, the same street is empty. Arora recalls his experience of the night that the Partition was enacted, which was spent hiding in a barn with his parents. As an invisible observer, I find myself forcibly tracking backwards into the dark barn. A wooden door swings shut in front of me and I turn left, finding a small child (Arora) crouching on the floor beside me. His mother and father are positioned behind me, both with anxious gazes. A rifle leans against the wall, next to a small table-like structure upon which small candles burn. Arora tells of his silent terror as sounds of violence erupted outside the barn throughout the night. I move closer to the candles as the tabletop structure morphs into a miniature scene of a small township on fire. As I stare at this scene, Ahmed tells of his own terror the same night, as he watched his entire village burn to the ground.

The following scene illustrates the most harrowing of Arora's memories—his train ride across Partition lines into India. As a user, I find myself positioned in the aisle of a moving train alongside stationary passengers, many of whom resemble wooden mannequins. The characters of Arora and his parents are more life-like, although, like the other figures, they are hard to see in the low light of the carriage. I find that I am holding an oil lamp in my hand, which I can move around to light up the space close to me. I move towards some of the mannequin-like figures and illuminate the details of their faces as well as the wooden seats that they are positioned upon. Arora's voiceover recalls how the train stopped for water, allowing his family members and other passengers to disembark. When they did so they were ambushed by hostile forces and all but Arora's father were killed. Arora survived by hiding behind a seat on the train. As the details of this massacre are shared, the viewable space on the train seems to shrink. Darkness descends and a bright palette of colour fades to red and black. The mannequins change into burnt and decayed forms that are draped over seats in poses of self-preservation. A lifeless male figure has fallen to the floor in the aisle, and lies with arms outstretched. As user, I illuminate these lifeless forms with the oil lamp, so as to make sense of this scene of horror. The scene is static for some time to enable this exploration. Continuing his voiceover narration, Arora tells Ahmed of a vision that he had in the aftermath of the massacre—of Krishna dancing on the head of the venomous snake demon, Kaliya. As he describes this, a visual representation of the vision appears in the darkened train carriage, further illuminating the scene.

The remaining scenes of the VR experience explore Ahmed's childhood experience of walking in a caravan towards Pakistan. This perilous journey ends with his entry into a refugee camp as a seven-year-old child. For the final scene, we return to the round table, where the two elderly men finish their tea. 'Did we cross paths?' they ponder. As the sound of birds chirping grows louder, the two men dissolve into streams of butterflies. The project then offers a moving rendition of *Subh-e-Azaadi*, a song written by the Pakistani poet Faiz Ahmad Faiz, the lyrics of which appear in multiple languages in the space surrounding me, encouraging contemplation on the human toll of the Partition. The inclusion of this song reflects the VR project's focus on reconciliation and healing. This focus is further evidenced by the equal time that is given to the men's respective stories, and the way that they are presented as friends rather than adversaries. Responsibility for the bloodshed of the Partition is firmly directed towards the British government in the opening paper theatre sequence; however, the two narrating characters display somewhat mellow attitudes towards the historical actions of their former rulers throughout the work. As a result, the men's individual stories provide powerful entry points into a larger narrative of human suffering and the quest for freedom.

Like the previous case study, *Child of Empire* adopts classical storytelling techniques, with voiceover narration guiding the user's understanding of most scenes. Featuring parallel narratives and flashback sequences, the work presents its narrative as a chain of causal events. These classical elements reflect the influence of cinematic storytelling on the work.

The environmental features of *Child of Empire* do however play an integral role in the transmission of narrative information to the user, in that (1) as is the case with screen media in general, mise en scene elements convey meaning and (2) the design of 360-degree space and the featured interactive devices invite the user to explore, interpret and invest in the situations that unfold. In terms of the former I note an impressionistic rendering of human figures and settings that emphasises the subjective memories of the narrators. Moreover, included colour schemes and objects underline both the impact of India's colonisation and the two narrators' childhood experience. Bright colour is used to represent a harmonious multicultural society that existed prior to British intervention (most notably in the opening moments of the paper theatre production, although this palette resurfaces in Arora's memory of life before the Partition). By contrast, life after the Partition is portrayed in dark tones and enveloped in shadows. The featuring of mannequins in the place of human characters emphasises the lack of agency granted to vast populations affected by the Partition-like mannequins, Arora's family is subject to manipulation by external forces. The decayed quality of these mannequins, which the user also notes when looking at the representation of their own hands, is a reminder of not only the devastating impact of the Partition, but of the time that has passed since this historical event.

In terms of the impact of spatiality and interactive devices, one can observe a project design that encourages user exploration of the various scenes to further understand the two narrators' subjective experience, an activity that accords with Jenkins' notion of environmental storytelling. The user is granted the ability to move around the various spaces that are depicted and can therefore make sense of the various objects embedded within environments through exploration. While in some moments the user exists in space alongside the depicted narrator/s (such as being at the table with the two elderly men, or in the barn alongside Arora and his parents), at other times they are left alone within a frozen or static scene to absorb and contemplate the impact of Partition events. The additional interactive devices—the shooting of colour in the street scene and the use of the oil lamp as a torch—allow the user to shape the appearance of the environment, fostering greater investment and immersion in the scenes. In the case of the train scene, the oil lamp is a device that encourages the user to actively seek out story details (by illuminating the faces of massacre victims, represented there as decaying mannequins). As such, the work fosters a powerful link between the subjective experience of the narrators and the embodied experience of the user.

On the Morning You Wake (to the End of the World)

Like *Child of Empire*, this chapter's final case study also seeks to convey subjective experience of a historical event. At 8.08 am on 13 January 2018, an emergency alert about a ballistic missile threat was mistakenly sent by text message to the 1.4 million citizens of Hawai'i. This terrifying alert granted them approximately 15 minutes to prepare for a nuclear strike that, if real, would decimate their surroundings. State officials announced their mistake some 38 minutes later, leaving citizens reeling from the false alert. *On the Morning You Wake (to the End of the World)* explores the ways that individuals reacted to the alert, and the chaos that erupted in its aftermath. First hand-audio testimonies and spoken word poetry is illustrated using volumetric video, computer-generated imagery and visual effects, offering representations of environments that, for 38 minutes in the minds of participants, were moments away from obliteration. My close reading will explore the first episode of the VR experience, titled *Chapter 1: Take Cover.*

The episode begins in darkness, before a series of swirling dots of light appear all around the user, like stars in a universe, or particles materialising in space. A female voice over delivers a poem written by one of the work's creators, activist, artist, and Professor of Native Hawaiian politics, Dr Jamaica Heolimeleikalani Osorio, which encourages contemplation on the beginnings of life. 'On the Morning You Wake to the End of the World [...] take your body back to the clay...', this suggests. The light particles rise up all around me and cluster into vague forms, like atoms creating matter. A landscape becomes discernible—mountains and a sea (see Fig. 4.5).

A moment later we transition to a hyperreal scene of a beach at dawn as Osorio's audio testimony recalls her activities on the morning that the

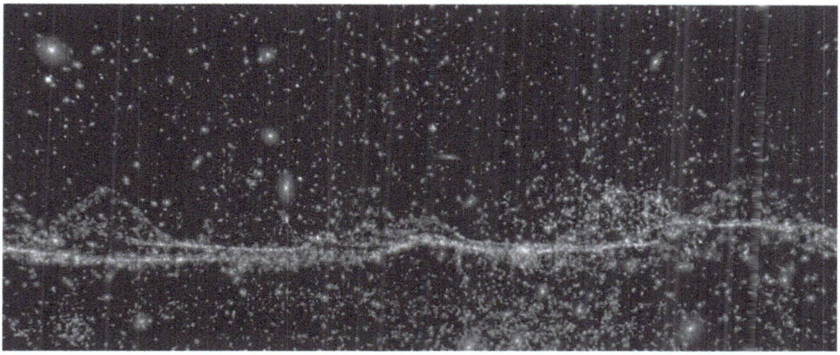

Fig. 4.5 A landscape take shape in *On the Morning You Wake (to the End of the World)*. (*© 2022 ARTE France, The British Film Institute and 38 Minutes Ltd*)

alert was sent. A rosy sunrise illuminates this scene, which is created through animation and volumetric video capture. A woman wearing athletic attire and a baseball cap (presumably Osario) squats next to one of several canoes that rest on sand adjacent to rocks and palm trees. It is 8.07 am in the morning. As an invisible and unacknowledged witness to the scene, I watch as she retrieves her mobile phone from a bag to take a picture of the multicoloured sky. She pauses as a text message is received. We then cut to a new environment—a hillside where several stone houses sit among luscious vegetation. The sky remains illuminated with the same colourful display. A realistically rendered man and a woman (Kauai couple Bruce Allyn and Cynthia Lazaroff) observe the sunrise from the balcony of one of the buildings. Like the other elements of this second environment, they are miniaturised in relation to my scale as an observer, meaning that they somewhat resemble dolls in a dollhouse. This difference in scale grants me a 'God's eye' perspective on the scene while also accentuating the two protagonists' situation of powerlessness in the moments to come. Lazaroff's audio testimony notes the beautiful but ominous sunrise on the morning that the alert was sent. 'Bruce said "I've got to go get the good camera and record it"', she recalls. I watch as the miniaturised figure of Allyn takes some photos from the balcony.

The following scene transitions us to the indoor environment of another resident, high school teacher Angie Anderson. In this bedroom environment I return to a viewing position that is scaled to offer a human perspective of events, therefore existing alongside the depicted character as an invisible observer. I watch as Anderson moves about the room, taking some final steps to ready herself for work, before her phone buzzes with the text message alert. Anderson stares at this message on her phone with a puzzled expression. As she does so, cracks appear in the walls of the realistically rendered scene. These quickly spread and then the entire room breaks up into a patchwork of uneven shapes, then smaller particles, as though obliterated by a nuclear strike at that moment.

At this point in the VR experience, the text message that residents received is displayed on a black screen: BALLISTIC MISSILE THREAT INBOUND TO HAWAI'I. SEEK IMMEDIATE SHELTER. THIS IS NOT A DRILL. Bruce Allyn's audio testimony fades in as I read this, expressing shock and fear. A moment later I'm returned to the scene of Allyn and Cynthia on their balcony, although I'm now located in the house behind them, watching from beyond an opened screen door with a human-scale perspective of the unfolding events. 'You initially can't even process it' Allyn exclaims. 'I realised if I am getting this message, everyone is getting it'. As Allyn and Lazaroff look out at the sun rising over the mountains in the distance, the landscape dissolves into light particles on a black background. The balcony breaks up into pieces and disappears from under their feet, leaving their bodies suspended in air (see Fig. 4.6). As with the preceding scene, this is a powerful representation of the protagonists' emotional and psychological experience in the moments after the alert message was received. The breakdown of the environment into something resembling atomic particles represents a possible future for the protagonists, this involving the destruction of their surroundings and everyone contained within these. The VR experience conveys a sense of their world physically disappearing as they contemplate the ramifications of the text message.

The following scenes of the episode further draw upon the technique of rendering environments as dot-like particles or in geometric shapes, which dissolve and disappear as the experience transitions from one environment to another. I hear witness testimony of chaos on roadways as citizens speed in cars to be with their loved ones in the aftermath of the alert's issue. I see children forced into underground drains by parents who sought

Fig. 4.6 The landscape is reduced to particles in *On the Morning You Wake (to the End of the World)*. (*© 2022 ARTE France, The British Film Institute and 38 Minutes Ltd*)

shelter. A man runs across a field with a young child on his back and another at his side, only to be refused refuge within a large building. One scene transports me to Princeton University (the only scene set outside of Hawai'i) where Dr Tamara Lilinoe Patton, a nuclear expert, is working in the library. Her solitude is broken soon after 8.08 am as her mobile phone chimes with a flurry of messages from family and friends in Hawai'i, all of whom desperately seek her advice on the alert. In voiceover narration, Patton recalls thinking that her friends and family had perhaps 15 minutes to prepare themselves before the missile would hit. As she contemplates the mass destruction that such a nuclear event would produce, the library environment breaks up into geometric shards of colour that float away into space. For the final scene of the episode, we return to the beach environment that was seen at the start of the experience; however this is now rendered as a series of coloured dots in black space. I watch as Osorio rows out into the ocean in her canoe, a lone figure in a vast, abstracted world. As for the opening scene of the VR experience, the rendering of this scene reduces the landscape to a series of small particles—space literally dematerialised around the protagonist.

The impressionistic rendering of the environment in this final scene and the episode more broadly encourages reflection on the precariousness of Earth and the danger of nuclear technologies. I would argue that this expressive approach to the representation of subject matter, which helps to communicate to the project's themes, is a significant contributor to the emotional impact of the work.

The notion of environmental storytelling would, however, appear less applicable to *On the Morning You Wake* than the previous case studies, given its limited interactivity. Similarly to *Child of Empire*, the project relies on voiceover narration and mise en scene as the two principal means through which narrative information is delivered but it is notable that the project offers less of a sense of agency to the user than *Child of Empire*. One can explore the virtual environment with 6DoF but has no further ability to interact with the represented documentary participants or environmental elements. As a result, narrative information is largely interpreted through the act of witnessing events rather than via more active play with environmental elements. This is not to say that the user can't explore the 3D environments that depicted in the work, but that this exploration is limited and does not include the ability to touch or move objects. As such there is limited opportunity for narrative to emerge through discovery.

One can also note that as the user is positioned as an invisible observer within each scene, there is no opportunity for them to engage in role-play as story participant. Whereas *The Changing Same* offers an experience that is akin to an enactment of narrative, casting the user as a character in the drama and featuring characters that 'break the fourth wall' to address them directly, *On the Morning You Wake* is experienced by a user, who is not acknowledged by story protagonists as 'being present' in the virtual environment. In other words, the user plays no active role as a character in the unfolding story. In sum, one can observe a favouring of classical storytelling approaches rather than spatial exploration of environments as a means towards narrative understanding.

Conclusion

This chapter has explored the use of expressive environments and interactive devices in virtual reality documentaries through a close reading of three room-scale projects. This analysis has revealed how non-realist approaches can be particularly adept for the historical documentary genre, considering how abstract or expressive environments can convey meaning related to the subjective experience of past events. The three projects that have received analysis in this chapter display a range of imaginative approaches to the design of 3D environments, and moreover, they consider the position of the user within these environments and their interaction with story agents as a means to further communicate project themes.

As the analysis above has demonstrated, the three works draw upon classical and environmental storytelling approaches to varying degrees. 'Embedded narrative' and 'enacted narrative' are two environmental storytelling concepts that emerge from the analysis. On the former, one can observe that the first and second case studies most clearly demonstrate how narrative might be embedded within objects in a VR story, however, it is notable that these objects are not 'presented redundantly across a range of spaces', as Jenkins theorises in relation to video games (p. 126) but are featured in specific scenes in a controlled manner. In the case of *The Changing Same*, objects and architectural structures representing periods of black history are depicted as floating fragments that the user must interpret to form a meaningful whole. For *Child of Empire*, the user is offered play with interactive devices that allow them to affect the environment (e.g. a torch that illuminates the contents of a train carriage), and so their physical exploration involves discovery of narrative elements in a more active sense. This controlled presentation of objects with narrative meaning is directly tied to the works' linear narratives, which feature a series of causal events in accordance with classical storytelling formats. *On the Morning You Wake (to the End of the World)* also features a classical storytelling structure, showing less obvious play with environment storytelling techniques than the other projects.

The enactment of narrative within the projects is likewise limited by the linearity of each documentary storyline, however we see something akin to the virtual environment functioning as a 'staging ground' for story in *The Changing Same*. This work features scenes that cast the user as a character in its unfolding drama, providing a first-person experience of racial prejudice. This approach, in which the user adopts the point of view of a felon and is addressed directly as such by other characters, might be likened to the 'enacted narrative' that is described by Jenkins, even though the user's role is somewhat passive (rather than engage in role-play, they can only observe as events take place). Despite the user's lack of agency, these scenes encourage an understanding of the depicted events through simulated, embodied experience.

The mix of classical and environmental storytelling approaches that is observed above reflect the influence of cinema and games on contemporary VR projects as well the ongoing challenge of combining an authored narrative with the interactivity that VR can offer.[9] Closed narrative structures, which are typical for documentary, do not permit the user to affect story outcomes, however as the case studies demonstrate, the user's experience of a documentary narrative can be varied, personal and embodied, based on their exploration of the environment and engagement with story agents.

To date, scarce academic scholarship has explored environmental storytelling for entertainment-based VR and it is hoped that this chapter encourages further discussion in this area. The case studies explored above demonstrate how VR, as a narrative medium, can be particularly well-suited to environmental storytelling as it allows users to explore fully realised 3D environments from multiple angles and user perspectives. This

[9] The problem of reconciling a pre-authored narrative with interactive elements is described as a 'narrative paradox' by Aylett and Louchart (2007). This suggests that highly structured stories are incompatible with forms of interaction that hand more authorial control of the narrative to the user.

can create a sense of immersion within a storyworld that is not possible with traditional screen media.

Considering this chapter's exploration of works featuring limited user interaction, further research might explore environment storytelling in the context of open-ended VR works featuring emergent narratives. Such works allow the user to generate narrative possibilities, as well as to draw narrative meaning, through their exploration and interaction with a virtual environment.

References

6x9: A virtual experience of solitary confinement. (2016). Dirs. Francesca Panetta and Lindsay Poulton. *The Guardian.*

American Documentary. (2021). "The Changing Same: An American Pilgrimage," An episodic virtual reality racial justice experience by Sundance and Emmy-winning innovators rada studio and scatter, premieres at 2021 Sundance New Frontier. https://www.amdoc.org/pressroom/changing-same-american-pilgrimage-episodic-virtual-reality-racial-justice-experience-sundance-and-emmy-winning-innovators-rada-studio-and-scatter-premieres-2021-sundance-new-frontier/

Aylett, R., & Louchart, S. (2007). Being there: Participants and spectators in interactive narrative. *Lecture Notes in Computer Science, 4871*, 117–128. https://doi.org/10.1007/978-3-540-77039-8_10

Barbot, B., & Kaufman, J. C. (2020). What makes immersive virtual reality the ultimate empathy machine? Discerning the underlying mechanisms of change. *Computers in Human Behavior, 111*, 106431.

Bellinck, T., & van Dienderen, A. (2019). "That's My Life Jacket!" Speculative documentary as a counter strategy to documentary taxidermy. *Critical Arts, 33*(1), 60–74.

Bevan, C., Green, D. P., Farmer, H., Rose, M., Cater, K., Stanton Fraser, D., & Brown, H. (2019, May). Behind the curtain of the "ultimate empathy machine" on the composition of virtual reality nonfiction experiences. In *Proceedings of the 2019 CHI conference on Human Factors in Computing Systems* (pp. 1–12).

Bruni, L. E., Kadastik, N., Pedersen, T. A., & Dini, H. (2022). Digital narratives in extended realities. In *Roadmapping extended reality: Fundamentals and applications*, 35–62.

Carson, D. (2000). Environmental storytelling: Creating immersive 3D worlds using lessons learned from the theme park industry. Gamasutra.com. Vol. 1.

Child of Empire. (2022). Dir. Erfan Saadati. Project Datsaan.

Clouds Over Sidra. (2016). Dir. Chris Milk. Milk VR

De la Peña, N., Weil, P., Llobera, J., Spanlang, B., Friedman, D., Sanchez-Vives, M. V., & Slater, M. (2010). Immersive journalism: Immersive virtual reality for the first-person experience of news. *Presence, 19*(4), 291–301.

Farr, L. (2008). Paper dreams and romantic projections: The nineteenth-century toy theater. In D. Denisoff (Ed.), *The nineteenth-century child and consumer culture* (pp. 43–62).

Fisher, J. A. (2022). Epistemic rhetoric in virtual reality interactive factual narratives. *Frontiers in Virtual Reality, 3*, 845489.

Habgood, J., Moore, D., Alapont, S., Ferguson, C., & van Oostendorp, H. (2018, September). The REVEAL educational environmental narrative framework for PlayStation VR. In *Proceedings of the 12th European conference on Game-based Learning* (pp. 175–183).

Hassan, R. (2020). Digitality, virtual reality and the 'empathy machine'. *Digital Journalism, 8*(2), 195–212.

Hunger in Los Angeles. (2012). Dir. Nonny De la Peña. Emblematic Group.

Jenkins, H. (2004). Game design as narrative architecture. *Computer, 44*(3), 11.

Jones, S., & Dawkins, S. (2018). Walking in someone else's shoes: Creating empathy in the practice of immersive film. *Media Practice and Education, 19*(3), 298–312.

Kool, H. (2016). The ethics of immersive journalism: A rhetorical analysis of news storytelling with virtual reality technology. *Intersect: The Stanford Journal of Science, Technology, and Society, 9*(3), 1–11.

Laurel, B. (1993). *Computers as theatre*. Addison Wesley.

McRoberts, J. (2018). Are we there yet? Media content and sense of presence in non-fiction virtual reality. *Studies in Documentary Film, 12*(2), 101–118.

Murray, C. D., & Sixsmith, J. (1999). The corporeal body in virtual reality. *Ethos, 27*(3), 315–343.

Murray, J. H. (1997). *Hamlet on the holodeck: The future of narrative in cyberspace.* Simon & Schuster/Free Press.

Nitsche, M. (2008). *Video game spaces: Image, play, and structure in 3D worlds.* MIT Press.

Nooney, L. (2013). A pedestal, a table, a love letter: Archaeologies of gender in videogame history. *Game Studies, 13*(2), 137.

Notes on Blindness. (2016). *Dirs.Arnaud Colinart, Amaury La Burthe, Peter Middleton, and James Spinney.* Archers Mark & Atlas V.

On the Morning You Wake (to the End of the World). (2022). Dirs. Mike Brett, Steve Jamison, Arnaud Colinart & Pierre Zandrowicz. Archers Mark & Atlas V.

Pietroben, A. (2021). "To rewrite the narrative together"—Michèle Stephenson, Joe Brewster, Yasmin Elayat (THE CHANGING SAME). https://www.xrmust.com/xrmagazine/stephenson-brewster-elayat-the-changing-same/

Renov, M. (1993). Toward a poetics of documentary. In M. Renov (Ed.), *Theorizing documentary* (pp. 12–36). Routledge.

Shapiro, L. (2010). *Embodied cognition*. Routledge.

Shibolet, Y. (2019). *Towards a framework for embodied narrativity*. Masters Thesis, Utrecht: University of Utrecht.

Shin, D. (2018). Empathy and embodied experience in virtual environment: To what extent can virtual reality stimulate empathy and embodied experience? *Computers in Human Behavior, 78*, 64–73.

Smith, H., & Worch, M. (2010, March). What happened here? Environmental storytelling. In *Game Developers conference in San Francisco*.

Soler-Adillon, J., & Sora, C. (2018). Immersive journalism and virtual reality. *Interaction in digital news media: From principles to practice* (pp. 55–83)

The Changing Same Episode 1: The Dilemma. (2020). Dir. Michèle Stephenson. Black Dot Films.

The Displaced. (2015). *Dirs. Imraan Ismail, Ben C. Solomon, and Dan Edge. The New York Times.*

The Unknown Patient. (2018). Dir. Michael Beets. VRTOV.

Topsfield, A. (1985). The Indian game of snakes and ladders. *Artibus Asiae, 46*(3), 203–226.

CHAPTER 5

Time, Space and the Body in *The Under Presents* (2019), a Multiplayer Virtual Reality Game

Introduction

In recent years, the gaming industry has focused considerable attention on leveraging VR technologies so as to create highly immersive gameplay experiences (Monteiro et al., 2018, p. 1). VR games come in a variety of genres and formats, but key to their success is the creation of a sense of presence—of being inside the virtual world of a game—which is fostered by a range of creative approaches and technological affordances. While research has explored the role of perspective on user experience in VR games (Denisova & Cairns, 2015; Kallinen et al., 2007; Gorisse et al., 2017), scant literature has examined the way that narrative structures and devices give rise to powerful emotional and embodied experiences in this context. Peng et al. observe that 'A growing number of VR games are providing players with the type of emotional challenge characterized by narrative materials and emotional ambiguities' (2019, p. 2); however, they note that this area has received little attention.

In response to this gap in literature, this fifth chapter explores narrative structures within the multiplayer VR game *The Under Presents* (Tender Claws 2019). Within this landmark VR experience that combines game mechanics with immersive theatre elements, players are transported to a vaudeville stage buried in the sands of a vast desert and asked to uncover the mystery of a stranded ship and its inhabitants, remnants of which litter the landscape. Inside this nightclub venue, in which a variety of

K. Dooley, *Virtual Reality Narratives*,
https://doi.org/10.1007/978-3-031-64965-3_5

performers stage shows, mask-wearing users can congregate to learn and cast spells that unlock the secrets of the world. Players lack the ability to speak and must instead communicate with one another through movement or the clicking of their fingers. For limited periods, the world of 'The Under' has also featured an array of speaking non-player characters (NPCs) performed by live actors, who engage players in improvised performance. Key to this game is the ability to engage with these NPCs, and with other players, to unlock the full potential of the world. In doing so, players traverse a variety of game spaces and loops in time, with minimal instruction to indicate their optimal path or options.

With reference to narrative theory for games (Aarseth, 2012; Ryan, 2009), the chapter will interrogate the narrative experience that *The Under Presents* offers, noting the project's combination of linear story, improvised 'live' moments, and open-world narrative elements. The chapter's narrative and phenomenological analysis is based on my first-hand experience as a player, as well as secondary accounts of game experience found in video captures posted to YouTube, a user-created Wiki (Fandom, n.d.) and other online sources. A focus of the chapter will be an exploration of the player's characterisation as a faceless, voiceless and genderless being who possesses high levels of agency and has the ability to negotiate space and time within the game's world. With reference to Ryan's emotional and strategic conceptions of space in digital narratives (2015), I will argue that the involvement of the player's body in this time and space manipulation is an innovation that capitalises on the affordances of VR as an intimate and embodied medium. As such, *The Under Presents* has much to teach us about the potential of VR game narratives.

The Growth of VR Games

While VR games have become more prolific in recent years, they have a history that traces back several decades and involves significant advancements over time. Following the development of Ivan Sutherland's *Sword of Damocles*, a head-mounted display (HMD) that provided an early AR experience in 1968, various research projects and games companies explored the potential of VR technologies in the 1970s and 80s (Sherman & Craig, 2018). Nintendo introduced the 'Virtual Boy' console in 1995, which used a stereoscopic 3D display to deliver a portable VR experience. However, due to several limitations, including player discomfort and lack of engaging content, this was a commercial failure (Boyer, 2009).

Companies such as VPL Research and SEGA also developed VR systems in the 1990s and 2000s, but their products were expensive and not widely accessible. VR entertainment was at this time held back by technical limitations, high costs and limited computing power.

The development of consumer grade VR headsets in the early to mid-2010s fostered a new wave of VR entertainment media, which has been showcased in festival settings and other venues around the world. This beginning of this latest wave of activity was marked by the introduction of the Oculus Rift HMD, a device that was developed via a successful Kickstarter crowd-funding campaign in 2012. Following the success of the Oculus campaign, other companies entered the VR market, with HTC Vive, Sony PlayStation VR, and Samsung Gear VR emerging as notable VR platforms. This period saw the release of several VR games and experiences, showcasing the potential of the technology.

In more recent years, VR has achieved what could be considered a more mainstream adoption in the area of gaming. The release of standalone VR headsets, such as the Meta Quest and HTC Vive Focus, has removed the need for a high-end PC to play games, thus making VR accessible to a wider audience. Other advancements, such as improved video resolutions and more ergonomic design, have enhanced the overall experience of VR games. Both indie developers and major game studios have embraced VR, producing experiences that span multiple genres and distribution platforms. Notable games include the popular *Beat Saber* (Beat Games 2019), which was released across Playstation, Windows, Oculus and other platforms. Set in a neon environment, this experience encourages players to slice blocks with a light saber in time to musical beats. Meanwhile *Half-Life: Alyx* (Valve 2020), a puzzle-solving game set in the Half-Life universe, and *Superhot VR* (Superhot Team 2016) offer highly immersive experiences in the first-person shooter genre. *The Elder Scrolls V: Skyrim VR* (Bethesda Game Studio 2017), the virtual reality adaptation of the popular open-world role-playing game (RPG) allows players to explore the substantial world of Skyrim in a more immersive way. Adopting a more light hearted tone, *Job Simulator* (Owlchemy Labs 2016) parodies various jobs in a comical way, allowing players to interact with virtual objects. These successful games are but a sample of a growing number of titles that offer diverse experiences in VR.

The Under Presents—An Overview

The Under Presents was developed and produced by independent, Los-Angeles-based studio, Tender Claws, led by Samantha Gorman and Danny Cannizzaro, in collaboration with the live performance troupe, Piehole. Being both a puzzle game and a computer-generated performance space, the game includes a variety of narrative elements and structures. As I've outlined elsewhere (Dooley, 2023), it begins with an approximately 20-minute introductory experience that can be accessed for free using a Meta HMD. This begins in a dark and waterlogged wasteland, where the player must put on gold bracelets and a mask before moving towards the ruins of a nightclub from which muffled music exudes. Guided by the MC, a non-human figure with a black tuxedo and misshapen gold mask, the player enters this building and navigates through rooms full of doors and clocks in order to enter the 'Main Stage' of the game. This first part of the game is an onboarding experience that unfolds with limited direct instruction. Firstly, the player adjusts to the game's unique method of locomotion, known as the 'Scrunch Teleport', which sees them literally reach out and pull space towards themselves. Secondly, the player navigates time loops where they are able to see earlier versions of themselves (as an animated, black cloaked avatar) exploring game spaces. Only by coordinating their actions over several iterations of time is the player able to progress to the Main Stage and access the full multiplayer version of the game.

The notions of coordinated action and jumps through time also underpin the player's experience of the 'Main Stage' and surrounding desert. This multiplayer environment provides the venue for encounters with both programmed and live actor NCPs. The Main Stage is a nightclub featuring a variety of vaudeville style acts that appear on rotation and is built in the ruins of a large ship submerged in the sand of a vast desert environment. Here, players converge, interact with objects laid out on tables and use these objects to cast spells. Some of these spells require player collaboration and can result in the rebuilding of mysterious ruins found in the exterior landscape, the acquisition of new masks or increased powers of mobility. While players are not able to speak, they can communicate via hand gestures in order to encourage movement through space and the completion of collaborative tasks. For limited periods of time since the game's release, the Main Stage and surrounding areas have featured a number of human and non-human NPCs played by live actors, who speak

Fig. 5.1 Two players engage with a live actor avatar (screen capture from the author's game play). *The Under Presents* (2019), Tender Claws, LLC

directly to players and engage them in improvisation (see Fig. 5.1). While this activity has added an additional layer of playfulness and intrigue to the game, it is not an essential element of game play.

Some of these NPCs also appear in the single player 'Time Boat' puzzle experience that sits at the heart of *The Under Presents*, although performances are programmed, rather than live, in this setting. This scripted narrative involves the crew and passengers of The Aickman, a research vessel that sets sail in a quest to retrieve radiation samples following a 1958 nuclear event. Before reaching its intended destination, the ship becomes stuck in an ice flow and is damaged, leading to the crew and passengers' deaths in a variety of circumstances. This storyline is first presented by the

Fig. 5.2 One of several photo booths located in the multiplayer area that transport the player to the Time Boat experience (screen capture from the author's game play). *The Under Presents* (2019), Tender Claws, LLC

MC, who holds a model of the ship in a bottle. By entering a number of photo booths set about the Main Stage area of the game world (see Fig. 5.2), the player can be transported onto the Aickman to experience the narrative in real-time in three acts and an epilogue. Within these scenes, the viewer can explore the ship as a body existing alongside characters as events slowly unfold, or remove their mask so as to access a god-like view of the ship and its participants. In this latter position, the viewer can run their finger across their mask to wind time forward and backwards and is therefore able to review or speed up events. While the happenings that unfold on the Aickman seem somewhat predetermined, it is possible for the player to perform actions at key moments over the three acts, which result in the saving of characters from death.

The summary presented above outlines the principal elements of *The Under Presents* but does not capture the full complexity of the game, which involves several other sideways experiences and locations that connect the various narrative elements. The multiplayer area of the game contains several spaces to be explored and puzzles to be solved, but there are no demands made of the player to follow these threads. One could find enjoyment by simply observing the live acts in the nightclub as a virtual body. The player's mask is their principal tool throughout the game. Further to taking it off in the Time Boat experience to control the flow of time, it is removed in the multiplayer area to cast spells. By working through the Time Boat experience and by exploring the multiplayer area, the player comes to understand the world of *The Under Presents* as a surreal, timeless and liminal space that is built out of the remnants of the Aickman.

The Under Presents was released in November 2019 for Steam VR, Oculus Rift, and Oculus Quest, while a later version, *The Under Presents Tempest*, also existed between July to September 2020.[1] This second iteration of the VR experience involved a staging of scenes from the same-named Shakespearian play by live actor-controlled avatars in the word of the Under. This resulted in an approximately 40-minute experience that was scripted but also influenced by audience participation. Performed in the early stages of the Covid-19 pandemic, *The Under Presents Tempest* responded to lockdown conditions by enabling a (virtual) live theatre experience when physical theatres were closed. On this subject Corts aptly notes that the 'performance stands out not only for its commentary on the pandemic, but for the potential it demonstrates for an experience unfettered from the constraints of the physical world both in body and place through VR' (2021, p. 236). Given the ephemeral nature of *The Under Presents Tempest*, the analysis to follow will explore narrative structures in the original game experience only. In conducting this analysis, I seek to explore the game's structuring of time and space, as experienced by the virtual body.

[1] *The Under Presents Tempest* shows ran daily from 9 July–30 September 2020. A short second run of performances occurred in March of 2021. See: https://tenderclaws.com/tempest for more information.

Narrative Structures Within *The Under Presents*

Drawing upon the affordances of contemporary VR technologies, *The Under Presents* is a somewhat hybrid experience that draws upon the narrative conventions of games, live theatre and cinema. A number of theoretical frameworks proposed by authors working in the area of interactive digital narrative (IDN) and game studies provide a useful lens through which to broadly consider the experience that it presents. First, I look to the two categories of interactive experiences that Ryan suggests fall within her definition of a narrative, this being 'a sequence of events involving thinking individuals, linked by causal relations, motivated by a conflict, and aiming at its resolution' (2009, p. 43). Writing on the poetics of interactive narrative, Ryan proposes the notions of 'narrative games' and 'playable stories' to explore the interplay between narrativity and interactivity within an IDN. The narrative game, she suggests, sees 'narrative meaning [...] subordinated to the player's actions' (p. 45). In other words, story elements enhance game play but are not produced through game play. By contrast a playable story sees 'the players actions [...] subordinated to narrative meaning', so that narrative is produced through the action of playing the game (p. 45). In terms of the former, Ryan cites the aforementioned *Half-Life* as well as *Max Payne* and *Grand Theft Auto,* all of which point the player towards goals that have parallels with real-life situations or fantasies. These narrative games represent a 'ludus activity' where pre-existing rules lead to states of winning or losing within a narratised world (p. 46). Conversely, within a playable story 'there is no winning or losing: the purpose of the player is not to beat the game, but to observe the evolution of the storyworld' (Ryan, p. 46). These types of experiences 'induce a much more aesthetic pleasure than narrative games because the player is not narrowly focused on goals' (p. 46). Within a playable story a narrative thus emerges as players explore their environment and discover its secrets.

The open-world environment of *The Under Presents*' Main Stage area best aligns with Ryan's description of a playable story seeing as there is no clear notion of winning or losing associated with the game's interactive devices. Rather, collaboration with other players or NPCs (through the casting of spells or the manipulation of time) results in revelations about the nature of the storyworld. Narrative unfolds slowly here, built up through the sum of many small details and player experiences. This model of narrative design encourages what Larsen et al. describe as 'communal ritual play', where engagement with other players and repeated play is needed to understand the full story being told (2023, p. 473). For this approach, full narrative disclosure 'is obtained through repetition, wherein players experience new pieces of content, different ways to solve similar problems, or find hidden objectives, making the multiple repetitions a somewhat new experience each time' (p. 473).

By contrast, the scripted Time Boat experience resembles a 'narrative game' (Ryan, 2009), with player input affecting the outcome of the story (the survival or death of the characters aboard the Aickman provides a notion of winning or losing). Further to these two principal offerings of the game, the player's experience in the Main Stage area is regularly interrupted by 'updates' from the MC. These programmed sequences (which might be referred to as 'cut scenes' due to their narrative rather than ludic value) reveal further details of the creation of The Under, or shed light on the various characters that inhabit the world. For example, the MC might appear on stage in The Under, to tell a story about one of the stage acts. At other points in the experience, the player might find themselves in a one-on-one situation with the MC, who provides lengthy monologues or even lectures on historical events within the diegesis. A video recording of the game that has been posted to YouTube captures a series of these monologues, including a lecture on the Aickman's doomed voyage (Kgm Student07, 2020). As can be seen in Fig. 5.3, the MC stands in front of a slide show projected on a screen and gestures at a map of the voyage. As a participant in this scene, the player is given control of a small device that advances the slides and must respond to the MC's instructions to activate this. Offering narrative details with minimal interactivity, these intermittent sequences defy categorisation according to Ryan's typology and more strongly resemble the scene of a film or a short act of theatre.

The categories of 'narrative games' and 'playable stories' can be further analysed with reference to Aarseth's work on narrative structures in video games (2012). Following on from the so-called ludology vs. narratology debate that appeared in an academic context in the early twenty-first century, Aarseth offers a model of narratological analysis that favours neither games structures or stories but rather sees both as mediated representations of human reality (p. 130).[2] As I have noted in Chap. 1, his analysis presents a framework that encompasses four key elements present in both

[2] It is beyond the scope of this chapter to offer a full summary of the ludology vs. narratology debate, which centred on the extent to which games could be considered as a narrative form. For more information see the section on Game Narratives in Chap. 1 of this book.

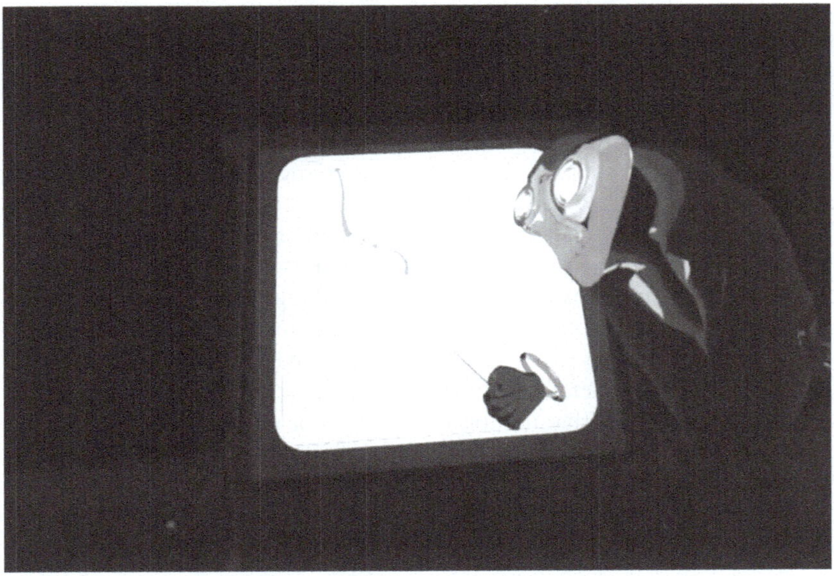

Fig. 5.3 The MC presents a slideshow on the Aickman's doomed voyage. (*The Under Presents* (2019), Tender Claws, LLC)

games and stories: places (worlds), things (objects), characters (agents) and events (p. 131). Aarseth firstly describes game worlds as physical or virtual structures that have clear boundaries and can be geometrically or topologically defined (p. 131). Unlike fictional worlds in films, game worlds rely on measurable space created through computer technology, offering concrete environments for players to explore. Additionally, game worlds consist of ludic spaces (playable areas) and non-ludic spaces (non-playable areas), with the scope of these areas varying depending on the game type (p. 131). Secondly, Aarseth categorises objects in a game world based on their malleability. These categories include static, non-interactable objects; static, usable objects; destructible objects; changeable objects; creatable objects and inventible objects. A player's level of agency is determined by these object qualities (p. 132). Thirdly, in terms of characters in games, Aarseth notes the possible incorporation of characters from other media. He proposes a classification system based on depth or shallowness, and malleability (p. 132). Characters might range from robots devoid of personality to complex individuals with detailed traits and backstories. A game may include a mixture of object and character types across these categories. Lastly, Aarseth interrogates events occurring in a game world, which he classifies in relation to 'kernels' and 'satellites' (p. 132). Kernels represent the essential events of a story, which make it recognisable (e.g. the wolf eating the grandmother in *Little Red Riding Hood*), while satellites are events that can be replaced or removed without altering the core essence of the tale. Based on these elements, he identifies four categories of events: fully plotted (pure story), dynamic satellites (playable story), dynamic kernels (multipath/quest games) and no kernels (pure game) (p. 132).

These useful classifications can be put together to determine the narrative and ludic elements, and emphasis, within a game. Aarseth suggests that works on the narrative-based end of the spectrum tend to have characteristics such as an inaccessible world, non-interactive objects, deep characters and a fully plotted sequence of events. On the other hand, games that prioritise ludic elements often include an open landscape, inventible objects, bots as characters and lack kernels (being thus pure game) (p. 132). The latter features fit with Ryan's category of 'playable story' and many of these can be seen to be at play in *The Under Presents*. Overall, however, the narrative structures of the VR experience do not align neatly with any single one of Aarseth's categories of events as I'll explore further.

The open world of *The Under Presents* features a number of spaces to be discovered and impacted upon through user exploration. Some of these spaces contain objects that are changeable or inventible. For example, by casting a range of spells and by working through various tasks, the player can conger new masks. At the same time, other objects within the storyworld (on the Time Boat and within the nightclub) are static and unchangeable, suggesting a predetermined narrative. In terms of character, I note the generic nature of the player's black cloaked and mask-wearing avatar (see Fig. 5.1), which will be analysed further below. While not a 'bot', this avatar lacks any individual character information or back story and thus functions as a generic 'body' through which the player can communicate with others. Conversely, NPCs such as the MC and the various crew of the Aickman do have distinct character traits and backstories. As such these characters offer a depth and lack of malleability that is quite different to the player as character. All of this suggests a sophisticated play between narrative and ludic elements. So too do events occurring in the game world, which include both 'kernals' that make the game recognisable, as well as 'dynamic satellites' that might be omitted without altering the core story. An example of the former is the scripted Time Boat experience, the ending of which can be altered slightly (characters can be saved from death) based on player interaction. This type of structure aligns with Aarseth's category of 'dynamic kernel', and is typical of multipath or quest games. Meanwhile, one example of the many 'dynamic satellites' in *The Under Presents* (what Aarseth calls a 'playable story') is the rebuilding of an observatory space in the desert surrounding the Main Stage of The Under. Two or more players working together in this space can transform the ruins into a fully realised building and obtain a star mask. This analysis demonstrates the complexity of the narrative structures in the VR experience, which might therefore be viewed to some degree as both a 'narrative game' and a 'playable story'. The classifications of narrative and ludic elements explored here, while useful, do not encompass some of the most notable aspects of *The Under Presents*, such as its experience of space, preoccupation with time, and the featuring of live actors in the virtual environment, all of which will be analysed further as a means towards articulating the specific qualities of the VR narrative.

Traversing Time Loops and 'Corporeal Space'

Several researchers have noted the distinctive properties of space in digital narratives (Aarseth, 2001; Murray, 1997; Nitsche, 2008; Ryan, 2015; Wolf, 2002). Aarseth suggests that 'what distinguishes the cultural genre of computer games from others such as novels and movies, in addition to its obvious cybernetic differences, is its preoccupation with space' (2001, p. 161), while Ryan suggests that video game space 'can be experienced both strategically and emotionally' (2015, p. 114). While both time and space have received significant attention within broader narrative theory (Wei et al., 2010), time within digital narratives has received less focus, which Ryan attributes to its more abstract nature. She observes that

> While we experience time by thinking about it, we experience space with our senses and with the movements of our body. We relate to space proprioceptively and kinetically. Space, unlike time, is visible, and we see space gradually unfold as we move, especially when we move at high speed. (Ryan, 2015, p. 119)

While this observation is applicable to digital media on a broad scale, I would argue that time is made visible in *The Under Presents*, and therefore deserves specific attention within a narrative analysis of this project. While intrinsic to the narrative, movements through time and space are also deeply connected to the player's corporeal experience of the game, as the manipulation of both elements can be considered an embodied activity.

The experience of a VR game involves the player's immersion in virtual space. Unlike a traditional video game, which positions the player in front of a screen, the VR game places their physical body in the virtual centre of a game experience, therefore encouraging them to physically turn around and explore a 360-degree landscape. Furthermore, the Meta Quest 2 and similar untethered Head-Mounted Displays (HMDs) provide what Saker and Frith refer to as 'coextensive space', wherein emerging design elements enable the integration of 'concrete reality' (2020, p. 1429). This means that the player's 'real-world' space and physical body has an impact on or corresponds to the virtual world depicted in the game (for example, taking a step sideways in the real world results in the player moving sideways in the virtual environment).

In *The Under Presents*, the player finds themselves in a number of surreal environments with few clues as to the opportunities that each location affords them. Rules of the game can be ascertained through interaction with other players (e.g. an experienced player might lead others towards an area of interest), or through clues embedded in the world's mise en scene. The latter can be described as a form of 'environmental storytelling' (Jenkins, 2004), where narrative information is distributed throughout the storyworld for the player to discover.[3] In this way, the player's bodily interaction with this space and its objects is central to narrative progression. Ryan's notions of 'emotional space' and 'strategic space' provide a useful lens through which to further interrogate the player experience of the game's various environments, before then exploring the player's experience of time.

Writing on digital narratives, Ryan observes two distinct conceptions of space. She suggests that the first, emotional space, is 'an experience of space associated with affective reactions. These reactions can be either positive, such as a sense of belonging, of security, of being home, or negative, such as repulsion, fear, or a sense of being lost' (p. 106). Ryan suggests that this type of space is best viewed from a horizontal perspective that mirrors normal human perception of the world and therefore 'comes closest to the lived, embodied experience that produces emotions'

[3] For more information on environmental storytelling, see Chap. 4.

(p. 106). As such it is a space that evokes the imagination, or contains stories and memories that are experienced by the interactor.

Whereas emotional space 'constructs the self as a relation to its environment', strategic space 'constructs the self as possibilities of action' (p. 107). For Ryan, this type of space is concerned with reaching goals or solving problems. As such, she suggests that strategic space 'is best represented in map view, as a vertical projection in which no object hides any other, because it is very important for strategic planning to see how objects relate to each other' (p. 107). As an example of this type of space, Ryan refers to squares on a chess board, which present paths for player action but have 'no intrinsic emotional value for the player' (p. 107). This is not to say that playing chess is an experience devoid of emotion but that the game space itself is not representative of this emotion.

On video games as a type of digital narrative, Ryan suggests that space can be experienced both strategically and emotionally, this involving an interplay between pursuing quests and the exploration of a world (p. 114). Writing on emotional space in open-world games in particular, she invokes the notion of flânerie, as explored by French poet Charles Baudelaire, to describe an experience of 'free wandering' within a game world, which may lead to random occurrences but also involves movement purely for the purpose of aesthetic appreciation. She observes that 'in a world design you do not have to accept all the tasks given to you by NPCs' (p. 114). Rather, space might be a site for socialising with other players or just a landscape to explore. The open-world game might then encourage flânerie whilst also offering strategic space to be traversed in the pursuit of quests.

This shift between free wandering and the pursuit of quests fits with my experience of space within *The Under Presents*. As a player, I have spent considerable time simply enjoying the ambience of the Main Stage or looking for secret locations or objects in the desert. The latter has not been driven by a need to fulfil any particular quest, but more so a desire to more fully understand the limits and nature of the storyworld. Within the Main Stage and surrounding desert area, my association with other players has had a social element. Although I have not been able to speak to other players, I have been able to wave at them, get their attention by clicking my fingers, share objects and/or follow them. On one of my early visits to The Under's nightclub, I found several players engaged in clumsy, improvised combat with swords and other tools on the dancefloor as one of the pre-programmed acts performed on the stage adjacent to us. Like the other players, I removed my mask, held it in front of my body and attempted to perform magic spells by manipulating objects placed on top of it. This action generated new objects, such as onions and other food stuffs to eat and drink. This experience continued for some time, during which I enjoyed exploring the nightclub environment and testing my powers in this space. When one player exited, I followed, eager to see where they might be headed. In the desert outside, this player pointed at a piece of paper on the ground, on which a spell formula was detailed. This was an invitation to pursue a quest, which I could take or leave. After noting the details of the formula, I wandered back to the nightclub to watch another act.

Even the Time Boat experience, as the most structured narrative sequence within the game, offers the player an experience of flânerie. As the virtual body, the player can explore the ship at their leisure, tuning in and out of different characters' conversations so as to get a sense of unfolding events. This involves moving along the Aickman's various decks, living quarters and operational spaces via a series of staircases and portals. When the ship becomes stuck in ice, the player can follow NPCs who dismount into the ice fields. The fact that the player has the ability to intervene in the narrative unfolding in this space is not immediately apparent, and so one might progress through the various acts as a pure observer. The rules associated with the quest to save characters are not self-evident, and may only be discerned by consulting the wiki for the game or another source of guidance.[4] It is noteworthy, however, that the player can obtain a god-like view of the events unfolding on the Aickman, by removing their mask. When doing so, the player finds themselves positioned in front of a miniature version of the ship, where they can not only view tiny versions of the various characters in space, but see themselves as a miniature standing static with their mask in hand. While this is not a 'map view' of the scene, it is closer to the vertical projection that Ryan associates with strategic game space. This viewpoint on the action, as well as the player's ability to scroll through time whilst occupying this viewpoint, affords them the ability to isolate specific moments when intervention may be consequential. For the experienced gamer, this god's-eye view of the game space may in itself function as a cue to engage in strategic action.

[4] A comprehensive wiki for *The Under Presents* can be found at https://the under-presents.fandom.com/wiki/The_Under_Presents. In this forum players share information about narrative and gameplay elements.

Further to this analysis of emotional and strategic space, I would argue that the most noteworthy aspect of the player's traversal of space in *The Under Presents* is related to the 'scrunch teleport' mechanic which sees them reach out their hand and literally 'pull' space towards their own body. This mechanic emphasises the player's navigation of space as an embodied activity that allows for rapid movement through the landscape. Co-director of the project, Samantha Gorman, describes this locomotion method as being tied to the time loops and 'tears in space' that are key to the narrative. She describes how

> We landed on a system where the player could reach out and pull the middle portion of the world towards them: as if reality was a spandex cloth you were tugging on. Then when the player lets go, the tugged part stays fixed and the rest of the world snaps toward you. On a technical level, this means that there is always a fixed anchor point in the player's field of vision. Only half of the world moves at once, first the inner field-of-view, and then the outer, so the player remains grounded. (Gorman quoted in Damiani, 2019)

The involvement of the player's body in this manipulation of space draws upon the affordances of VR technology (in this case hand controllers and head tracking within the HMD) to create a sense of presence in the virtual environment. Drawing upon these devices and technologies, the player is positioned as the central axis around which the 360-degree game world revolves. The scrunch mechanic means that they *move space* rather than move through space, as an embodied activity. One might ponder whether the nature of this action calls for a new conception of space that is specific to the VR game. While Ryan's description of emotional space is related to 'affective reactions', this notion does not seem sufficient to describe space that first and foremost, is experienced through movement of the body. I therefore adopt the term 'corporeal space' to describe space that is experienced by the HMD-wearing player as a physical body and virtual avatar located within a 360-degree virtual environment. While in relation to game experience this space might have emotional or strategic properties, it is space that is manipulated by a player located at the centre of a storyworld, whose bodily movement and action—the twisting of their body, the movement or their head, arms and hands—physically conjures space.

At the heart of this concept of corporeal space in *The Under Presents* lies the simultaneous experience of the player as a physical body in real life and as a virtual avatar, creating and engaging with space in interactive 3D virtual reality (VR). This diverges from non-VR games, where, as noted by Ash (2009, p. 2116), interactions with the image's space are limited by the constraints of a control pad. In contrast, *The Under Presents* utilises the VR interface, granting the player's physical body control over the creation of space. This phenomenon aligns with the earlier mentioned idea of 'coextensive space' by Saker and Frith (2020, p. 1429), which explores a symbiotic relationship between the physical and digital realms. Such a notion implies that game spaces facilitated by VR technology can conjure an illusion of physicality that accords with the experience of 'real' space.

Further work is needed to explore the validity and broader application of the notion of 'corporeal space' in the context of contemporary VR projects; however, when it is considered in light of other narrative-based VR games, it would appear apt. The single player game, *Virtual, Virtual Reality* (Tender Claws in 2017), for example, casts the player as a virtual labourer who must assist AI clients, and demands that they undertake physical challenges in a variety of simulated environments. Space within these environments can be physically warped by a player seeking to jump between worlds, and is constituted by the player's moving avatar. To take another example, the social VR game *Gorilla Tag* (Another Axiom 2021) puts players in the bodies of virtual gorillas and demands that they thump their arms so as to knuckle-walk on the ground. The player's corporeal experience of movement through space is here aligned with that of a real gorilla as they attempt to tag or avoid being tagged by other players, fostering a non-human point of view. Meanwhile, the casual VR game *Bait!* (Resolution Games 2019) positions the interactor beside a lake with a fishing rod and asks them to swing their arms so as to cast the rod and catch fish. As the interactor moves to their best vantage point, their view of the environment changes accordingly. For each of these diverse games, space is constituted by the movement of the player's real body, which is mirrored in the virtual environment, foregrounding an embodied experience of narrative.

As Flavian et al. (2019) observe, the high levels of embodiment that are generated by immersive technologies can establish a symbiotic relationship between humans and technology. This propels users into a state where the technology seamlessly enhances their capabilities (allowing them to rapidly traverse a landscape, as occurs via the scrunch teleport mechanic in *The Under Presents*, for example). This phenomenon calls for the careful consideration of how interactive devices and user interfaces can extend the

VR user's natural abilities (i.e. how their perceptual or motor skills might be enhanced) and moreover, how this can assist in the delivery of narrative.

Further to the notion of corporeal space, one could argue that the manipulation of time be considered an embodied activity in *The Under Presents.* The notion of the 'time loop' appears in multiple ways within the game, considering narrative structures, game mechanics and player experience. Firstly, the looping of time, as a game mechanic, is presented in the introductory sequence when the player must coordinate their actions over several iterations of time in order to enter the Main Stage area. Secondly, as described above, the player can physically control the passing of time during the Time Boat experience, and moves across time periods between this experience and that of the Main Stage area. The aforementioned photo booths act as an entry point for jumps backwards in time, while a gift shop located in the desert provides a re-entry point to the Main Stage area. With these devices and architecture, the game not only foregrounds the player's spatiality within the scene but also makes the passing of time, and shifts between time, visible. As Wei at al. argue in relation to video games more broadly, 'time and space can be seen as separate—but not unconnected—aspects of game design and experience' (2010, p. 2). In their exploration of the representation of time in video games, Wei et al. look to Arsenault and Perron, who argue that 'the temporal dimension of gameplay prevails on its spatial characterization' (2009, page). In other words, one might note the passing of time based on changes to the appearance of game space as interactions occur. Certainly, one can see this representation of passing time at play during the Time Boat sequence when the player winds time back and forward, noting the movement of characters and the Aickman's gradual disintegration. However, I would argue that the player's physical ability to manipulate time with their fingers, as well as to jump between the Main Stage area and Time Boat experience via the photo booths, makes time visible in a way that goes beyond spatial characterisation and rather, is the result of the player's bodily experience. I will further explore this notion with reference to different presentations of time within the storyworld.

A 'Real-Time' Experience of Narrative Events

As a VR game, *The Under Presents* has an experiential quality, which means that narrative events can be experienced in what feels akin to 'real-time'. Several researchers have proposed typologies of time frames or time schemes in video games, with some overlapping categories (Hitchens,

2006; Juul, 2005; Wei et al., 2010; Zagal & Mateas, 2007). To further explore the presentation of time in *The Under Presents*, I draw upon Juul's dual structure typology, as well as Zagal and Mateas' work for the Game Ontology Project. These frameworks provide a means to analyse the presentation and specificity of time that is described above.

Juul theorises two time schemes for games: play time and fictional time (2005). Play time refers to the time the player takes to play the game (the physical time that passes while the player is engaged in playing). Conversely, fictional time refers to the time of events that unfold in the game world. Adopting this classification, one might note that fictional time in *The Under Presents* is somewhat varied. The Time Boat experience has a fixed timeline and order of events that unfold with a series of ellipses between the three acts. By contrast, the Main Stage and its surrounds exist in a time vacuum. As a player it is clear that, in this location, you are in a time after the Aickman's voyage, but it is not clear when (or where) exactly this later world exists. Within the Time Boat experience, play time resembles real-time if the player experiences the unfolding narrative on the deck of the vessel alongside the NPCs. If the player removes their mask, however, and thus activates their god-like view of the ship, they can manipulate the unfolding of the narrative in time. Play time is then no longer equal to real-time. The ability to manipulate time allows for the player to replay events or view events out of sequence. This activity is based upon the player's clear understanding of the fictional time associated with the Aickman's voyage, which is drawn from the narrative structured in three acts.

Similarly, the Main Stage offers a real-time experience of the various nightclub events as well as engagement with other characters. While the player experience of this space is informed by the Time Boat's narrative, there is less sense of fictional time here. A player that logs off the game app might return a day later to find that little has changed. Other players' actions within the multiplayer space mean that limited objects within the environment are temporarily rearranged (e.g. table dressings within the nightclub might be disturbed) but there is no sense that this change is associated with a movement in time, or a shift in the overall narrative. Play time equals real-time, which foregrounds player experience within the landscape.

The notion of 'real-time' receives attention in Zagal and Mateas' analysis of the temporality of games, which is situated in the context of their Game Ontology Project, a hierarchical framework developed to help describe the various structural elements of games (2007). These authors adopt a relationist approach to explore 'the relationships between events, and thus to relationships between state changes in the world' (p. 517). This results in four proposed temporal frames: real-world time (established by events that take place in the physical world), gameworld time (events that take place within the represented game world), coordination time (events that coordinate the actions of multiple players and agents), and fictive time (the application of sociocultural labels to events, and to historical narratives) (pp. 518–519). Zagal and Mateas suggest that it is common for video games to possess multiple temporal frames, either simultaneously or across different levels.

Their notion of fictive time has parallels with Juul's fictional time and covers the experience of time passing within a game world, as marked by day/night cycles, changes of the seasons or the inclusion of narrated event sequences. As explored above, we see this in the Time Boat narrative that plays out in three acts and an epilogue. More interesting for this analysis is Zagal and Mateas' notion of real-world time, which is established with reference to the player's physical surroundings or body outside of the game. This is a more expansive notion than Juul's 'play time' as it addresses the way that events in a game may 'depend on specific labelled times in the real world, or on the passage of specific real world durations' (p. 518). An example of this temporal frame in *The Under Presents* is in the introductory sequence where the player must coordinate their actions so as to progress to the Main Stage area. Alarm clocks feature in this sequence as a reminder of the limited time that is available to complete the task in each iteration. In *The Under Presents*' Main Stage area I observe a crossover between real-world time and gameworld time as gameplay actions, as well as events in the virtual environment, play out with real-world time as their only reference.

It is worth noting that the events in *The Under Presents*' multiplayer area continue even if the individual player takes no action. On this subject, Zagal and Mateas suggest that gameworld time can invoke a sense of 'liveliness' if gameworld events 'continue to occur even when the player is not actively participating in the world' (p. 518). In *The Under Presents*, this notion of 'liveliness' has been reinforced by the appearance of live actors in the multiplayer area. For example, as a player, I have engaged in somewhat random wandering in the desert areas around the nightclub, and have discovered groups of players engaging with live actor NPCs. In one instance, I entered the Gift Shop setting that is some distance across the desert from the Main Stage, finding a laughing, miniature skeleton NPC who was throwing drinks to the floor around an assembly of players. By staying in the nightclub, I could have avoided this activity entirely, and without consequence in terms of my future engagement with the game. This example demonstrates how one can visit the multiplayer world of The Under as one would a real-world destination, and stay for as long as is desired, encountering different players and NPCs (live or pre-programmed) each time. The navigation of time and space within this virtual environment is in this way an embodied act, experienced by the player as an active participant at the centre of the storyworld, and resembling a 'real-world' interaction.

Live Actors, Players and Intimate Experience

Further to the notion of 'liveliness' that is drawn from the presentation of gameworld time in *The Under Presents*, I would argue that the live actor NCPs that have appeared in the game for limited periods bring a sense of liveliness and spontaneity to the multiplayer area. The individual player's association with these NCPs draws upon the conventions of immersive theatre to foster a personal and intimate experience of the game world. This is created through affective interactions between the NCPs and players as generic, virtual bodies, and also through player to player association, which can result in the successful casting of spells and the discovery of new spaces. These interactions not only contribute to the player's understanding of the storyworld but are sites for the creation of playful mini-narratives that foster a sense of connection.

As the latest wave of VR entertainment has gathered steam in recent years, a number of practitioners have explored game worlds and online platforms (e.g. VRChat) as a venue for a type of immersive theatre.[5] This follows the success of high-profile location-based immersive theatre productions, such as British company Punchdrunk's various productions of *Sleep No More*. The term 'immersive theatre' encompasses a broad group of practices that enable audience participation in a theatre performance. White suggests that it includes 'performances which use installations and expansive environments, which have mobile audiences, and which invite audience participation' (2012, p. 221). On a similar note, Alston describes

[5] See Chap. 7 for an analysis of several projects incorporating live actors that have been created in VRChat.

an immersive theatre production as one where the audience might 'refashion' or 'co-produce' a theatre performance (2016, p. 7) by roaming and interacting with performers. Whereas traditional theatre creates a space for the spectator to observe and reflect, Alston suggests that immersive theatre might lead the audience member to introspection 'as attention is turned toward an experience that is produced within the body' (Alston, p. 9). Central to this type of theatre performance is the notion of 'immersion' that is manifest through the spectator's location being inside the world of the performance (White, p. 221). *The Under Presents* (and *The Under Presents Tempest*) can be considered seminal works in this regard due to their incorporation of immersive theatre practices in a VR game environment.

White suggests that immersive theatre productions may offer a coherent narrative or a more dream-like experience, but are likely to involve exploratory spaces (p. 221). As the analysis above demonstrates, *The Under Presents* offers both a coherent backstory (The Time Boat) and a 'timeless' multiplayer space where narrative is encountered through discovery or generated through interaction with others. My experience of player participation in the Main Stage area has parallels with White's description of audience participation in performances of Punchdrunk's *Sleep No More*:

> Typically an audience will move from place to place, either individually or in small groups, movement that often accelerates as performers follow narrative paths and spectators pursue them. The feeling that there is more to see in the next room, and that there is always a danger of missing something, propels this movement. The moment-to-moment 'what happens next?' of conventional narratives is replaced by the 'where is he going?' and 'what's in the next room?'(White, p. 225)

This description suggests that the audience members of *Sleep No More* are actively involved in the generation and delivery of a narrative. I would suggest that similarly to what is described by White, the player's experience of interaction with live actor NCPs in *The Under Presents*' multiplayer world results in a narrative experience underpinned by encounters in space. As with *Sleep No More*, players in *The Under Presents* tend to flock towards and follow live actor NPCs who might engage them in an improvisation or reveal details of the broader storyworld. The discovery of a live actor NPC in the environment not only adds an element of novelty to the game, but fosters a sense of intimacy and connection with the storyworld and other players, which is drawn from a shared, ephemeral experience. At these moments narrative is generated through player interaction with the NCPs, meaning that the player themselves becomes a storytelling tool.

For example, on one of my visits to the multiplayer area, a live actor adopting the avatar of a female flight attendant appeared in the desert outside of the nightclub and encouraged me and five or six other players to follow her towards the wreck of a small plane. This was half submerged in the desert some distance away. On arrival at the wreck, we were encouraged to enter the plane, take a seat and buckle our seat belts. The flight attendant spoke as if the plane was functional, her dialogue suggesting that she had come from a parallel universe or an earlier time. Most of the players did as she requested, while one stood by and listened. Part of the fun of this experience was her banter with individual players. As a participant in the improvisation I was directly addressed by the NCP or, in other words, I was *recognised* as a participant in the storyworld. At this moment I felt less a game player than a character in the unfolding narrative, although that character was very much 'me'. This notion of the player as character is explored by Scriven in the context of multiplayer online games, who suggests that a player might be seen as a 'subject in the game world and a crucial part of the fictional narrative of the game world' (2018, p. 194). Speaking on these moments of live actor improvisation with players, co-director Gorman comments that

> The barrier of the stage is removed and the audience is placed within the narrative. In The Under itself, players may encounter live actors and (are) occasionally pulled aside for a "one-on-one" experience. The idea of intimacy, feeling chosen and being 'seen' is important. (Gorman quoted in Damiani, 2019)

Both my experience and Gorman's comments suggest that *The Under Presents* offers a performative space for both players and actors that abounds with narrative threads. As such, player experience is informed by personal encounters in space, which can offer a feeling of connection to the storyworld.

The live actor NCPs that appear in *The Under Presents'* multiplayer space are varied and numerous, fulfilling a range of narrative functions. The game's wiki lists more than 100 different characters, including humans, cats and other animals.[6] Some of these characters are drawn directly from the Time Boat experience, and therefore create a link to the 'earlier time' linear narrative that is presented as a single-player experience. Other characters, such as the airline hostess, bring narrative detail and colour to the multiplayer space. Aarseth's analysis of character in video game narratives suggests that these characters reflect a high level of authorial control of the game narrative, seeing as they are predefined characters with high levels of details and depth (2012, p. 132). While narrative structures are most certainly the result of authorial control in *The Under Presents*, I would argue that the live actor characters' central purpose is to enable player engagement and input into the game world's narrative through affective encounter. To further evidence this claim, I look at a player video posted to YouTube, which captures an encounter with two live actor NPCs named 'Princess Dumpster Truck, Mother of Dragons' and 'Kitanya Von Mousetrap' (beezysmeezy, 2020). These characters, who have the appearance of cats wearing crowns or headdresses, speak to players assembled in a desert space. Princess Dumpster Truck calls herself 'the princess of all trash in The Under', and encourages players to sniff a large dragon egg that she holds. Kitanya Von Mousetrap, her older sibling, helps to direct players as they work collectively to hatch a dragon from the egg. Over the course of around 19 minutes this improvised, interactive performance that informs players' understanding of the game world plays out. The relationship between the two live actor NPCs and many others are outlined on the extensive wiki site for *The Under Presents*, where one can also access embedded YouTube videos of the various characters interacting in the game world. As with other live actor NPCs, the two cats have defined appearances, mannerisms and relations, which are captured on the wiki site.

While the speaking NCPs of *The Under Presents* are rich in nature, the player's non-verbal, black cloaked avatar is somewhat generic. Most notably, this avatar lacks a face that might communicate a sense of an emotional status or personality. Rather, the gold mask covers this area. As previously mentioned, by adopting various gameplay strategies, the player has the ability to alter the scale of their virtual body, or to replace their generic gold mask with a more customised version. They might also acquire a hat to wear, although ultimately their appearance remains somewhat like that of other player characters. According to Aarseth, character

[6] See https://the-under-presents.fandom.com/wiki/Live_Actor_Characters

malleability is characteristic of a more user-controlled narrative experience (2012, p. 132), although I note that in the context of this specific game, character malleability is limited. One could argue that the generic appearance of the player's avatar creates a space for the player to inhabit the game as themself. As a faceless being they are not aligned with a predefined character or any sociocultural status but are able to relate to other players as an undefined and anonymous entity.

The game's interaction design grants the player the ability to physically interact with others through hand gestures and the exchange of objects, which also fosters a sense of intimacy. A player might attempt to grab an object held by another player or a live actor, leading to tug of war-like battles that stretch their arms beyond their normal capacity. This sounds unpleasant, but my experience of this phenomenon has been otherwise. Gorman emphasises the importance of this 'multiplayer grabbing' that becomes a way for players to communicate:

> To encourage this we also added the ability to send haptic vibration pulses down your arms. Pull the index trigger whenever you're holding an object and all other remote players holding the same object will see and feel a pulse snake its way to them. This plus the (finger) snapping [...] start to develop a vocabulary players can use to communicate creatively. (Gorman quoted in Damiani, 2019)

Further to Gorman's suggestion that these haptic technologies provide a means of communication, I would suggest that they provide a means towards player bonding through shared bodily experience. Scriven's work on the embodied sense perception of online multiplayer games (2018), as informed by the work of Alfred Shultz (1967), provides a point of comparison that can help to understand this phenomenon. Adopting a phenomenological perspective to describe the experience of playing a non-VR game, Scriven describes how his experience of a 'corporeal Other' (a fellow player) is entirely mediated by audio-visual technologies and hardware such as a keyboard, thus preventing a direct apprehension of 'their embodied self or their subjective experiences' (2018, p. 200). This mediation means that his perception of the other player is based on their actions only, as represented in audio-visual format by the computer interface. By contrast, the player's experience of other players and live actors in *The Under Presents*, while still mediated by digital technologies, does permit an understanding of the fellow player as an embodied Other. The player's physical body is involved in this understanding, as can be evidenced in a review of the game by Devon Baur (2021). Baur writes of his experience playing the game alongside live actors during a Covid-19 lockdown:

> Standing in my living room, over a month into quarantine, I lifted my hands and hugged a muted and masked stranger [...]; and while I never felt their touch, I know that somewhere out there they lifted their arms and, for that small moment, we were not alone. (Baur, 2021, p. 108)

I would argue that the player's use of their physical body to manipulate their avatar, and their ability to grab and exchange objects, provide a means of embodied, subjective encounter. This phenomenon not only increases the player's sense of presence and immersion in the storyworld but means that the generation of narrative becomes a personal and somewhat shared, affective experience. This means that, further to positioning the player as the axis around which the game world revolves, *The Under Presents* offers interactive devices that foreground the player's corporeality in terms of how they experience and contribute to unfolding narrative threads.

Conclusion

As a game that provides a venue for immersive theatre performances, *The Under Presents* uses VR technology to foster an innovative and complex narrative experience. In this chapter I have analysed the narrative structures that are present within the game, noting a mix of open-world and quest experiences that encourage player engagement in the generation of story. I have noted the way that the storyworld's various characters, objects, settings and events allow for a sophisticated interplay between narrative and ludic elements, leading to the creation of a personal and intimate player experience. Moreover, I have highlighted the way that the player's avatar design and interactive possibilities (to communicate via bodily gestures rather than by speech) foster an embodied experience of the storyworld. This latter aspect gets to the heart of VR storytelling by fostering a player's deep immersion in a storyworld that is experienced as a series of affective encounters.

Moreover, I have argued that the player's manipulation of time and space in *The Under Presents* can be considered an embodied activity mediated by the VR HMD and hand controllers. The elasticity of time and space is not only the central theme of the project, but also informs player interaction with the storyworld—the way that they pull space towards themselves using the scrunch mechanic or the way that they might wind time back or forward using their fingers on a mask. Further to identifying overlapping emotional or strategic spaces within the game world, I have proposed the term 'corporeal space' to address this constituting role of the player's body in the 360-degree VR environment. This concept reinforces the notion of a narrative journey that is literally in the hands of the player and results from their physical manipulation of spatial and temporal components.

While the investigation of VR game narratives presented in this chapter centres on a single case study, I believe that there is much to be learned here about the potential of VR to create powerful emotional and embodied narrative experiences. Throughout the history of gaming, there exists a rich tradition of non-VR games that incorporate physical bodily movements and experiences into their game play (e.g. arcade car racing games or the Nintendo Wii); however, my analysis demonstrates how the VR game takes this corporeal experience into new terrain by creating the illusion of the player's physical body at the centre of an enclosed diegetic world.

Several years on from its release, *The Under Presents* continues to attract new players and maintains its status as a cutting-edge VR experience. There are many aspects of the game that deserve further research, such as its actor interfaces and complex cast of characters. Emerging as it did, in the months before Covid-19 spread across the world, *The Under Presents* offered a mysterious game world for multiplayer investigation and a live performance venue taken up by actors who were no longer able to perform in physical spaces due to lockdowns. It continues to provide an indication of what innovative narrative-based VR games can offer.

Note: Parts of this chapter were presented at the 2023 International Conference on Interactive Digital Narrative (ICIDS) in Kobe, Japan. This earlier paper, which was published as conference proceedings, has been revised and expanded.

References

Aarseth, E. (2001). Allegories of space: The question of spatiality in computer games. In R. Koskimaa (Ed.), *Cybertext Yearbook 2000*. University of Jyväskylä.

Aarseth, E. (2012, May). A narrative theory of games. In *Proceedings of the international conference on the foundations of digital Games* (pp. 129–133).

Alston, A. (2016). *Beyond immersive theatre*. Palgrave Macmillan.

Arsenault, D., & Perron, B. (2009). In the frame of the magic cycle: The circle(s) of gameplay. In B. Perron & M. J. P. Wolf (Eds.), *The Video Game Theory Reader 2* (pp. 109–131). Routledge.

Ash, J. (2009). Emerging spatialities of the screen: Video games and the reconfiguration of spatial awareness. *Environment and Planning A, 41*(9), 2105–2124.

Bait! (2019). Resolution games.

Baur, D. (2021). The Under Presents by Samantha Gorman and Danny Cannizzaro. *Theatre Journal, 73*(1), 106–108.

beezysmeezy. (2020). *The Under Presents: Princess dumpster truck, mother of dragons* (YouTube video). Published August 25. https://www.youtube.com/watch?v=j0B7WBaNgRo

Boyer, S. (2009). A virtual failure: Evaluating the success of Nintendo's Virtual Boy. *The Velvet Light Trap, 64*, 23–33.

Corts, A. (2021). The Under Presents: The tempest by William Shakespeare. *Theatre Journal, 73*(2), 236–238.

Damiani, J. (2019). 'The Under Presents' is a novel exploration of VR and live immersive theatre. *Forbes*. https://www.forbes.com/sites/jessedamiani/2019/11/19/the-under-presents-is-a-novel-exploration-of-vr-and-live-immersive-theatre/?sh=7dfaa8d87455

Denisova, A., & Cairns, P. (2015, April 18–23). First person vs. third person perspective in digital games: Do player preferences affect immersion? Paper presented at: CHI'15. Proceedings of the 33rd Annual ACM Conference on Human Factors in Computing Systems, Seoul, South Korea. New York, NY: ACM.

Dooley, K. (2023). Traversing Space in The Under Presents (2019), a VR Game. In *International conference on Interactive Digital Storytelling* (pp. 442–453). Cham.

Fandom. (n.d.). *The Under Presents* Wiki. https://the-under-presents.fandom.com/wiki/The_Under_Presents

Flavián, C., Ibáñez-Sánchez, S., & Orús, C. (2019). The impact of virtual, augmented and mixed reality technologies on the customer experience. *Journal of Business Research, 100*, 547–560.

Gorisse, G., Christmann, O., Amato, E. A., & Richir, S. (2017). First- and third-person perspectives in immersive virtual environments: Presence and performance analysis of embodied users. *Front Robot AI, 4*, 1–12.

Hitchens, M. (2006). Time and computer games or "no, that's not what happened". In Proceedings of the 3rd Australasian conference on Interactive Entertainment, pp. 44–51.

Jenkins, H. (2004). Game design as narrative architecture. *Computer, 44*(3), 11.

Juul, J. (2005). *Half-Real: Video games between real rules and fictional worlds.* MIT Press.

Kallinen, K., Salminen, M., Ravaja, N., Kedzior, R., & Sääksjärvi, M. (2007). Presence and emotion in computer game players during 1st person vs. 3rd person playing view: Evidence from self-report, eye-tracking, and facial muscle activity data. Paper presented at: Proceedings of the Presence, pp. 187–190.

Kgm Student07. (2020). The Under Presents: MC monologues. (YouTube video). Published January 22. https://www.youtube.com/watch?v=oLA7rE1ztHg

Larsen, B. A., Junius, N., & Carstensdottir, E. (2023, October). Communal ritual play: Repetition and interpretation of game narratives across communities. In *International conference on Interactive Digital Storytelling* (pp. 472–488). Springer Nature Switzerland.

Monteiro, D., Liang, H. N., Xu, W., Brucker, M., Nanjappan, V., & Yue, Y. (2018). Evaluating enjoyment, presence, and emulator sickness in VR games based on first- and third-person viewing perspectives. *Computer Animation and Virtual Worlds, 29*(3–4), e1830.

Murray, J. H. (1997). *Hamlet on the holodeck: The future of narrative in cyberspace.* MIT Press.

Nitsche, M. (2008). *Video game spaces: Image, play, and structure in 3D worlds.* MIT Press.

Peng, X., Huang, J., Li, L., Gao, C., Chen, H., Tian, F., & Wang, H. (2019, May). Beyond horror and fear: Exploring player experience invoked by emotional challenge in VR games. In *Extended abstracts of the 2019 CHI conference on Human Factors in Computing Systems* (pp. 1–6).

Ryan, M. L. (2009). From narrative games to playable stories: Toward a poetics of interactive narrative. *StoryWorlds: A Journal of Narrative Studies, 1*, 43–59.

Ryan, M. L. (2015). Emotional and strategic conceptions of space in digital narratives. In *Interactive Digital Narrative* (pp. 106–120). Routledge.

Saker, M., & Frith, J. (2020). Coextensive space: Virtual reality and the developing relationship between the body, the digital and physical space. *Media, Culture & Society, 42*(7–8), 1427–1442.

Schutz, A. (1967). *The phenomenology of the social world.* Northwestern University Press.

Scriven, P. (2018). The phenomenology of the "other" in computer game worlds. *Games and Culture, 13*(2), 193–210.

Sherman, W. R., & Craig, A. B. (2018). *Understanding virtual reality: Interface, application, and design.* Morgan Kaufmann.

Gorilla Tag. (2021). Lead designer: Kerestell Smith. Another Axiom.

The Under Presents. (2019). Dirs. Danny Cannizzaro & Samantha Gorman USA: Tender Claws.

Virtual, Virtual Reality. (2017). Dirs. Danny Cannizzaro & Samantha Gorman. Tender Claws.

Wei, H., Bizzocchi, J., & Calvert, T. (2010). Time and space in digital game storytelling. *International Journal of Computer Games Technology, 2010*, 1–23.

White, G. (2012). On immersive theatre. *Theatre Research International, 37*(3), 221–235.

Wolf, M. J. (2002). *The medium of the video game*. University of Texas Press.

Zagal, J. P., & Mateas, M. (2007). Temporal frames: A unifying framework for the analysis of game temporality. In *Situated play, proceedings of DiGRA 2007 conference*, pp. 516–522.

CHAPTER 6

Between Storytelling and Storyliving: User Customisation of Virtual Reality Narratives

Introduction

In 2017, as a new wave of narrative-based virtual reality experiences were showcased on online news sites, at film festivals, conferences and in other venues around the globe, the term 'storyliving' gained traction as a means of describing the embodied user experience that these works offered. Writing in the context of immersive journalism for the Google News Lab, Maschio used the term to describe 'a significant formal shift from traditional storytelling mediums to VR', which involved a diminished centrality of 'telling' (2017, p. 9). Rather, Maschio suggested that the user would enter a VR story as a digital entity, learning through engagement and embodiment, 'as though they lived it' (p. 9). This notion emerged from a user study of participants who experienced a range of VR projects. The phenomenon of 'storyliving', Maschio argued, calls for a reconception of narrative structure with a VR experience, favouring the three experiential phases of 'initiation', 'exploration', and 'making sense', rather than traditional linear notions of 'beginning', 'middle' and 'end' (p. 10). As Greenwald notes, the overall message of Maschio's Google News Lab study related to VR's potential to deliver 'powerful advertising and journalistic messages' seeing as stories could be experienced in 'deeper and potentially longer lasting ways' (2017). Consequently, the concept was evoked in broader discussions of brand management using immersive media (Rose, 2018).

K. Dooley, *Virtual Reality Narratives*,
https://doi.org/10.1007/978-3-031-64965-3_6

In an article published five years after Maschio's study, Vallance and Towndrow move away from the journalistic context to align the notion of VR storyliving with a broader narrative experience that is 'not structured or pre-generated, but unfolds as the participant experiences the emerging, semi-authored virtual environment, providing imaginary visions of personal histories' (2022, p. 4). Considering the potential future technological advancements of VR, their use of the term relates to a narrative that is shaped by a high level of user input, which raises questions in regard to authorial control.

The problem of reconciling pre-authored plot structures with real-time user action and interaction in a virtual environment has been described as a 'narrative paradox' by Aylett and Louchart (2007, p. 116). who observe that the more freedom a user is given to affect a narrative, the harder it becomes to deliver a story with conclusive plot elements (Aylett & Louchart, 2003, p. 5). Vallance and Towndrow describe a pre-authored approach that involves highly structured plot devices as 'external authorship' and suggest that it dilutes the concept of storyliving (2022, p. 2). They thus argue for a 'semi-authored virtual environment' (p. 4) that allows the user to become an active participant in an unfolding drama. The affordances of VR then allow the user to 'go beyond witnessing (a story), and become personalized by the virtual circumstance in order to subsequently dispense a deliberate experience' (Vallance & Towndrow, p. 2).

VR Storyliving is an enticing concept but questions remain as to how it might be approached by a creator at a practical level. Maschio's suggestion that it should involve less story 'telling' suggests a radical departure from traditional models of narration, while Vallance and Towndrow would seem to argue for a narrative experience that can be personalised for the user. One might also question whether the concept is better aligned with certain VR technologies and platforms, considering the spectrum of possibilities for interaction that currently exist.

This sixth chapter seeks to investigate these areas through the analysis of two recent narrative-based VR projects: *Lustration* (New Canvas 2022) and *Fire Escape* (iINK Stories 2019). These award-winning works insert the user into mysterious storyworlds where they are directly addressed by characters. Moreover, they feature a range of interactive devices, such as branching narratives and selectable vantage points of plot action, which encourage the user to tailor their narrative experience.

In relation to the tailoring of a product or service, one might experience processes of personalisation or customisation. The terms 'personalise' and 'customise' are often used interchangeably but they have specific meanings. Following Nguyen et al. (2020) one can define personalisation as offering 'a system driven way of delivering information in a pre-planned format based on an assessment of individual characteristics or preferences' (p. 32). In the context of a narrative-based VR experience this might involve dynamically changing content, layouts, or narrative paths based on real-time information about the user. Conversely, customisation refers to a user-driven approach to the tailoring of information, which is undertaken by an active interactor (p. 32). This could involve an individual's selection of content from a set of available options to create an experience that interests them. Both of these approaches to tailoring might enhance a user's experience of a story and thus make it more emotionally impactful and memorable.

The two case studies listed above offer fictional stories with predetermined plot structures that are delivered using game engine technologies. The first project, *Lustration*, is a short series created with native VR painting and animation software, *Quill*. Written and directed by Australian First Nation creative Ryan Griffen based on his comic series of the same name, this project follows the journey of a number of characters who navigate the afterlife in a world known as 'The Between'. Each episode is told from a different point of view, and moreover, within episodes the user can switch between a number of predetermined vantage points. As well as allowing the user the ability to align themselves with different characters, they can switch back and forth between 'The Between' and 'the land of living', which affects their understanding of plot action.

The second case study, *Fire Escape*, similarly grants the user the ability to select their vantage point on an unfolding story. Set in a Brooklyn apartment block, this Hitchcock-esque murder mystery positions the user as a witness and detective who can tune into the eight separate narratives of their suspicious neighbours, to discover the identity of a murderer. As the various narrative threads develop, the user is put into direct contact with the murderer via a phone device and can shape the outcome of the story via their response to a series of prompts.

Considering both the predetermined plot structures and variable story elements that these two VR experiences offer, I will seek to explore the narratives that they foster with user input. To aid in this project I will consider several frameworks and conceptual models for understanding interactive narrative (Aylett & Louchart, 2007; Ogle, 2019) as well as the System, Process, Product (SPP) model of narrative production theorised by Koenitz (2010, 2015). This latter model observes a user's engagement with an interactive narrative system (the overall project delivered via hardware and software), a process that results in a narrative experience (a product) that may differ from one user to another. With reference to this and other models, I present a close analysis of my experience of both projects, noting moments where I was able to tailor my narrative experience. In doing so, I will argue that the two projects, as examples of interactive digital narratives (IDNs), offer user-customised experiences that encourage some measure of 'storyliving'. This is achieved through the offering of multiple story strands, which might be selected based on user interest or identification with characters. I start this investigation with a further discussion of storytelling and storyliving so as to explore the diverse nature of contemporary VR narratives.

Storytelling and Storyliving in VR

The latest surge of virtual reality technologies has presented fresh avenues for presenting digital narratives with enhanced levels of immersion and interaction. Considering the VR experiences of the last decade, one can observe a spectrum of interactivity ranging from 360-video works (sometimes referred to as 'cinematic virtual reality') to 'room scale' works requiring hand controllers or other devices. As I have noted elsewhere (Dooley, 2021), entertainment-based VR works can be roughly categorised into two groups when considering the viewer's capacity to navigate and affect 360-degree space while wearing a head-mounted display (HMD). Firstly, there are works characterised by three degrees of freedom (3DoF), which enable the viewer to look upwards and downwards and rotate left and right from a fixed, central axis. In this scenario the viewer is essentially placed within a spherical scene that is typically created using an equirectangular video file presented in either monoscopic (2D) or stereoscopic (3D) format. This classification of VR, which emerged circa 2014 in tandem with the advancement of high-quality 360-degree cameras and affordable HMDs, provides a user experience that is reasonably limited in terms of interactivity but is the most accessible due to the lower costs associated with the creation and viewing technologies. The second category of works offer six degrees of freedom (6DoF), which affords the user the same capabilities as 3DoF works but also grants them the ability to shift the central axis. This additional freedom allows the user to move forward and backward, left and right, and up and down within a potentially reactive environment, requiring real-time rendering by game engine technology. Both of these types of experiences enable interactive digital storytelling by allowing the user to choose their field of vision within 360-degree space (and thus fostering a particular understanding of narrative events) while the latter category may afford the user opportunities for additional engagement. While 3DoF and 6DoF technologies offer distinct experiences in relation to user movement within a virtual environment, narratives delivered in either format can be augmented with additional interactive devices (e.g. the inclusion of 'hotspots' that react to the user's gaze).

Thus, VR narratives offering either 3DoF or 6DoF to the user can be considered as interactive but one might question whether the term 'storyliving' might be levelled one of these formats in particular. Following Laurel (1991), I define 'interactivity' in this context as relating to the user's ability to be 'engaged in the ongoing flow of the representation' of a work' (1991, p. 20). Aylett and Louchart suggest that 'characteristic of VR is that the role of the subject (i.e. the user) to whom the narrative is communicated is, in terms of interaction, "active" in the unfolding of the narrative as opposed to its "passive" role in most of other classical narrative media (i.e. the spectator)' (2003, p. 3). The term 'active' as it is used here relates to a user who participates in the building of a narrative experience through their positioning *within* a 360-degree storyworld, rather than as a spectator placed in front of a rectangular screen.

In his Google News Lab ethnographic study, Maschio gathered consumers' perceptions of VR by showing them a range of experiences in 3DoF and 6DoF formats. As Maschio notes, some practitioners have advocated for a definitive differentiation between 360 live-action video and computer-generated content; however, the participants of his study considered both to exist on a spectrum of VR (p. 7). In their responses, they do not appear to differentiate between the forms of interaction that these experiences offer, meaning that the storyliving concept is applied broadly across all VR media by Maschio. By contrast, Vallance and Towndrow would seem to have a more interactive, game engine-driven format in mind when they argue for experiences that are 'time-independent process-oriented' as storyliving (p. 4). Similarly, Aylett and Louchart propose a 'process view of narrative' for VR, this involving 'a dynamic system building itself from the interactions of its own narrative elements and factors' (2003, p. 7). In common with Vallance and Towndrow, this process view considers the user, and his/her behaviour, as a resource for the creation of story and sits in opposition to 'authorial and structural narrative approaches' (Aylett & Louchart, 2003, p. 7).

With this differentiation between a structural narrative approach and 'story as process' in mind, I note that the terms 'storytelling' and 'storyliving' do not describe mutually exclusive activities. As a noun, the former relates to the activity of telling or writing stories,[1] while the latter, as posited above, describes a user experience of 'lived' story within a virtual environment. One could argue that some measure of storytelling is required to create the parameters for a narrative experience that emerges even almost completely as a result of user interaction, but as Maschio suggests, that traditional models of narrative need to be reconsidered in light of this user engagement and embodiment. This argument is in fact shared by Vallance and Towndrow who refer to 'narrative storyliving in VR as a way of understanding the intersecting space between storytelling and storyliving' (p. 3). It must be noted that these authors' conception of storyliving is somewhat aspirational, and looks to advancements in artificial intelligence as a means to fully realise the notion. In the case study analysis below, I investigate this interplay between storytelling and storyliving, which might involve the personalisation and customisation of an authored narrative. Before proceeding; however, I present an overview of models for interactive storytelling that offer guidance for this study.

Narrative Theories and Models for IDNs

Over the last three decades or so, scholars have explored models of interactive storytelling in the context of games, virtual reality and digital media more broadly, noting a range of possibilities for user interaction with story. Scholarship in the multidisciplinary field of interactive digital narratives (IDN) is of particular benefit to this chapter's investigation. This research area explores how the specific affordances of digital media (fostered by technologies such as computers and the internet) challenge existing concepts in narrative theory, such as the notion of unified plot structures and authorship (Koenitz, 2010, p. 176). Seminal texts by Laurel (1991), Murray (1997) and Ryan (2001) interrogate and reflect upon the interactive qualities of digital media following advances that occurred in the

[1] The Collins Dictionary defines storytelling as 'the activity of telling or writing stories', and suggests that the term originated around 1700–1710. See https://www.collinsdictionary.com/dictionary/english/storytelling

1980s and 1990s. Like these older texts, recent scholarship on narrative-based VR and digital storytelling more broadly understands IDN as 'a form of expression that tightly integrates interactivity and narrative' (Koenitz, 2010 p. 177).

In my analysis below I will refer to several texts that provide roadmaps for understanding interactive narrative structures (Aylett & Louchart, 2007; Koenitz, 2010, 2015; Ogle, 2019). The models presented within these texts adopt varying but somewhat complementary perspectives on interactive narratives as processes or systems. Firstly, I look to Aylett and Louchart who discuss user roles in relation to 'storyfication' (the process through which a narrative is internalised by the user) (2007). This comes following an experiment that attempts to resolve the aforementioned 'narrative paradox', through the offering of emergent narrative, which is defined by the authors as 'the creation of story-like experiences in real-time using interaction between intelligent synthetic characters as a generative mechanism' (2007, p. 116). Aylett and Louchart suggest five spectator or user positions on a spectrum of interactivity for digital narratives. At the most non-interactive end of the spectrum lies the conventional film audience or spectator, while conversely the most interactive position involves a 'freely participating character' who is involved in a generative or emergent narrative (p. 119). The three intermediate positions, labelled 'non-participant control', 'non-participant influence', and 'participant control points' sit between these two poles. The former involves high levels of author control, while the 'non-participant influence' position might interleave interactive and non-interactive phases, thus offering the user some degree of authorial responsibility. The latter position, 'participant control points', relates to branching narratives that allow user input into a story's direction. The authors describe these participant control points as allowing 'a set of pre-authored possibilities to be navigated […] thus isolating interactive possibilities from non-interactive story-elements' (p. 120). They suggest that interactivity is the determining influence on the user experience of a narrative and that these various positions 'result in basic differences in the storification process' (p. 120).

Aylett and Louchart's classification of five positions finds its reflection in Ogle's suggestion of 15 visual models aimed at enhancing interactive storytelling within innovative cinematic mediums (2019). These models similarly encompass a spectrum from no interactivity to emergent narrative. Ogle observes the dearth of literature addressing the intricacies of scripting for the immersive and interactive qualities inherent in new cinematic formats (p. 4). In response, she advocates for the integration of 'model thinking' as a valuable tool to guide the creation of interactive storytelling systems. Although the title of Ogle's article implies that her proposed interactive storytelling models herald novel forms of filmmaking, the content of her discourse delineates a 'new domain' that assumes diverse terminologies such as interactive cinema, cinematic virtual reality (CVR), interactive film, interactive drama, interactive storytelling, interactive narrative and interactive digital storytelling (IDS). The article also acknowledges the loosely associated concepts of virtual reality (VR) and augmented reality (AR) more broadly (p. 5).

Two of the models within this framework that hold particular pertinence when discussing the attributes of the immersive case studies below are the '360-Degree Interactive Video Model' (2019, p. 15) and the 'Intersections Model' (p. 16). The former aligns with a 360-Degree Video offering 3DoF, yet it distinguishes itself by incorporating interactivity that goes beyond the basic control of the viewer's gaze (p. 15). Ogle proposes that this model likely involves interactive elements aimed at facilitating discovery or exploration, leading to a singular narrative conclusion; however, multiple narrative endings are conceivable (p. 15). On a similar note, Ogle's 'Intersections Model' has a focus on plot, featuring a main story that stands alone; however, secondary backstories that are also standalone might be tied to this main story (p. 16). To access these secondary stories, the user might use interactive 'jumping points' that are predefined. Ogle suggests

> The main story has one outcome, one ending. The secondary/backstories also have one outcome, one ending. The viewer's understanding of the overall story depends on how in-depth they choose to go into the secondary/backstories. Therefore, the viewer may only get a partial secondary/backstory. The main story, however, is seen in full, as the 'jumping points' are only available after that segment of the main story has been viewed, and the viewer returns ahead of the next scene in the main storyline. (Ogle, 2019, p. 16)

The model of interactivity offered here results in a non-linear narrative constructed from linear elements, as each backstory, as well as the main story, has a predetermined outcome. As Ogle notes, this model bears some resemblance to Ryan's 'Vector with Side Branches' (2015, p. 167), although for Ryan, such a model does not weave the branching narratives directly back into the narrative. Rather, Ryan sees the 'side branches' as a means to introduce background information or additional details. Ogle's '360-Degree Interactive Video Model' and the 'Intersections Model' both offer user experiences that could fall within Aylett and Louchart's 'non-participant influence' position, seeing as pre-authored narrative segments and moments of interactivity can be interweaved. The latter would however also appear to cross over into the 'participant control points' position seeing as the user can select different paths through secondary stories.

The models of interactive storytelling that are explored by these authors can be further understood with reference to the System-Process-Product (SPP) model outlined by Koenitz (2010, 2015, 2023). The SPP model emerges from a strand of IDN scholarship that considers the design and development of interactive 'systems' (computer applications and related hardware such as a keyboard, mouse or VR HMD). As digital entities, IDN systems encompass an array of latent narratives that materialise through user engagement—an operational 'process' culminating in a realised narrative output or 'product' (Koenitz, p. 180). In other words, the system contains 'the protostory, the sum of all potential narratives that can be instantiated with a given artefact' (Koenitz et al., 2020, p. 11). The term 'instantiated' captures the notion that a myriad of distinct narrative experiences might spring forth due to the user's involvement, as can be seen to occur within narrative-based virtual reality encounters. Notably, the SPP model moves away from models associated with the traditional and formal examination of literature and cinema within the field of narratology, and rather, 'takes the systemic, dynamic character of IDN works as its central characteristic' (Koenitz et al., 2020, p. 10). This builds on the 'cognitive turn' in narratology—a viewpoint that perceives narrative not solely as an attribute of specific artefacts, but as a cognitive process (Koenitz et al., 2020). There are some parallels in this process with Aylett and Louchart's aforementioned notion of 'storyfication' as the internalisation of a narrative by a user. In the analysis below, I draw upon the SPP model of analysis to isolate and interrogate the component parts of the described VR experiences, such as their procedural components and assets.

In their publication discussing the creation of interactive narratives for virtual reality (VR), Fisher et al. (2022) examine VR experiences developed using game engines. They introduce a novel research agenda that offers insights into issues related to interaction, including aspects like 'scripting the body, movement as action, environmental storytelling, and guiding user gaze' (pp. 675–678). These writing challenges are classified according to the SPP model, with a strong emphasis on user experience design. According to the SPP model, scriptwriting entails a multifaceted approach. Firstly, writers are prompted to perceive the system as a repository of 'protostory' elements, focusing on how they can employ media assets, software, and hardware combinations to actualise their creative vision (Fisher et al., p. 679). This exploration involves dissecting the interactor's demeanour, gestures, body language and orientation as fundamental components of an IDN protostory. Additionally, it involves a consideration of how hardware will respond to user input (p. 679). Secondly, at a process level, the model prompts writers to contemplate the interactor's engagement levels and embodiment within the experience. It encourages the identification of optimal paths through the narrative and techniques for directing the user's attention (p. 680). Lastly, at a product level, writers are encouraged to reflect on aspects like replay value and strategies for utilising the end product to foster a deeper comprehension of the narrative (p. 681). In summary, the authors assert that the SPP model effectively delineates the distinct stages involved in conceptualising, implementing and engaging with an interactive VR experience that scriptwriters need to account for (p. 675). Consequently, the SPP model can serve as a 'compositional scaffold' for structuring VR writing endeavours (p. 680).

Further to offering guidance for writers of VR interactive narratives, the agenda proposed by Fisher et al. presents a framework for the analysis of VR narratives according to the SPP model. Drawing upon the ideas presented by these authors, in the analysis to follow I will interrogate the two case studies in terms of the experience they offer, considering the user in relation to the protostory and instantiated narratives. This will involve consideration of character and storyworld as well as user interface (UI) and narrative design, and the posing of questions about attention guidance. An adoption of the SPP framework, as well as those outlined by Ogle and Aylett and Louchart, allows for further consideration of the customisation of VR narratives, and of the overlaps between storytelling and storyliving.

Case Study Analysis

Lustration

Following the successful reception of a pilot prototype in December 2020, Australian production Company, New Canvas, released *Lustration* on the Meta platform between March and May in 2022. Derived from a comic book bearing the same title, the four-part, noir-style animated series follows a collection of characters whose narratives are enigmatically interwoven. At the centre of this narrative are Gallus and Bardolph, two protectors of 'The Between', a realm that dead people enter to lustrate or cleanse themselves before moving on to the afterlife. Gallus and Bardolph are tasked with removing (by shooting) evil people who do not belong in The Between, however, in Episode One, we see that Bardolph is losing faith in this mission. This puts both Gallus and Bardolph at risk of punishment from their superiors, two white haired men named the Cheribums who represent a powerful corporation. In Episode Two we meet Detective Elizabeth Pine, an atheist and hardened cop inhabiting 'the land of the living' who is investigating the death of a conspiracy theorist with knowledge of The Between. When Aliria, a ghost who is stuck in The Between, materialises in Pine's apartment, the detective is forced to reconsider her beliefs. Episode Three introduces Malcolm, a recently deceased man and the father of Aliria, who like his daughter, has slipped into The Between as a drifter. Seeking to find his daughter, Malcolm finds a guide in the form of Stone, a rogue former protector. In the final episode we discover that Bardolph had previously hidden one of the targets that he was supposed to remove from The Between. Having left Gallus in a safe house, he shoots one of the Cheribums when confronted. Episode Four concludes with this cliffhanger, meaning that the various narrative threads remain open at the end of the series. Considering the complexity of the story and these multiple story threads, the analysis that follows is limited to Episodes One and Two.

Episode One of *Lustration* begins with an onboarding screen that resembles the page of a comic book (see Fig. 6.1). Onboarding can be defined as 'the process followed to guide users to understand technically and conceptually how to participate in a VR experience' (Whittaker, 2023, p. 2). This might involve practical instructions as well as stylistic elements that foster an initial understanding of the virtual environment. For *Lustration*, the comic style still frame outlines the way that the user should

Fig. 6.1 Onboarding instructions and user interface for *Lustration* (screen capture taken by the author). (Courtesy of New Canvas)

use the project's user interface (UI)—a rectangular window attached to the left hand controller—that features a series of buttons related to different 'cameras'. When clicking on these cameras with their right controller, the user can select different points of view within the story or jump between stories unfolding in parallel worlds. The UI also features buttons that allow the user to pause, advance or rewind the experience to certain points in the narrative. Given the sometimes-simultaneous action that occurs across parallel worlds, the rewind button is particularly important, as it allows the user to access story information that they might have missed on their first viewing. Whittaker suggests that the onboarding process involves an 'invitation to immersion', and suggests a comprehensive framework that considers platform, place, time, genre and users as part of this process (p. 13). One can observe that *Lustration*'s onboarding screen is platform specific and gives an indication of the genre of work; however, information about the time and place of the story is not presented until the episode begins in earnest. This onboarding screen appears at the start of each of the four episodes, thus accounting for users who may view the series out of sequence.

After I click the play button, Episode One begins in an empty warehouse space, where The Oracle, a lone aboriginal character, sits playing a tabletop video game. The user is granted six degrees of freedom (6DoF) within this roomscale scene (and throughout the series), meaning that they can rotate their body and take steps to explore the environment. The Oracle speaks to me directly, welcoming me to The Between and explaining the logic of the world, which he has inhabited for 60,000 years. This establishes The Between as a timeless place that somewhat resembles the land of the living, albeit without a living human population. This friendly but somewhat indifferent character functions as a guide of sorts, delivering an overview of the lustration process that occurs in The Between. While listening to this information, I experiment with the four camera positions that are offered, finding that these move me closer or alternatively, further away, from the protagonist of the scene. In effect, the ability to teleport using these camera positions provides a quick and easy way to move around the virtual environment, and can be complemented by the more subtle movement of my physical body to shift my vantage point of the action. I eventually settle on a position that sees me in close proximity and in front of the Oracle, so that I might study the video game that he plays.

This opening scene could be considered to function as a continuation of the onboarding process, seeing as it involves no significant action but allows the user time to experiment with the UI. As such, the scene aligns with Machio's 'initiation' stage of storyliving in VR, in which 'the viewer becomes accustomed to his or her new environment' (p. 10). Although the user is not given a virtual body that appears within *Lustration*, they find themselves being directly addressed by The Oracle in this scene, which helps to foster a sense of social presence in the storyworld or 'the illusion of "being there" with another' (Nash, 2018, p. 127). The remainder of the series does not include this direct address, leaving the user in a more objective position of witness to the unfolding events.

After some moments, the experience progresses to a second scene, which introduces the anguished Bardolph and his younger offsider, Gallus, in a yellow-tinted park. Camera A offers a distanced view of both characters in this scene, while Camera B favours Bardolph (see Fig. 6.2) and Camera C favours Gallus. By selecting either of the latter two camera positions, the user can physically align themselves with one of the characters and obtain a better view of their facial expressions. Gallus smokes a cigarette and questions Bardolph's depressed mood as they wait for a target that they must eliminate to arrive. Camera D, however, takes the user into a parallel storyworld (the land of the living) where this target is murdered under the cover of darkness. Once dead, he appears in The Between,

Fig. 6.2 Bardolph and Gallus wait for a target to appear. Screen capture from *Lustration*, Episode One. (Courtesy of New Canvas)

where he is shot once again by Bardolph. On my first viewing of this sequence, I flicked between camera positions to see how the two parallel words were connected. My interest in Bardolph and Gallus' conversation meant that I missed the target's assassination in the land of the living; however, I later replayed this parallel scene in full so as to better comprehend the story thread. On this second viewing I heard the target's ravings about a conspiracy in the afterlife, and realised that his knowledge of this realm was the reason for his murder. This replay also confirmed the moment of the target's death as the central event that connects the two worlds.

In the episode's third scene, we see Gallus in the living room of his city apartment where he is visited by the Cheribums. They are suspicious of Bardolph's behaviour and warn Gallus that this could lead to his downfall alongside that of his partner. Cameras A, B and C allow me to move closer or further away from the various characters within this living room. Meanwhile Camera D takes me into the corridor outside of Gallus' apartment. This corridor is initially empty but midway through the scene, Bardolph arrives and approaches the apartment front door. He pauses before he enters, hearing the voices of the occupants, and learns that Gallus has been ordered to report on his whereabouts. The perspective offered by Camera D aligns the user with Bardolph whereas Cameras A to C focus on Gallus' experience. I initially flick between all camera positions but then replay the scene from the perspective offered by Camera F so as to hear the full dialogue between Gallus and his superiors.

The final scene of Episode One sees Bardolph and Gallus driving on a deserted highway in an outback location at night. Cameras A, B and C offer perspectives from within the car as they converse, these being more or less aligned with either character, while camera D positions the viewer over the bonnet of the car. The two characters' conversation can be heard from all of these positions, while the latter offers a clearer view of the landscape outside of the car. Gallus tells Bardolph that he has been threatened by their superiors. He urges his partner to change his attitude. Suddenly a white clothed woman (Aliria) who is suspended in the air over the road collides with the car, smashing the front windscreen. The car grinds to a halt. 'Is she a target?', asks Gallus. 'A drifter', replies Bardolph. The episode concludes with their contemplation of this incident.

This outline of Episode One evidences the highly structured plot devices that are featured throughout *Lustration*. The project's protostory elements (outlined below in Table 6.1) offer a series of intersecting, linear

Table 6.1 Protostory elements in *Lustration* based on SPP analysis model (Koenitz, 2023, p. 87)

Element	*Functions*	*Lustration*
Procedural components	Provide rules like physics systems, societal rules, spatial configurations, interaction processing and also generative components	360-degree virtual environments, ability to choose vantage points, switch between parallel narrative sequences, fixed sequence durations
Assets	Provide static material for narrative design	Pre-authored, linear narrative sequences presented within virtual environments, multiple characters and settings, visuals and sounds, 2D assets for UI
UI	Enable agency through interaction	Control panel with camera system, fast forward/rewind function Point and click with hand controller First-person view of events from within the storyworld, 6DoF spatial movement, no interaction with objects
Narrative design	Arrangement of content, mechanics of the relationship between elements	Four episodes of fixed duration, parallel narratives within episodes, variable camera vantage points Game engine enables switching between camera views or parallel narratives
Narrative vectors	Parts of the narrative design to guide the user and create specific effects	No guidance to suggest optimal camera positions or timing to switch between parallel narratives, rewind button allows 'missed' information to be accessed

narratives, which lead to a single ending; however, the overall story is experienced differently by each user, depending on the camera perspectives that they choose at any particular moment. Using the SPP model, one might consider the project's interactive 'system' to involve an application that can be accessed using the Meta Quest 2 HMD and hand controllers (a combination of software and hardware). The project's assets include linear story threads that unfold in 360-degree virtual environments as well as the 2D UI.

At a process level, the user is enabled to select their preferred viewing perspective, which is perhaps based on an interest in particular characters or the desire to explore the 360-degree space of the scene from another perspective. I would argue that the multiple camera positions offered through *Lustration*'s UI encourage somewhat random switching between different perspectives on the user's first viewing, seeing as the direction that the narrative and the ways that the various cameras foster an understanding of this, cannot be foreseen. Seeing as it is not physically possible to absorb parallel story threads in a single playthrough, a user that adopts this approach will be delivered a narrative experience that feels somewhat incomplete. By this I mean that important narrative information will appear to have been missed or they may feel that they have not taken the optimal path through the experience. The replay and fast forward function remedies this situation, allowing the user to select certain moments in the episode that they would like to see from another perspective and to access additional plot details. Thus, in this way *Lustration* offers a predetermined narrative and limited interactive devices while engaging the user in the process of storytelling, which results in a customised 'product' or narrative experience. As part of this process, the user internalises the narrative based on their interaction with the various characters and the camera system.

The user's ability to negotiate space from different perspectives in *Lustration* somewhat aligns with Machio's proposed second experiential phase of storyliving: 'exploration' (p. 10). He suggests that

> Once the viewer has been initiated, he or she explores the space, sometimes beyond the narrative, to seek out salient details. Emboldened by this sense of agency, he or she acts on their instincts and finds pleasure in their sense of control. Their body is the central medium for interacting with and finding significance in the virtual space. (Maschio, 2017, p. 10)

With this quote in mind, one can note that by placing the viewer within the 360-degree space of each scene and granting them the ability to walk around and/or switch camera perspectives, *Lustration* offers a somewhat interactive and visceral experience of the narrative, although this is contained within a set of predetermined parameters. The user must turn their head to explore space, can crouch down or move sideways to change their viewpoint of the scene and/or navigate the UI to switch between positions, demonstrating agency as an active participant in the experience. The various camera positions and rewind/fast forward buttons (as protostory elements) enable an exploration of space as well as of narrative threads by the user as a body. The characters and plot devices featured within the work are however, very much aligned with traditional storytelling models, drawing heavily on tropes associated with film noir in particular.

As an interactive narrative system, *Lustration* somewhat aligns with Ogle's '360-Degree Interactive Video Model' seeing as the camera system enables a level of interactivity that extends beyond the user's ability to rotate their gaze in the virtual environment. This interactivity facilitates discovery or exploration but leads towards a singular narrative conclusion. On a similar note, the project somewhat aligns with Aylett and Louchart's 'participant control points' position on their proposed spectrum of interactivity for digital narratives, seeing as the user is able to navigate a set of pre-authored possibilities via the camera system. Aylett and Louchart suggest that a typical example of this model involves branching narratives, which they consider to be 'a minimally interactive form of participation' (p. 120). This involves the navigation of pre-authored possibilities through user decision making at specific choice points, which isolates 'interactive possibilities from non-interactive story-elements' (p. 120). While the camera system offered by *Lustration* allows the user to jump between narrative threads, I note that there are no predefined moments for them to do this, as is typical of branching narratives, which allows important narrative information to be missed.

To take another example of this phenomenon in *Lustration*, I will examine a scene set in Detective Elizabeth Pine's open plan apartment in Episode Two. At the beginning of the scene we see Pine sitting at her dinner table, working through case files for the murder that occurred in the land of the living in Episode One. The project's interactive system offers six different camera positions within this scene. Cameras one to three offer different viewpoints of Pine as she works. Meanwhile cameras four to six offer a view of the apartment in the parallel world of The Between. The latter world is more dimly lit, has a slightly darker colour palette and contains a series of floating light orbs. I flick through each of the viewing positions that are offered in the first 30 seconds of the scene, finding that Pine is the only character present. Settling on camera two (in the land of the living), I observe as Pine gets up from the table and moves to the nearby kitchen. A large window that reveals a night-time cityscape is positioned above the kitchen sink, where she stops to fill a glass of water. Suddenly the window ripples and Aliria bursts through it, crashing into Pine and knocking her unconscious to the floor. Aliria then disappears from the land of the living and becomes present in The Between, as can be seen via cameras four to six. For the remainder of the scene I flick between the two parallel worlds, observing as Pine regains consciousness and phones a friend for help. In parallel time, one can observe Aliria as she negotiates Pine's apartment in The Between. Towards the end of the scene Aliria finds a photograph of a man resembling Bardolph on Pine's bookshelf (see Fig. 6.3). She seems to recognise him. This moment hints at further links between *Lustration*'s various characters, which are not resolved in the initial series. A user who is jumping between the six camera positions could easily miss this moment, should they have chosen to focus on cameras one, two or three at this time. The scene thus offers two parallel narratives that are interconnected and leaves the user to select their preferred thread, or to replay the scene and view both threads in turn. In either case, the user navigates pre-authored narrative structures, customising their narrative experience via their choice of camera, but not affecting the underlying story.

Fig. 6.3 Aliria explores Detective Pine's apartment in The Between. Screen capture from *Lustration* Episode Two. (Courtesy of New Canvas)

Fire Escape

Following a successful festival run, this VR experience was released to the public via the online Steam platform in April 2020.[2] Similarly to *Lustration*, the project draws upon tropes associated with an established cinematic genre; in this case, the murder mystery. Displaying the influence of Alfred Hitchcock's thriller, *Rear Window* (1954), the series unfolds across three 20-minute episodes, the first of which begins at 8 pm on Thursday, 1 October. In Episode One the user finds themselves positioned on the balcony of a New York apartment complex with a voyeuristic view into the windows of their eight neighbours. They can look around with 3DoF from this fixed position and further interact by clicking on the various windows, which magnifies their view of each neighbour and tunes them into individual audio tracks associated with the separate apartments. This method of interaction effectively changes the user's view from an extreme wide shot of the apartment complex to a medium shot of the selected apartments so that the details of various characters' stories can better be studied. The user watches as the landlord, Jared Mendel, gathers the various tenants of the building in his penthouse apartment to announce his eviction plans. Suddenly a fire alarm sounds, and as the tenants scramble out of the building, Jared is murdered by an unknown assailant.

A second significant character in this drama is ASMR Sweetie who lives downstairs and appears to be romantically involved with Jared. Throughout the series, she speaks directly to the user via phone calls that can be answered using the project's smartphone-like UI. As is the case in the opening episode of *Lustration*, this direct address fosters a sense of social presence for the user. Although the user cannot speak back into this phone, they can make emoji-based responses to questions posed by ASMR Sweetie and other callers, which impact upon the story's direction. These emoji choices sometimes activate branching narratives at key moments within the series, which lead to two possible endings. At other moments they are a means for the user to receive a somewhat personalised response from the character they are in dialogue with, albeit this being from a set of predetermined possibilities. For example, in the user's first conversation with ASMR Sweetie, she asks if they are lonely. The emoji that the user selects in response influences ASMR Sweetie's next line of dialogue. At the end

[2] *Fire Escape* is listed as an 'adventure game' on the online distribution platform, Steam. See: https://store.steampowered.com/app/1224480/Fire_Escape/

of Episode One, the user receives a warning not to trust this character from an unknown male caller.

Episode Two, which begins at 10 pm on the same evening, involves police investigation of the murder. Users can zoom in on two detectives' conversations with the various tenants or observe their conversations amongst themselves, all of which offer clues as to the identity of the murderer. While the user has agency to explore the individual stories of the tenants using the magnification tool, there are key story moments where their attention is forcibly directed by the narrative system so that important story beats are not missed. For example, when the two detectives surmise the progress of their investigations into the murder inquiry, the user is given no option but to listen to this conversation. This episode concludes with a further hint at ASMR Sweetie's involvement in the crime.

The third episode, beginning at 10.20 pm, unveils the unknown caller—a disgruntled former tenant—as Jared's killer. The user's interactions with this character via the mobile phone UI have the potential to implicate them in his final action of setting fire to the apartment building. For example, during a phone call, the killer and arsonist poses the question: 'Are you ready to light the spark with me?' The user can respond positively or negatively via an emoji.

The residents seek refuge from the flames atop the apartment complex, forming either a group of dissenting individuals or a tightly knit community of survivors, representing two distinct outcomes of the narrative. The specific conclusion encountered by the user is shaped by their interpretation of the characters' dynamics, which has been conveyed to the system through their emoji reactions.

As an interactive digital narrative system, the game engine-driven experience of *Fire Escape* can be seen to offer a collection of 'protostory' elements (Koenitz et al., 2020) that are delivered via a HMD and hand controllers (see Table 6.2). The project's assets include a main menu, a compelling murder mystery narrative with two possible conclusions and a collection of intertwined subplots that may or may not be accessed by the user. These subplots revolve around the individual backstories and actions of the characters involved. Once the user reaches the conclusion of the experience, they have the option to navigate back to the main menu and replay episodes, restarting from specific five-minute intervals. Given the user's capacity to tune into distinct apartment settings within the episodes, it becomes possible to relive the experience multiple times, unveiling fresh details with each playthrough. In other words, a variety of narrative

Table 6.2 Protostory elements in *Fire Escape* based on SPP analysis model (Koenitz, 2023, p. 87)

Element	*Functions*	*Fire Escape*
Procedural components	Provide rules like physics systems, societal rules, spatial configurations, interaction processing, and also generative components	360-degree virtual environment, fixed user position on balcony, ability to 'magnify' windows to experience parallel narratives, 'real-time' narrative sequences
Assets	Provide static material for narrative design	Main menu, pre-authored, linear narrative sequences presented within outdoor apartment block and individual interior apartment settings, multiple characters, sounds, instructional text, 2D assets for UI
UI	Enable agency through interaction	Point and click with hand controller as phone First-person view of events from within the storyworld, 3DoF
Narrative design	Arrangement of content, mechanics of the relationship between elements	Three episodes of fixed duration, Core narrative and selectable secondary parallel narratives within episodes, Defined branching narrative 'choice points' Interaction with characters via phone (answering phone calls and inputting emoji reactions)
Narrative vectors	Parts of the narrative design to guide the user and create specific effects	Perusal of secondary narrative material provides insight into subplots, response to prompts leads to two possible endings, possible user alignment with the antagonist

experiences or 'products' might be instantiated based on the user's process of interaction with the system.

After purchasing *Fire Escape* via Steam, I experienced it several times, and was therefore able to explore the subplots associated with the apartment tenants in some detail. The diverse characters that are featured in the various windows include a heavily pregnant young woman, a seemingly affluent business woman and her younger partner, and a method actor pretending to be a police officer. I found their rich and sometimes overlapping stories to be interesting in their own right, whilst also providing information relevant to the main storyline of Jared's murder. My focus on different characters in various playthroughs meant that I instantiated a unique narrative experience each time, even if the main murder plot remained somewhat consistent.

Like *Lustration*, the project's interactive narrative system somewhat aligns with Ogle's '360-Degree Interactive Video Model' seeing as it features 'storytelling devices that draw the viewer's attention to relevant parts of the story, [...] the clear establishment of objects of interactivity, what interactions will be used and how they will move the story forward' (2019, p. 15). Considering the latter, I note that onboarding instructions appear throughout Episode One (e.g. there is instructional text that is displayed on screen) providing an understanding of the various interactive devices. Additionally, as a 3DoF experience *Fire Escape* offers a freedom of visual perspective. Although the user is fixed to their balcony position, they can rotate their view and thus adopt the role of a fellow apartment tenant, albeit as a mostly passive voyeur. The project does not, however, grant the user 'the allowance of time to visually explore', which is one of Ogle's criteria for the above-named model (p. 15). On this subject I note that once each episode begins, it is not possible to 'pause' the unfolding narrative to explore the setting, as is the case with *Lustration*. In other words, an exploration of space, as separate from narrative elements, cannot be undertaken by the user. As such the project does not entirely fulfil the criteria for Machio's 'exploration' phase of storyliving, even though the user's body remains 'the central medium for interacting with and finding significance in the virtual space' (p. 10) As outlined in Table 6.2, the controlled delivery of pre-authored plot elements throughout the project is a feature of its narrative design, even though the user has some agency to affect these.

Perhaps more fitting then as a conceptual model enabling analysis, is Ogle's 'Intersections Model', which involves a main story and several connected secondary stories that may also stand alone (Ogle, 2019, p. 16). As mentioned above, Ogle suggests that this model of interactive storytelling has 'predefined "jumping points" (where the viewer can jump to a secondary story)' which are accessed by interaction (p. 16). *Fire Escape* features such a device to transition the user between the main narrative (Jared's murder) and the individual tenant subplots. As described above, these jumping points manifest as apartment windows, intentionally crafted to offer 'magnification' during specific moments, granting users the liberty to delve into particular narratives. However, when crucial information related to the main storyline is conveyed, this capacity to zoom in on a user-selected storylines vanishes to ensure that essential plot developments are not overlooked. Although the intricacies of individual character stories contribute to a more profound comprehension of the overarching narrative, they are not essential for grasping the fundamental plot.

There are some similarities between this model and Aylett and Louchart's above-mentioned 'participant control points' position, seeing as the user is able to navigate a set of pre-authored possibilities via the window magnification. Further to this interactive device, the emoji responses that give rise to two possible endings offer a further opportunity for the user to assert agency over their narrative experience. These devices isolate 'interactive possibilities from non-interactive story-elements' (Aylett & Louchart, p. 120), ensuring that a coherent overall narrative is instantiated.

Discussion and Conclusion

The description and analysis above demonstrate the bringing together of narrative structures associated with cinematic and/or comic book forms with novel interactive devices in both *Lustration* and *Fire Escape*, which gives rise to experiences that are responsive to user input. As IDNs, the two projects offer the user the opportunity to affect their experience of the narrative, although the scope of the user's influence on the eventual story outcomes is limited. In other words, the 'product' that is instantiated through user negotiation of 'protostory' elements in either project generally includes non-negotiable narrative structures. Given that both projects deliver highly structured and predetermined narratives, one might question the degree to which their respective user experiences deliver a measure of storyliving. The highly authored nature of both stories conflicts Vallance and Towndrow's definition of the phenomenon, even if both projects actively engage the user in the plot's 'unfolding layers' (p. 2). Neither project sees the user 'become' the story; however, they do situate the user *within* the storyworld and allow them to directly interact with characters through first-person address. Moreover, both projects' UIs allow the user to drive the narrative to its conclusion through interaction (by choosing various narrative threads). I would argue that this constituting role of the user within the virtual environment is key when considering one's ability to 'live' a story through immersive experience. Writing in a documentary context Nash posits that, 'in locating the spectator imaginatively "within" a simulated space, albeit with varying degrees of intensity, VR creates an experience of physical "navigation" fostered via the turn of their head or the movement of a mouse' (2018, p. 97). This involves a shift from the representation of story to the simulation of experience, which one could consider enabling 'lived' story. Such a shift seems applicable to the two projects that are interrogated above and more broadly speaking to VR storytelling across genres and platforms as a 360-degree medium.

Maschio's notion of storyliving does not explicitly take aim at any specific genre of VR storytelling; however, the applicability of this concept to non-fiction media, in particular, becomes apparent when considering his final proposed stage of a 'storyliving' experience: 'making sense' (p. 10). This stage involves the user's transition back to 'reality' after an experience concludes, where they '(draw) on prior life experiences, (seek) out information to provide additional context, and (incorporate) the perspective they've experienced into their worldview' (p. 10). Such a phenomenon seems more fitting when considering documentary experiences that explore social or political issues, rather than the dramatic, fictional narratives of *Lustration* and *Fire Escape*. I would argue that both of the analysed projects do however offer a 'dramatic expansion of perspective' by providing selectable vantage points of unfolding action, which is key to Maschio's notion of 'living the story' (p. 20).

The potential for storyliving in both projects, I would argue, is tied to the user's ability to tailor their narrative experience, therefore becoming an active participant in the process of storytelling, as well as an observer located within the virtual environment. One can observe that as an interactive narrative system *Fire Escape* offers a user experience that is both personalised and customised. The former involves the user's receipt of personalised character dialogue based on the responses they input into the system while the latter concerns their selection and navigation of subplots. *Lustration* likewise offers the ability to customise the narrative experience by choosing vantage points of the action and the ability to replay content, but does not offer personalised narrative threads. As previously mentioned, the personalisation of narrative threads in *Fire Escape* occurs within limited and pre-established parameters, resembling a type of branching narrative. I would suggest that the limitation of the narrative personalisation and customisation featured here is a result of the 'narrative paradox' discussed by Aylett and Louchart (2007). In other words, given the highly structured and somewhat traditional plot structures that are featured in both works, forms of interaction that hand more authorial control of the narrative to the user are not possible. This is evidence that, as Vallance and Towndrow contend, 'storytelling in VR may not yet generate a fluid, context independent, interactive narrative' (p. 2); however, developments in AI might herald a solution to this problem in future.

Regardless of the limitations surmised here, I would argue that the two case studies display novel approaches to combining an authored narrative with interactive elements. Going forward I would argue for further consideration of storyliving in relation to a user's immersion in a VR fictional storyworld, their engagement with interactive devices and their internalisation of a narrative.

References

Aylett, R., & Louchart, S. (2003). Towards a narrative theory of virtual reality. *Virtual Reality, 7*, 2–9.

Aylett, R., & Louchart, S. (2007). Being there: Participants and spectators in interactive narrative. *Lecture Notes Comp. Sci., 4871*, 117–128. https://doi.org/10.1007/978-3-540-77039-8_10

Dooley, K. (2021). *Cinematic virtual reality: A critical study of 21st century approaches and practices*. Palgrave Macmillan.

Fire Escape. (2019). *Writers Sam Butin, Navid Khonsari, Vassiliki Khonsari, Andres Perez-Duarte*. Director Navid Khonsari. iNK Stories: USA. Three episodes.

Fisher, J. A., Vosmeer, M., & Barbara, J. (2022). A new research agenda: Writing for virtual reality interactive narratives. In *International conference on interactive digital storytelling* (pp. 673–683). Springer.

Greenwald, M. (2017). *From storytelling To VR 'storyliving': future marketing communications*. Forbes. Published July 31. https://www.forbes.com/sites/michellegreenwald/2017/07/31/from-storytelling-to-vrstoryliving-future-marketing-communications/#34ffa5b235e2

Koenitz, H. (2010). Towards a theoretical framework for interactive digital narrative. In R. Aylett, M. Y. Lim, & S. Louchart (Eds.), *Interactive storytelling: Third joint conference on interactive digital storytelling* (pp. 176–185). Springer.

Koenitz, H. (2015). (2015). Towards a specific theory of interactive digital narrative. In H. Koenitz, G. Ferri, M. Haahr, D. Sezen, & T. I. Sezen (Eds.), *Interactive digital narrative* (pp. 91–105). Routledge.

Koenitz, H. (2023). *Understanding interactive digital narrative: Immersive expressions for a complex time*. Routledge.

Koenitz, H., Eladhari, M. P., Louchart, S., & Nack, F. (2020). INDCOR white paper 1: A shared vocabulary for IDN (Interactive Digital Narratives). *arXiv preprint arXiv:2010.10135.*

Laurel, B. (1991). *Computers as theatre.* Addison-Wesley Publishing Company

Lustration VR. (2022). *Dir. Ryan Griffen.*

Maschio, T. (2017). Storyliving: An ethnographic study of how audiences experience VR and what that means for journalists. *Google News Lab.* https://newslab.withgoogle.com/assets/docs/storyliving-a-study-of-vr-in-journalism.pdf

Murray, J. H. (1997). *Hamlet on the holodeck: The future of narrative in cyberspace.* MIT Press.

Nash, K. (2018). Virtually real: Exploring VR documentary. *Studies in Documentary Film, 12*(2), 97–100.

Nguyen, M. H., Bol, N., & King, A. J. (2020). Customisation versus personalisation of digital health information: Effects of mode tailoring on information processing outcomes. *European Journal of Health Communication, 1*(1), 30–54.

Ogle, G. (2019). Screenwriting for new film mediums: Conceptualizing visual models for interactive storytelling. *Journal of Screenwriting, 10*(1), 3–27. https://doi.org/10.1386/jocs.10.1.3_1

Rear Window. (1954). *Writer John Michael Hayes.* Director Alfred Hitchcock, 112 minutes.

Rose, M. (2018). Technologies of seeing and technologies of corporeality: Currents in nonfiction virtual reality. *World Records, 1*(1), 1–11.

Ryan, M.-L. (2015). *Narrative as virtual reality 2.* Johns Hopkins University Press.

Ryan, M.-L. (2001). *Narrative as virtual reality. Immersion and interactivity in literature and Elec-Tronic media.* The Johns Hopkins University Press.

Vallance, M., & Towndrow, P. A. (2022). Perspective: Narrative storyliving in virtual reality design. *Frontiers in Virtual Reality, 3,* 779148. https://doi.org/10.3389/frvir.2022.779148

Whittaker, L. (2023). Onboarding and offboarding in virtual reality: A user-centred framework for audience experience across genres and spaces. *Convergence,* 13548565231187329.

CHAPTER 7

Virtual Reality Narratives Live Online: Immersive Theatre in VRChat Worlds

Introduction

In recent years, several globally accessible social VR platforms such as VRChat and RecRoom have grown in popularity. These platforms allow users to enter customised 3D virtual environments as full body avatars with speech, eye tracking and hand movement abilities. Adopting these avatars, users can join communities, play games or engage in social activities such as watching a movie or attending a party, similarly to how they would in real life (Freeman & Maloney, 2021). Perhaps the most successful of these social platforms is VRChat (abbreviated as VRC), which in December 2023 had an estimated 20 million players (Play Tracker, 2023), the majority of whom have accessed the application using a standalone Oculus Quest device (Lee, 2022). The platform was released in 2017 by game distribution service Steam and can also be accessed by desktop users through its website (vrchat.com) Kim notes VRC's appeal to both experienced and first-time developers of 3D virtual worlds, observing the way that 'users have pioneered various roles for their own interests and skill sets, ranging from 3D modelling avatars, community moderation on Discord, to hosting and live streaming talk shows on secondary media platforms like Twitch and YouTube' (2021, p. 11). This widespread appeal is reflected in the sheer number of community-created VRC worlds: more than 25,000 and counting as of October 2022 (VRChat, 2022).

K. Dooley, *Virtual Reality Narratives*,
https://doi.org/10.1007/978-3-031-64965-3_7

As well as providing an indication of what the Metaverse (an online virtual world where people can work, socialise and play) might look and feel like, VRC provides a venue for the evolving medium of immersive theatre. The term 'immersive theatre' is used to refer to a broad collection of practices that involve audience participation in the performance of a theatre work. Alston suggests that 'one of the main differences between performances that involve an immersive and/or participatory mode of audience engagement and other kinds of theatre is that audiences both refashion and co-produce theatre performances' (2016, p. 7). This 'co-production' means that the audience is asked not just to observe and reflect, but to roam and interact with performers, an experience that might lead to introspection 'as attention is turned toward an experience that is produced within the body' (Alston, p. 9). The potential of immersive theatre has been highlighted by the success of shows such as British company Punchdrunk's *Sleep No More*, which debuted in New York in 2011, and the Guild of Misrule's *The Great Gatsby,* (the longest running immersive theatre performance to have graced London's West End), both of which were affected by COVID-19. When the pandemic forced theatres and other performance venues to close, it left a void for interested audiences and performers of immersive theatre. As a result, a number of theatre collectives and artists looked to digital technologies as a means to continue their practice while in lockdown. The result is an abundance of live performances in VRC and on other platforms as practitioners experiment with crafting and delivering immersive theatre in a virtual setting. Notably, live theatre in VRC allows both performers and spectators to have a shared, embodied experience from the confines of their own (separate) homes. This new variety of theatre has persisted, despite the reopening of physical venues as the COVID-19 pandemic wanes, and continues to gather steam.

This chapter explores recent developments in immersive VR theatre, posing questions about narrative experiences that involve real-time interaction with virtual actors in a VR environment. The chapter will explore several performances staged on VRC, such as *Scarecrow VRC* (K'Arts AT, 2020), by South Korean creator Smgmoo Lee and *Finding Pandora X* (Double Eye Studios, 2020). The former originated as a one-on-one VR immersive theatre experience that pits the user against a swarm of evil firebirds, while the latter is set in the times of ancient Roman theatre and asks its virtual audience to assume the role of the Greek Chorus. In my analysis of these works I consider both creator aims (as evidenced in interviews) and audience accounts of the experiences. The chapter's central case study is *The Severance Theory: Welcome to Respite*, produced by the

US-based Ferryman Collective (2021), a critically acclaimed 40-minute experience that casts one audience member as Alex, a child that experiences dissociative personality disorder, as he/she struggles against an evil force known as 'The Shadow'. Other audience members assume the role of invisible entities that have the power to protect Alex. This experience includes voting devices, meaning that the audience can influence Alex's story. Like *Scarecrow* and *Finding Pandora X*, *Welcome to Respite* includes complex game mechanics and visual effects to encourage user interaction with live actors and other story agents.

The chapter will examine the way that *Welcome to Respite*'s narrative is constructed, considering onboarding and offboarding sequences (the methods by which performers prepare participants to enter and exit the virtual VR world) as well as the story itself. My close reading and narrative analysis of the experience is complemented by interviews with four of its creators: co-writer and director Lyndsie Scoggin, producer and performer Deirdre V. Lyons, producer Stephen Butchko and special effects/animation and co-sound designer Christopher Lane Davis. Considering the ephemeral nature of live theatre in VRC, these interviews grant me an awareness of devices and story threads that I might not have experienced first-hand when participating in the work and allow me to understand the way that technical and logistical factors have impacted on the development of story. With reference to existing literature on immersive theatre (Baía Reis & Ashmore, 2022; Dixon, 2006) and social VR worlds (Freeman et al., 2022; Freeman & Maloney, 2021), I will argue that this VR work offers the user a 'personal' experience of a pre-authored narrative delivered through live performance, where one-on-one engagement with actors fosters high levels of engagement and feelings of immersion.

On 'Liveness' in Immersive, Digital and VR Theatre

Theatre, as an art form, is defined by live performance. This is what separates it from media such as film (and non-live television), which offers pre-recorded performances that have been pieced together from edited source material. Unlike film actors, theatre actors perform a role from beginning to end in a fixed period, with no opportunities to correct mistakes (or at least they cannot do so until the following performance). In the case of classical theatre, this calls for improvisation when unseen events disrupt the delivery of a scripted narrative, while for immersive theatre, improvisation occurs in response to spectator interactions, creating or altering a narrative. As Phelan posits, 'Without a copy, live performance plunges into visibility—in a maniacally charged present—and disappears into memory, into the realm of invisibility and the unconscious where it eludes regulation and control' (1993, p. 148). Perhaps with this in mind, Reason argues that '"liveness" has increasingly become seen as something consumed when attending theatre performances, a commodity specifically purchased by audiences, [...] especially in contrast to non-live performances' (2004). This view suggests that the ephemeral nature of theatre, and the uniqueness of each performance, is the art form's most exciting and sought-after quality.

The notion of liveness is complicated by the integration of digital material into a theatre performance. The liveness of actors is obvious to an audience sharing a physical performance space with other bodies, while the appearance of actors through mediating technologies such as video and VR may be less so. Davis notes that 'in live drama work and performance, participants and performances receive different forms of feedback through all the human sensory channels in what might be called "synchronous" time' (p. 511); however, mediating technologies may restrict this feedback. In the case of VR theatre in online worlds, actors and audiences may inhabit completely different physical spaces, entering a virtual world as avatars, but yet a sense of liveness is generated through real-time interaction and improvisation. This notion accords with Auslander's suggested features of 'liveness', these also including real-time connections and feedback in mediated as well as classic live performance (2006). Auslander's definition can be applied to a broad range of theatre practices that involve digital interfaces and tools. These might include physically present performers, the co-presence of physical and digitally mediated actors or works that unfold in entirely virtual realms. In the case of live theatre in VRC, virtual bodies (avatars) are gathered in a virtual space, where they react to real-time events and interaction with performers. Before isolating the specificity of narrative produced in this context, I consider a range of VR theatre trailblazers, noting their innovative interactive and immersive features.

A Brief History of VR in Theatre and Performance Contexts

As VR technologies have developed, a number of practitioners have explored their potential in live theatre and performance contexts. Notable experiments in this arena date back to the 1990s, generally involving site specific experiences. While innovative, these projects were often costly and logistically challenging affairs, meaning that they were experienced only by small audiences in art festival settings (Baía Reis & Ashmore, 2022, p. 8). Looking back at this early work, Corts suggests a preoccupation with 'the seamless delivery of video, an experiment that required the use of supercomputers to merge images' (2022, p. 127). These new techniques and technologies provided artists with an expanded toolbox to foster audience interactivity, expanding the possibilities for immersive theatre and performance.

In his study of early trailblazing works, Dixon observes that 'rather than exploring futuristic worlds and ideas, artists […] predominantly utilized the technologies to create environments and experiences that correspond to the natural, the ancient, and the primordial' (2006, p. 24). As examples, he cites Brenda Laurel and Rachel Strickland's *Placeholder* (1993) and Char Davies' *Osmose* (1994–1995) as two particularly influential works. The former was an interactive two-person VR experience produced through the Banff Center's Art and Virtual Environments Project in Alberta, Canada. Powered by 11 computers and utilising more than 25,000 lines of code (Dixon, p. 28), *Placeholder* allowed two users to explore and play in three connected virtual environments, each inspired by natural landscapes of the Banff region. Wearing headsets, the users could walk around and listen to spatialised audio, including verbal narration from 'the goddess', which was spoken by a live performer. Additionally, sensors were attached to the users' bodies enabling full body tracking (rather than just head or hand tracking) in the virtual environment. Within each setting, users were encouraged to adopt the perspective of a non-human body: a fish, crow, spider or snake, guided by the goddess. As Dixon outlines, this allowed them to not just move close to other creatures, but to 'exchange "embodiments"', by becoming creatures (p. 29). Llanura suggests that *Placeholder* presented a unique experience to each user, as the narrative was constructed in response to their behaviours and action in the virtual environment (2015). The project demonstrated VR's ability to offer non-human points of views, and despite its short exhibition life at Banff in 1993, has received significant academic attention.

The latter project, Davies' *Osmose*, was a real-time VR experience featuring 3D environments and spatialised sound experienced through a head mounted display (HMD). For this corporeal experience, the user was also fitted with a motion tracking vest that monitored movement (from the waist up) and breathing so that the work's stereoscopic imagery could respond to these elements (Dixon, p. 31). Wearing these devices, the user found themselves in a forest and other natural settings, these providing 'a spatio-temporal arena in which mental constructs of the world can be given 3D form and be kinaesthetically explored through full-body immersion and interaction' (Davies, 1998, p. 65). Stern describes how users 'literally breathe(d) generative, image-based life into Davies' 3D world, and navigate(d) it using the simple angling of their torsos' (2013, p. 33). Through the work Davies aimed to not only communicate a vision of the world, but to demonstrate 'the medium's potential to enable us to experience our place in the world afresh' (Davies p. 65). This was achieved through embodied immersion that was ground-breaking at its time of creation.

Other notable early VR performance works include Australian Jeffrey Shaw's *The Legible City* (1988), and Michael Benayoun's CAVE installation *World Skin* (1998) (DeLahunta, 2002, p. 107). Following these and other experiences, was UK-based Blast Theory's *Desert Rain* (1999), which according to Dixon, delivered a more revolutionary VR performance event (p. 48). As a collaboration with the Computer Research Group, an advanced VR computer lab at Nottingham University in the UK, this experimental production used complex technologies to explore the 1991 Gulf War. Part installation and part video game, this takes the form of a 30-minute experience for six players who are given a mission to complete in the virtual world. The experience begins with each player being led into a room where they remove coats, set aside their personal possessions and put on a 'blue, hooded jacket uniform' (Dixon, p. 49). Following this physical 'real-world' experience, they move to a main installation space and engage the collaborative task of finding human 'targets' in a virtual environment. As Dixon notes, this part of the experience may generate a sense of anxiety for the player, as it is not clear what will happen once targets are located, and whether players will be asked to kill them (p. 49). Successful groups locate the targets in a bunker space, at which point a real-world live performer emerges and leads players to a mock motel room. In this space they are presented with video footage of the targets that they have captured, which reveals them as real people whose lives were affected by the Gulf War. The result is an experience that implicates the six players in combat games, this posing questions about the 'unreal' nature of war.

The period between the late 1990s and early 2010s saw continued although less notable experimentation with VR and performance, with innovation hampered by high costs and necessarily lengthy development periods. Dixon comments that work of this time was produced 'with considerably less impact and fervor' (2007, p. 3), while Popat suggests that 'interest in VR waned in favour of "mixed reality" in digital arts and performance, where virtual and physical elements combine within the artwork or environment' (2016, p. 358). Another factor that affected the growth in this area related to the unscalable nature of VR experiences, a problem that has persisted in relation to the current wave of VR. Dixon notes that 'classic' VR experiences from the 1990s were 'highly individual and improvisational, and require(d) sufficient time for users to orient themselves and explore' (2006, p. 51). This meant that the overall length of an experience could not be controlled or fixed as is the case for a film or classical theatre production, a factor that prevented high turnover of audiences.

The growth of the internet in the late 1990s may have also influenced a decline in interest in VR theatre, with online platforms providing an increasingly popular venue for performance. Dixon considers the theorisation of internet communication as a form of virtual performance of the self, this meaning that '"digital performance" is rationalized by many as being already ubiquitous, embracing multiple communicational and presentational aspects of electronic everyday life' (2007, p. 3). According to this view, theatre is not just produced in explicit online venues but also in a range of 'everyday' places, such as chatrooms, on blog sites and through online games (Dixon, p. 3). In terms of the latter, one might consider the performative aspects of online role-playing game *World of Warcraft* (launched in 2004) or online open-world game *Second Life* (launched in 2003).[1] The latter allows desktop users to build content and interact with others in a multiplayer environment. Early versions of *Second Life* offered features that now also appear in VR social platforms such as VRC

[1] For a discussion of performance in *World of Warcraft* and *Second Life* see Parker (2014).

(including the ability to customise avatars and communicate via voice), although the platform was not accessible via VR head mounted display goggles.[2]

The technological developments of the 2010s fostered another wave of innovation by VR practitioners, allowing for the combination of high-quality audio-visual material (live-action or computer-generated), theatrical and game elements. This is reflected in works such as Academy award-winning filmmaker Alejandro G. Iñárritu's *Carne y Arena* (*Flesh and Sand*, 2017), which features material filmed in 360 degrees. Based on true accounts, this location-based VR installation allows users to experience a refugee's journey across the US border from Mexico. Like the aforementioned *Desert Rain*, this three-part experience starts in a physical room where participants are asked to remove their shoes and put their personal items into a locker. They then put on VR goggles, headphones and a backpack (containing a computer) and are immersed in a cinematic virtual reality sequence that sees them led across a harsh desert landscape. This unfolds in a large physical space where participants roam barefoot while wearing a headset. In the final section, the participant encounters a video art installation in a third space, which reflects on the stories of refugees who fled to the United States from a variety of homelands. The experience thus combines physical experience with on-site facilitators who are part-performer and part-docent, pre-recorded video and reactive VR elements. In making this work, the director aimed to explore the possibilities of 360-degree imagery, as he comments

> My intention was to experiment with VR technology to explore the human condition in an attempt to break the dictatorship of the frame, within which things are just observed, and claim the space to allow the visitor to go through a direct experience walking in the immigrants' feet, under their skin, and into their hearts. (Iñárritu quoted in LACMA, 2022)

This quote captures the director's desire to involve audience members in a predetermined narrative as active participants, which he contrasts with his previous practice as film director. While impactful, it should be noted that this work, like those of the 1990s, is costly to mount and access is limited to in-person participants.

[2] It is now possible to access *Second Life* using a VR headset but the platform is not optimised for this point of entry or experience.

Other practitioners have created theatrical experiences in fully immersive online worlds resulting in greater audience accessibility. A landmark VR experience that takes this approach is US-based studio Tender Claws' *The Under Presents* (2019), an animated, multiplayer game that continues to intermittently feature live actors, accessible via an Oculus Quest HMD (see Chap. 5 for an analysis of this project). In the dreamlike world of this application, the player roams freely in a reactive, post-apocalyptic landscape so as to unlock the mystery of a shipwreck transformed into a nightclub. The player's virtual body is a faceless black figure with mask, cape, and hood, which glides through the vast environment. Although unable to speak, the user can communicate with other players using hand signals, as facilitated by HMD hand controllers. Working collaboratively with other players, the user casts spells that unlock secrets of the land, give them special powers (such as flight) and/or change their avatar's appearance. A separate user interface enables live performers to appear in the land of *The Under* as avatars, adopting one of several predetermined characters to engage players in short improvisations. This facet of the work was drawn upon most heavily in a variation of the main experience, *The Under Presents: Tempest*, which delivered an interactive narrative experience based on the Shakespearean play of the same name in late 2020 and 2021. In both experiences, the audience can affect the narrative through interaction with the environment, live actors and other players. In this sense story making is a collaborative affair led by the user's virtual body.

While *The Under Presents* was designed before the onset of COVID-19, it was during the pandemic that its popularity soared, seeing as it could be accessed remotely by a seemingly unlimited number of players. This influential work demonstrated the huge potential of immersive VR theatre, fostered by the Oculus Quest's ability to offer six degrees of freedom to the player (the ability to interact with objects and move freely within a 360-degree environment) without being tethered to a mainframe computer. Writing on this and other recent VR theatre works, Corts rightly suggests that 'rather than merely imitating [...] physical world performances, [...] virtual immersive theatre productions can challenge our notion of what both the physical and virtual body can experience' (2022 p. 128). In the case of this experience, the player's virtual body transcends the limits of the physical body through play with scale, multiplicity and interaction with space.

As previously mentioned, the COVID-19 pandemic caused major disruption for performance makers around the globe leading to widespread experimentation with new technologies to connect with audiences. In the wake of the pandemic, several practitioners have retained an interest in VR technologies as a means to broaden their audience reach, this perhaps involving in-person and remotely accessible theatre performances produced in parallel. One such example is the US Actors Theatre of Louisville's production of Charles Dicken's *A Christmas Carol*, which was presented on stage and in virtual reality using real-time motion capture and game engine technology (Gochfeld et al., 2022). In this production, a single actor played the role of Dickens, both narrating the story and portraying many of the characters. In their analysis of the work, Gochfeld et al. describe how 'the director wanted to explore how XR (extended reality) technologies could help bring an audience closer to the experience of Scrooge as he confronts his demons and finds redemption' (2022). Like *The Under Presents*, this production demonstrates the way that XR technologies can productively expand the practice of theatre makers, enabling them to connect with audiences in a range of geographical locations. Both of these productions support Garson's suggestion that VR theatre productions 'might finally break the geographic stronghold NYC and other metropolises have on the theatre and performance sector, and allow American theatre to finally decentralize, and perhaps even create a digital Broadway' (2022, p. 16). Garson's analysis of VR theatre notes a number of influential works staged on social platforms such as VRC. I will now explore key works in this area, noting their narrative structure and interactive devices.

Live Theatre in VRChat

The online worlds of VRC offer theatre creators a globally accessible venue to gather participants for real-time experiences. By tapping into an established communication platform, creators are able to focus their attention on content creation; however, as Gochfeld et al. observe, this occurs within defined parameters (2022). For example, the optimisation of the platform for stand-alone headsets such as the Oculus Quest means that there is a limit on how many participants can enter a particular 'instance' (a virtual setting or scene) as well as the complexity of visual materials that can be featured in a scene. The combined assets associated with a VRC environment must accord with a maximum file size that informs the scope of the creator's world building.

Prior to attending a live theatre experience in VRC, the participant is required to register an account with the platform, selecting a username and avatar. Like Montemorano, one might consider this avatar to be 'a digital surrogate for the physical self' that is both a communication requirement but also a form of self-expression (2020, p. 6). Avatars offer an opportunity to experiment with one's representation, and in VRC can take a variety of human or non-human forms. For some VRC theatre experiences, the participant must adopt a custom designed avatar, taking on the role of a predetermined character. In either case, the participant becomes a type of performer as they respond to the prompts of live actors and other forms of interaction, as is typical of immersive theatre.

One early interactive and immersive experience to be staged in VRC was *Scarecrow VRC* (K'Arts AT, 2020), by South Korean creator Sngmoo Lee. This project debuted at the Sundance Film Festival in 2020 as a one-on-one VR immersive theatre piece with an on-site live performer. In this original format, a single participant was fitted with various haptic devices (including one that produced temperature effects) as well as a HTC Vive Pro HMD. The experience then located them into a virtual field, where they were required to help a life-like scarecrow fight off a swarm of angry fire birds. This expressive but non-verbal scarecrow character was played by a live performer who was equipped with a motion capture suit and face tracking technology. One participant describes the interaction that the experience offered:

> It began with small interactions, like the actor physically plucking a flower from the palm of my hand. Once the birds began their attack however, these light touches became much more aggressive as the character sought shelter behind my back and clutched my shoulders in fear. As wave after wave of firebirds rained down on us from multiple directions, the scarecrow served as my spotter, physically redirecting me towards incoming attacks. (Melnick, 2020)

As this account of the experience demonstrates, the participant's 'real-world' contact with the live performer's body was experienced within the virtual space, creating a multisensory experience of a scripted story. The original version of *Scarecrow* concluded with the defeat of the firebirds and a restoration of order in the virtual world, at which point the scarecrow hugged the participant. After removing their HMD, the participant was able to meet the live performer in their physical rather than digital form.

In response to COVID-19, *Scarecrow* was reimagined in VRC for the 2020 Raindance Film Festival as an experience for up to two participants.

In this version, the live actor and participants occupy the VRC world as avatars. Although no physical contact between live actor and participant is possible, the scarecrow nonetheless responds to participant movements and encourages interaction. One participant describes her experience:

> After a little bit of fiddling, our scarecrow teaches us how to draw in the air, creating swirls of color in the air or majestic life-sized angel wings. I draw a three-dimensional heart over the scarecrow's chest; he seems to smile as he draws one over mine. [...] It's what makes immersive art and entertainment so compelling: to see and be seen; to feel the presence of others and to have your own presence felt in return. (Yu, 2020)

This participant testimony demonstrates the way that *Scarecrow VRC* draws upon new interactive tools associated with the social platform, such as the ability to add visual material by drawing. This activity functions as a means to unite actors and audience through collaboration. Creator Sngmoo Lee suggests that Scarecrow VRC creates the opportunity for actor and participants to form a powerful bond: 'We get to know each other, and to interact with each other. We become very meaningful friends in a very limited time and then have to say goodbye' (quoted in Raindance Immersive, 2020). Returning to Alston's description of immersive theatre poetics, I would argue that the participant's interaction with the virtual actor in *Scarecrow VRC* creates a sense of 'co-production' of the narrative, which increases feelings of bodily presence (as avatar) in the virtual world.

A second notable theatrical experience to be delivered in VRC is *Finding Pandora X* (Double Eye Studios, 2020), which won 'Best Immersive VR User Experience' on its debut at the Venice Film Festival. Set in the times of ancient Roman theatre, this larger scale production hybrid that features live Broadway actors asks its virtual audience to assume the role of the Greek Chorus. The creator's synopsis of the multiparticipant experience suggests that 'With the passing of ages, the Gods of Mount Olympus have faded away until only two remain: Zeus and Hera. Now they are in danger of disappearing if they can't recover the box of hope that Pandora removed' (Double Eye Studios, 2022). While the project loosely revolves around the quest to locate Pandora, the inclusion of branching narratives means that groups of participants have varying interactive experiences, as one participant recounts:

> Thanks to the branching narrative, each group experiences a different story throughout the experience. At one point during my performance, for example, several members of our group split up to explore an epic city while the rest of us joined Zeus for a few drinks at the base of Mount Olympus. (Melnick, 2021)

Over the course of *Finding Pandora X*, participants are asked to perform simple tasks as individuals or in groups. Narrative co-creation occurs through considerable actor improvisation in response to participant input and unforeseen technical challenges (Melnick, 2021). The experience begins with a period of onboarding as another participant describes:

> The experience starts with you outside the Olympus, and you get greeted there by Hermes, (who) will teach you the basics of the experience, so how to wear your avatar, [...] how to move, how to change the settings of VRChat, etc ... (Skarredghost, 2020)

This onboarding process establishes the live actor's dual role as a performer and a docent who helps participants to negotiate VRC's features. In this role, the performer must juggle multiple concerns, so as to ensure that participants' experience of the work is optimised. As one of the production's live actors comments 'In VR you have the difficult task of not only using the acting part of your brain but simultaneously conjuring your inner technician' (Winslow Kashani quoted in Melnick, 2021). This brief exploration of *Finding Pandora X* captures the complexity of live VR theatre production, which I will explore further in relation to this chapter's principal case study.

The Severance Theory: Welcome to Respite

The Severance Theory: Welcome to Respite (2021), produced by the US-based Ferryman Collective and CoAct Productions, is an approximately 45-minute experience that brings together animation, sound design and live theatre elements in a VRC environment. Based on an in-person immersive theatre experience for one participant that ran in Los Angeles in 2019, the project was adapted for VRC, where it can be experienced by up to ten remotely located participants. Based on true stories, the work explores Dissociative Identity Disorder (DID) through the eyes of a seven-year-old gender-neutral child named Alex. Formerly known as

Multiple Personality Disorder, DID is a mental health condition that involves problems with memory and identity, characterised by the 'ongoing coexistence of relatively consistent but alternating subjectively separate identities' (Kluft, 1996, p. 337). People affected by DID because of past trauma may have several separate identities referred to as 'alters' (alternate personalities). *Welcome to Respite* allows the audience to explore Alex's jumbled memories of a disturbed childhood. Triggered by a visit to the family home some years after their mother's death, Alex is taken back in time to re-experience life with their mum and dad. As the three characters have dinner and then prepare for bed, an antagonist force known as 'The Shadow' emerges, who threatens to overcome Alex. Two live actors play the roles of Mum and Dad, while one audience member (a premium ticket holder) is cast as the DID affected Alex. Up to nine additional spectators adopt the roles of invisible and silent 'alters' who can shape Alex's journey. While the two actors and the audience member playing Alex adopt custom avatars, communicating through speech and bodily gestures, the alters' interaction within the storyworld is more limited. Before presenting an analysis of *Welcome to Respite*'s narrative structure and devices, I will outline my experience of my work.

The Onboarding World

My experience of *Welcome to Respite* played out in three parts, the first of which involved onboarding (an introduction to the VRChat world). I experienced *Welcome to Respite* in the role of an alter character in June 2022 using a Quest 2 HMD. Prior to the performance, I received instructions on how to enter a specific VRC world from the Ferryman Collective via email. As an avatar of my own choosing, I followed these instructions and found myself in a 360-space that resembled a giant child's bedroom (see Fig. 7.1). By giant, I mean that the setting and its contents were enlarged, so that as an avatar, my size was equivalent to that of several scattered toys (a blue rocket, a plastic tape recorder, some coloured crayons) rather than a human being. This play with the scale of the audience's virtual body can be realised relatively easily through design choices in VRC, whereas it would involve considerable expense for an in-person production, this being one advantage of completely online immersive theatre.

Several other participants and two actors as avatars were also present, and it soon became clear that this was a lobby or onboarding space where the actors could prepare audience members for the main experience. In

Fig. 7.1 The bedroom onboarding space. (Courtesy of the Ferryman Collective)

the minutes that followed, one actor helped me to adjust my VRC settings to become an invisible 'alter' character. Another actor posing as a toy bear led a series of short activities that helped participants to understand the mechanics of interactive devices to come. We learned the rules of the experience, how to throw an object, and how to mute ourselves. *Welcome to Respite* co-writer and director Lyndsie Scoggin and co-producer and live actor Deirdre V. Lyons describe the nature and importance of this onboarding:

> The onboarding room (is) a training tool [...] the little toy friends that are in there will take the audience members around and ask them questions For example, one of them (concerns a) colouring book. The bear says 'I love to colour. My favourite thing to colour with is crayons. But Alex always likes to colour with markers. What's your favourite thing to colour with?' And then bubbles will pop up in front of (the participant) with crayons or markers. (Scoggin, 2022)

> Onboarding is incredibly important in immersive theater traditionally, to allow audiences time to relax into the right mindset. [...] We want the audience already thinking about their childhood, to start laying out the breadcrumbs that they will follow as the story unfolds around them [...] Actors are there to greet them, put them at ease, get them talking. If audiences

> want to go off and explore the space, climb the blocks they are free to do so. (Lyons, 2022)

Scoggin describes the audience's introduction to a voting mechanic that appears in a later section of the experience, while Lyons describes the manner through which 'alter' participants become acclimatised in the VRC environment. I would argue that one-on-one interaction with the live actors is key to both processes. As a participant, I enjoyed the personalised welcome and care that I received in this lobby space and felt that this heightened my connection to the storyworld. While this onboarding process drew attention to the fact that, as a physical being, I was located in my office and wearing a HMD, it nonetheless felt immersive due to the interplay between my avatar and those of the performers. The use of audio in the VRC world helped to foster this sense of immersion. As Garson describes 'similar to the "real" world, audio in this context works based on proximity: if an audience member is close to someone else in VR, they will hear them more clearly than if they are further away from them' (p. 11). But moreover, immersion was created through the various activities that called for the engagement of my real body to produce effects for my avatar in the virtual world.

During this onboarding process, the participant who would play Alex was taken aside and prepared separately. Alex's gender can be either male or female and is aligned with the participant who plays the role (see Fig. 7.2). Upon Alex's return to the lobby in a custom avatar, the toy bear signalled that the main experience was about to begin. Participants were led towards a giant Etch A Sketch where the two actor avatars walked through a door that appeared on its screen. A burst of shooting stars and a musical score signalled the transition to another setting.

The Main Experience: Back to the Family Home

The majority of the experience that followed took place in the setting of a two-storey house (Alex's family home). Some framing at the beginning of this 'main experience' sets up Alex's situation: Following their mother's death, Alex finds that details of their childhood are hazy. This suggests possible trauma. They return to the family home to experience a childhood memory. For the sake of clarity, I'll outline my recollection of this experience in the present tense.

Fig. 7.2 Behind the scenes of *Welcome to Respite*—the audience member playing the character of Alex can choose the skin tone of their avatar. (Courtesy of the Ferryman Collective)

As an invisible 'alter' character, I watch as 'Mum' arrives by car and ushers Alex through the front door of the house. I follow close behind. Once inside, mum plays old music and begins to prepare mac and cheese for dinner. She asks Alex a series of questions, receiving ambiguous, short answers in response. I take the opportunity to explore the house's main living area on the ground floor. Several floating blue icons (memory orbs), which are not visible to Alex appear in this setting. By hovering over each one, I can read text relating to Alex's memories, which hints at past traumas. Some moments later, Dad arrives at the house. He jokes and dances with Mum, and then pours himself a drink. A comment from Mum suggests that his drinking is problematic, which adds to a growing tension between the characters.

Dad and Alex climb the stairs to the attic. In this dark environment, they use a projector to cast the image of stars on the walls. This attic room is the same environment as was featured in the lobby, although its scale is now aligned with the real world. Dad recounts the story of Alex's birth (a fond memory) and suggests that Alex has been missing for the summer. An argument erupts between Mum and Dad. At this point, I am granted the ability to vote for Alex's next action. Should he continue to interact with his parents or hide? I vote for the former and Alex stays in their company. (This is one of several 'voting points' for the alter characters.) The argument dies down and suddenly Alex is alone in the dark. Red lines appear around them. A disembodied voice tells Alex that they are worthless. The alter characters are encouraged to move closer to Alex for protection.

Back downstairs, the family sits down for dinner, after which it is time for Alex to go to bed. Another voting opportunity arises for 'alters': does Alex want Mum to sing a lullaby or Dad to read a book before bed? I vote for the latter. As Alex settles into bed, the parents talk in the adjacent bathroom, mentioning Alex's appointment with a therapist the following day. Suddenly a demon with red eyes known as 'The Shadow' appears in Alex's bedroom, a physical embodiment of 'night terrors'. The impending arrival of The Shadow is signalled by a siren-like soundtrack that builds in volume. Co-sound designer Davis describes this as an 'entirely discordant' sound element: 'you hear it a couple of times subtly through the show, but then it comes to full fruition at the end' (Davis, 2022). At this point, as an 'alter', I'm encouraged to pick up and throw digital stars at The Shadow, to try to protect Alex, but this doesn't work. The Shadow engulfs the room and the environment swirls into a mass of colour before fading to black. This final narrative sequence draws upon the cinematic potential of VRC, featuring strong visual elements and an emotive soundscape. The affordances of VR are vital in the creation of emotional impact, as Lyons notes: 'The night terrors Alex experiences are much more terrifying than (they could appear) in real life. We can freeze Alex to the bed, have a monster come out of the closet and the whole house stretch in impossible ways' (2022). By moving away from the realism of earlier scenes, this fantasy-like depiction of The Shadow functions as means to visualise Alex's anxiety. As Garson notes, the 'special effects with visual and audio clues in VR (attempt) to express outwardly what someone with DID may go through internally' (p. 13). This highlights the distressing and debilitating impacts of DID and encourages empathy and understanding.

Behind the Scenes and Offboarding

Welcome to Respite is designed to be run by two actors ('Mum' and 'Dad') who are simultaneously performers and stage managers; however, as Lyons describes, another team member is usually on standby to provide technical support.

> Onboarding is such a challenge that we often have another team member […] on Zoom to help any audience members who have logged on to troubleshoot. […] They also monitor the email should any audience request help that way and they are on Discord in voice chat updating one of the actors (about) what is happening with the audience and when the show should start. The actor playing 'Dad' is hiding out behind the block castle [in the lobby space] in an invisible avatar, […] accept(ing) invite requests from audience members who are wanting to get to the same digital space as everyone else, sometimes searching for the audience usernames and sending them invites. (Lyons, 2022)

This outline of duties for the actor the playing 'Dad' demonstrates the complexity of the VRC actor's multifaceted role. This is further evidenced by Producer Stephen Butchko's description of how, throughout the show, 'the actors wear one earpiece that is connected to the headset for performing and another earpiece in the other ear that is connected to Discord for behind-the-scenes communication' (2022). As participants enter the lobby space, the two actors add the role of docent to their job description, ensuring that user experience will be optimised. As stage managers for the main experience, they work with an interface that allows them to trigger interactive devices for participants. At the same time, they engage in voice-acting and puppeteering of their full-body avatars to deliver a semi-improvised performance throughout. Lyons describes how audiences are generally 'polite and interested in following the social cues they are given', however, the performers can access a 'recall button' if participants stray from strategic locations. This and other behind-the-scene tools augment their abilities to steer participants as they might in a 'real-life' immersive theatre experience.

To conclude the experience of *Welcome to Respite*, the participant is transitioned into a 'credits gallery', a public VRC world where they can access further information about DID, the production and the performers of the show. Co-writer and director Scoggin suggests that this world is 'an educational tool' that allows interested parties to source resources, potentially leading to greater impact for participants (2022). The gallery also functions as a 'decompression space' (Garson, p. 15) where participants can reconfigure their VRC settings, reflect on the experience in the form of their original, self-selected avatar, and prepare for their exit.

One of the live performers leads participants through the world, pointing out its features. This gallery is somewhat similar to a physical space in which audience members might mingle with performers following an in-person immersive performance. As such, it provides one last opportunity for participants to engage with performers in a one-on-one manner. After thanking the performer, I explored the multiple rooms of this world and then logged off, somewhat sad to be leaving. Within the three stages of this affective and educational experience I had felt that, as a participant, I was acknowledged and valued by the production team. My final experience in the credits gallery, where I could speak with one of the actors, reinforced this feeling. I would argue that this offboarding world, like the onboarding lobby, offers component parts of a narrative experience centred around the participant. Further analysis of work's narrative structure and devices builds a case for this view of the work.

Narrative Structures: The Participant's Journey

As the overview presented above suggests, *Welcome to Respite* presents a loosely scripted linear narrative that is propelled by user input and interaction. The two live actors playing the role of Mum or Dad guide participants through the experience, engaging in moments of improvisation while also ensuring that story beats are delivered. Seeing as the character of Alex is the work's central protagonist, the participant playing this role becomes the central performer, while other participants adopt secondary performative roles. Baía Reis and Ashmore describe this participant experience as like 'being "inside" a video game [...]. They are the performer, they are a character. Their actions and participation will have some impact on the production as a whole and will also impact their own physiological reaction to the experience they are embarking on' (2022, p. 13). This description of live VR theatre aligns it with older immersive theatre practices but also stresses the digital and ludic nature of performance in a virtual space.

Like Baía Reis and Ashmore, one might consider this narrative experience as something akin to a 'Hero's journey' (Campbell, 1949) with the participant (as performer) occupying the position of hero. As noted in this book's introduction, this model that underscores countless feature film and video game narratives sees a story protagonist thrust into an extraordinary world following the onset of a disturbing force: 'A hero ventures forth from the world of common day into a region of supernatural wonder: fabulous forces are there encountered and a decisive victory is won: the hero comes back from this mysterious adventure with the power to bestow boons on his fellow man' (Baía Reis and Ashmore, p. 13). Considering the three sections of *Welcome to Respite* (onboarding, main experience and offboarding) I would argue that a personalised 'hero's journey' is experienced by the participant. As Bucher suggests, the 'inciting incident' (or disturbing force) is the moment that the participant puts on their VR headset and begins the experience (2017, pp. 160–161). By entering into the VRC world, the participant leaves behind their everyday reality, undergoing preparations for a journey (onboarding), enabled through one-on-one interaction with performers. While the storyline presented in the main experience does not involve a 'victory', the participant as performer undergoes a series of challenges and interactive moments that are an opportunity to learn about DID, before having an opportunity to 'decompress' in the offboarding world. They then exit VRC (a return to the ordinary world) with a potentially deepened understanding of the condition.

While the character of Alex is at the centre of *Welcome to Respite,* I would argue that the 'alter' characters also experience this narrative arc. As secondary characters, they are positioned alongside the protagonist as observers with some interactive abilities. Writing on point of view in narrative-based VR experiences, Larsen argues for the utility of a 'sidekick' position in which user's 'get to go along for the ride, to talk to A.I. characters and to be an integral part of the protagonist's journey' (p. 79). Such an approach, he rightly suggests, 'allows screenwriters the necessary narrative control, while audiences still get full presence and interactivity to the point where it does not overly side-track the story' (p. 79). I would argue that, as invisible observers and supporters of Alex, the alters occupy this 'sidekick' role. The inclusion of discoverable 'memory orbs' gives them the opportunity to discover backstory story content for themselves, while voting mechanics and requests for physical action (throwing stars) create a further sense of agency. The inclusion of these game-like elements, which are also present in the onboarding section of the work, opens up ludic spaces for the participant. While for the narrative trajectory of the main experience, these actions are somewhat inconsequential, I would argue that their impact on the participant's broader experience of the work in three parts is substantial in the way that they bring the physical body into play.

Welcome to Respite thus presents a linear narrative propelled by affective encounter. As Kim suggests in regard to VRC encounters more broadly, these encounters take place between the body and VR technology but also between 'the body-in-VR and the socio-technical world of VRChat, composed of an assemblage of 3D artifacts, music, text, videos, UI, voices, and avatars animated by users' (2021, p. 32). As is the case with other forms of immersive theatre, the narrative could not unfold without the input of participants as performers. However, for VR theatre, this input is driven by a form of embodiment that draws upon the unique affordances of VR technologies. Baía Reis and Ashmore describe this affective encounter as a 'metasensorial experience of whimsical nature that is sensorially, symbolically and aesthetically very close to a lucid dream' (p. 23). It begins when the participant becomes an avatar, 'an anthropomorphic process enabled by the combination of the illusions of immersion, presence, and plausibility that culminates with the appropriation of a virtual body' (p. 23). In this form the participant becomes a performer alongside the live actors, with all parties contributing to a co-production of story.

The Virtual Body as Storytelling Tool

When audience members enter and exit *Welcome to Respite*, they do so as an avatar of their own choosing. As such, the onboarding and offboarding sections involve a gathering of a variety of self-selected virtual bodies that can mingle with each other and respond to the live actors. However, for the main narrative experience, these avatars are removed or replaced, an action that facilitates the delivery of narrative. Given *Welcome to Respite*'s ludic qualities, Aarseth's analysis of character in video game narratives provides a useful lens through which to analyse the variety of avatars that appear in the experience. Aarseth suggests that characters 'can be classified in terms of their depth/shallowness, and their malleability/potential for player control' (2012, p. 132). A rich character (displaying high levels of detail and depth), he argues, reflects authorial control of a game, as the player is being asked to identify with a predefined character. Conversely, 'malleability and user control limit authorial affordances' (Aarseth, p. 132). With this in mind, I would argue that the avatars featured in different sections of *Welcome to Respite* reflect varying levels of authorial control of the narrative experience.

VRC avatars are rich in their design and may even resemble 'recognizable characters with distinct personality traits and character-specific emotes' (Montemorano, 2020 p. 23). By adopting a specific avatar, the user determines the eyes through which they will see and be seen, a decision that shapes their experience on the platform. In other words, the user has control of their experience. Freeman and Maloney suggest that the four aspects of aesthetics, gender, race, and age/maturity provide a means for social VR users, as avatars, to perceive and interact with one another (2021, p. 24). In this sense, each participant's avatar is a self-selected storytelling tool that provides cues for others. Moreover, Freeman and Maloney find that social VR users often choose avatars that reflect their offline identity, even when constructing platform specific forms of self-presentation (p. 24). Based on this research, it would seem likely that participants experience the onboarding and offboarding sections of *Welcome to Respite* in virtual bodies that reflect their real-life identities, likes and/or preferences. These avatars allow them to bring elements of themselves into the performance, while also contributing to their perception of the environment and other characters. For example, a tall avatar will see the world differently than a short one, and a humanoid avatar may be treated differently to a monster avatar by other participants.

Conversely, as mentioned above, the main section of *Welcome to Respite* sees one participant adopt a custom avatar, while additional participants become invisible 'alters'. While the audience member who adopts the role of Alex has some power to customise this avatar, choosing a skin tone 'that most aligns with how they see themselves' (Lyons quoted in CoAct Productions, 2021), it must be noted that this is an avatar with significant depth that reflects the production team's authorial control of this main experience. Via the Alex avatar, the participant sees the world from the height perspective of a seven-year-old child (the result being, for example, that the adult characters appear to tower above them, just as they would in real life). Moreover, the mechanics of the avatar shapes the participant's abilities to move within the virtual environment, creating the conditions of their embodied encounter with other characters. In a similar sense, the invisibility of the 'alter' characters shapes these participants' experience of the work.

While Alex's journey is based on a predetermined trajectory, the participant playing this role nonetheless has the ability to contribute to the unfolding narrative through their interplay with the live actors. The Mum and Dad characters guide Alex through each scene but there is room for Alex's response to alter the tone of the work. Scoggin observes that 'every Alex is different, every person is going to react differently in a situation, they might laugh it off, they might get nervous. [...] (It) is an opportunity for us as performers, or whoever is performing to improvise around that' (2022). Lyons recalls one example of this improvisation: 'We even had an audience member say during a show, "Wow, you are really bad parents," and we rolled that into the story, agreeing with him and telling them that we are really trying to get better, and the show continued' (Lyons, 2022). As this example demonstrates, Alex's behaviour within the main experience shapes the live actors' approach and all of the other participants' experience of the story.

Further to the concept of participants' virtual bodies as storytelling tools, one can examine the ways that the two live actors' bodies contribute to the narrative experience. Parker rightly notes that avatar bodies are not as expressive or flexible as real human bodies (2014, p. 159), while Lyons speaks of a loss of 'a lot of micro expressions, body language and other forms of human communication' (2022) but nonetheless, actor movements and gestures contribute meaning to a scene. More important however, is the expressive qualities of the actor's voice, which speaks directly to participants, allowing them to feel 'seen' in the virtual world. Lyons suggests that *Welcome to Respite* creates opportunities 'to explore intimacy and quiet moments between the performers and audience' (2022). Considering my own experience of the production, I would argue that these quiet moments occur across all three sections of the work, through personalised, one-on-one contact with the live actors.

Furthermore, combined with responsive movement, the actor's personal address creates a deep sense of immersion for participants. Kim makes the point that social VR worlds see social media and online voice or video teleconferencing converge, this creating a 'unique blend of voice chat and visual media technologies in social VR [...] predicated on not only immersion, but real-time immersion' (2021, p. 28). On a related note, Corts describes the powerful effect of live actor responsiveness:

> When my virtual hand reaches out to touch a performer or player who responds to that touch, my brain perceives the experience as reality. [...] This perception collapses the distinction between the physical and virtual worlds, allowing the user to experience even the most outrageous of worlds as real. (Corts, p. 133)

Thus, in the case of *Welcome to Respite*, each participant's experience of the narrative is generated through the immersive and embodied encounters with virtual actors, in self-selected or custom designed avatars that reflect different degrees of authorial control. While the participant who adopts the role of Alex has the greatest ability to influence the unfolding of events, the 'alter' characters also have some ability to affect storyline through the voting mechanic. For all participants, the work provides an affective experience of DID, seen through the eyes of an avatar, which may lead to a new way of thinking.

Conclusion

In this chapter I have explored the ways that three VRC theatre productions—*Scarecrow*, *Finding Pandora X* and *Welcome to Respite*—offer their participants a live and personalised experience of a pre-authored narrative. These works combine complex game mechanics and visual effects with immersion fostered by live actors' direct address. Like earlier VR experiences such as *Placeholder* or *Desert Rain*, VRC theatre productions allow participants to experience the world through different eyes. But while the location-based nature of these older works limited their audience scope and reach, the online platforms of VRC allow creators to connect with global participants. Moreover, VRC theatre offers audiences an experience that is not bound by real-world constraints. Participants as avatars, can 'free themselves [...] from the physics of the real world', limited only by the imagination of theatre artists working in this area (Fung et al., p. 74). This opens the possibility for a new type of immersive theatre practice that is broadly accessible and potentially cheap to develop.

The examples of live theatre in VRC that have been explored in this chapter were all originally developed with other forms of delivery (completely in-person or hybrid VR/in-person) in mind. The onset of COVID-19 led to their reconceptualisation in VRC, meaning that the works demonstrate the way existing immersive theatre narratives can be successfully translated for delivery in a completely online platform. Key to this task is the consideration of interplay between participants and live actors' virtual bodies. For all three productions, a sense of intimacy, connection and acknowledgement is fostered through live, direct contact with actors, participation in game-like activities and the ability to explore fantastical environments. As this chapter is written, a new round of experimental productions that have been conceived of and produced specifically for VRC are being shared with global audiences. One can imagine that, as VR technologies continue to develop, so too will the possibilities for VR theatre makers to immerse participants in otherworldly and potentially transformative narrative experiences.

References

Aarseth, E. (2012, May). A narrative theory of games. In *Proceedings of the international conference on the foundations of digital Games* (pp. 129–133).

Alston, A. (2016). *Beyond immersive theatre*. Palgrave Macmillan.

Auslander, P. (2006). Afterword: Is there life after liveness? In S. Broadhurst & J. Machon (Eds.), *Performance and technology: Practices of virtual embodiment and interactivity* (p. 2929). Palgrave Macmillan.

Baía Reis, A., & Ashmore, M. (2022). From video streaming to virtual reality worlds: An academic, reflective, and creative study on live theatre and performance in the metaverse. *International Journal of Performance Arts and Digital Media, 18*(1), 7–28.

Bucher, J. (2017). *Storytelling for virtual reality: Methods and principles for crafting immersive narratives*. Routledge.

Butchko, S. (2022). Personal Interview conducted via email, 23 August.

Campbell, J. (1949). *The hero with a thousand faces*. Pantheon Books.

CoAct Productions. (2021). *Behind the scenes of welcome to respite*. YouTube. Published August 25. https://www.youtube.com/watch?v=C3-q5A923Ow&t=300s

Corts, A. (2022). The Under Presents: The potential of the real in virtual theatre. In *The changing face of VR: Pushing the boundaries of experience across multiple industries* (p. 127).

Davies, C. (1998). Osmose: Notes on being in immersive virtual space. *9*(2), 65–74. https://doi.org/10.1080/14626269808567111.

Davis, C. L. (2022). Personal Interview conducted via Zoom, 15 August.

Davis, S. (2012). Liveness, mediation and immediacy–innovative technology use in process and performance. *Research in Drama Education: The Journal of Applied Theatre and Performance, 17*(4), 501–516.

DeLahunta, S. (2002). Virtual reality and performance. *PAJ: A Journal of Performance and Art, 24*(1), 105–114.

Dixon, S. (2006). A history of virtual reality in performance. *International Journal of Performance Arts & Digital Media, 2*(1).

Dixon, S. (2007). *Digital performance: A history of new media in theater, dance, performance art, and installation*. MIT press.

Double Eye Studios. (2022) *Finding Pandora X (website)*. https://www.double-eye.co/finding-pandora-x

Finding Pandora X. (2020). *Dir. Kiira Benzing*. Double Eye Studios.

Freeman, G., Acena, D., McNeese, N. J., & Schulenberg, K. (2022). Working together apart through embodiment: Engaging in everyday collaborative activities in social virtual reality. *Proceedings of the ACM on Human-Computer Interaction, 6*(GROUP), 1–25.

Freeman, G., & Maloney, D. (2021). Body, avatar, and me: The presentation and perception of self in social virtual reality. *Proceedings of the ACM on Human-Computer Interaction, 4*(CSCW3), 1–27.

Fung, S., Jacobson, K., & Pike, J. (2022, January). PXR2020: Re-seeing the possibilities of theatre in virtual, augmented, and mixed reality. *Canadian Theatre Review, 189.*

Garson, C. (2022). The severance theory: Welcome to respite (2021) by CoAct productions and ferryman collective. Show review. *Miranda. Revue pluridisciplinaire du monde anglophone/Multidisciplinary peer-reviewed journal on the English-speaking world* (25). http://journals.openedition.org/miranda/45673

Gochfeld, D., Coulombe, A., Yeh, Y. J., Lester, R., Fleming, R. B., Meicher-Buzzi, Z., & Tarr, A. (2022). A tale of two productions: A Christmas Carol on stage and in VR. *Proceedings of the ACM on Computer Graphics and Interactive Techniques, 5*(4), 1–9.

Kim, A. S. (2021). *Virtual worldmaking: A phantasmal media approach to VRChat.* Doctoral dissertation, Massachusetts Institute of Technology.

Kluft, R. P. (1996). Dissociative identity disorder. In *Handbook of dissociation* (pp. 337–366). Springer.

LACMA. (2022). *Alejandro G. Iñárritu: CARNE y ARENA [Virtually present, physically invisible].* Los Angeles County Museum of Art. https://www.lacma.org/art/exhibition/alejandro-g-inarritu-carne-y-arena-virtually-present-physically-invisible

Larsen, M. (2018). Virtual sidekick: Second-person POV in narrative VR. *Journal of screenwriting, 9*(1), 73–83.

Lee, J. (2022). A study of VRChat: Player interaction in metaverse. https://www.gamedeveloper.com/blogs/a-study-of-vrchat-player-interaction-in-metaverse-

Llanura, P. (2015). *"Placeholder" virtual reality and perception.* https://ucsd-vis159.wordpress.com/2015/03/19/placeholder-virtual-reality-and-perception/

Lyons, D. V. (2022). Personal Interview conducted via email, 23 August.

Melnick, K. (2020). Sundance: Immersive theater piece scarecrow had me hugging a live actor in VR. *VR Scout.* https://vrscout.com/news/sundance-scarecrow-vr-theater-with-live-actor/

Melnick, K. (2021). 'Finding Pandora X' is live VR theater at its absolute finest. *VR Scout.* https://vrscout.com/news/finding-pandora-x-live-vr-theater/

Montemorano, C. (2020). *Body language: Avatars, identity formation, and communicative interaction in VRChat.*

Parker, J. R. (2014). Theater as virtual reality. *Nonverbal Communication in Virtual Worlds*, 151–174.

Phelan, P. (1993). *Unmarked: The politics of performance.* Routledge.

Play Tracker. (2023). Vr chat - Insight. https://playtracker.net/insight/game/2704

Popat, S. (2016). Missing in action: Embodied experience and virtual reality. *Theatre Journal*, 357–378.

Raindance Immersive. (2020). *Raindance Immersive | Scarecrow interview in VRChat (YouTube video)*. Published November 10. https://www.youtube.com/watch?v=y3h1GqEbjzY&t=24s

Reason, M. (2004). Theatre audiences and perceptions of 'liveness' in performance. *Participations: Journal of Audience and Reception Studies, 1*(2). https://ray.yorksj.ac.uk/id/eprint/912/1/1_02_reason_article.htm

Scarecrow. (2020). *Dir. Sngmoo Lee.* K'Arts AT.

Scoggin, L. (2022). Personal Interview conducted via Zoom, 19 August.

Skarredghost. (2020). *Finding Pandora X review: A nice VR interactive theater performance.* https://skarredghost.com/2020/11/14/finding-pandora-x-review-vr/

Stern, N. (2013). *Interactive art and embodiment: The implicit body as performance.* Gylphi Limited. http://www.immersence.com/publications/2013/2013-NStern.html

The Severance Theory: Welcome to Respite. (2021). CoAct productions and ferryman collective: Los Angeles.

The Under Presents. (2019). Dirs. Danny Cannizzaro & Samantha Gorman USA: Tender Claws.

VRChat. (2022). Over 25,000 community created worlds and growing. https://hello.vrchat.com/#:~:text=Over%2025%2C000%20Community%20Created%20Worlds,is%20the%20place%20to%20be.

Yu, K. (2020). Follow this 'SCARECROW' into the dark (review). *No Proscenium.* https://noproscenium.com/follow-this-scarecrow-into-the-dark-review-73ddfee9b7ad

CHAPTER 8

Conclusion: Virtual Reality Narratives as Embodied Encounters in Space

Introduction

This book's study has sought to interrogate the specificity of virtual reality (VR) as a narrative format. In doing so it has profiled and explored a number of entertainment-focused VR projects that have been produced and exhibited in the last five years. Further to providing a sample catalogue of innovate and/or prize-winning work, the book has offered a close analysis of these VR projects, which has been informed by theoretical models and scholarship drawn from disciplines such as narratology, literature, film, theatre and games studies, computer science and interactive digital narrative (IDN). Moreover, it has adopted a phenomenological approach to the study of these VR texts, which seeks to account for the experience that they offer to the user. The projects that have been studied feature varying degrees of interactivity for their audiences and have drawn upon the conventions of a range of older media, such as film, theatre and games. The specificity of VR has been approached through discussion of its affordances as an embodied medium: the sense of presence that it can foster for the user and its system-generated immersive qualities. As the various chapters have demonstrated, VR technologies offer exciting possibilities for artistic expression and narrative representation that foregrounds user agency and input.

A number of industrial events have impacted on the direction of virtual reality storytelling during the writing of this book. Following the

The original version of the chapter has been revised. A correction to this chapter can be found at https://doi.org/10.1007/978-3-031-64965-3_9

K. Dooley, *Virtual Reality Narratives*,
https://doi.org/10.1007/978-3-031-64965-3_8

developments associated with the current wave of VR that are outlined in the introductory chapter, it has been interesting to observe how speculation regarding the impending arrival of the metaverse has created further traction for VR. In October 2021, Facebook (the parent company that owned Facebook, Instagram and WhatsApp) rebranded as Meta, a move that signalled CEO Mark Zuckerberg's intention to create a shared online virtual 3D space for users. This change was accompanied by an announcement that the company planned to spend $10 billion on the metaverse. Other companies developing metaverse products at this time included the Lego Group, Epic Games, Roblox, Sony and Microsoft, pointing to a bright future for VR. By 2023, however, hype around the metaverse had been replaced with that of artificial intelligence, following the growing use of products such as Open AI's language-learning model, ChatGPT, and image generators Dall-E (Open AI) and Midjouney (a Discord Bot). While Meta's 'Horizon Worlds' metaverse platform was met with a lukewarm response from users (see, for example, Hachman, 2022; Heath, 2022), VR technologies have continued to advance on the back of AI developments, offering more opportunities to storytellers. As of late 2023, one can contend that a new wave of VR headsets is on the horizon, marked by the anticipated release of the 'Apple Vision Pro' in 2024, which promises an era of 'spatial computing' (Apple, 2023). With this development and other technological advances in mind, one can remain excited about VR's potential as an immersive and interactive narrative medium.

Key themes have emerged across the chapters of this book concerning (1) VR as a spatialised storytelling medium, (2) user-focused approaches to VR narration and (3) VR as interactive digital narrative (IDN). Before returning to the research questions that underpinned this study (as listed in Chap. 1), I will take a moment to unpack these threads, noting the ways in which they foreground the notion of embodiment.

Virtual Reality as Spatialised Storytelling

As a 'frameless' form of visual media, VR presents moving images that completely encapsulate the user, meaning that a narrative can be told all around them. In terms of this 'spatialised storytelling', I have noted how VR projects engage their audiences in the distribution of information across all quadrants of 360-degree space, the use of attention guidance techniques to ensure that narrative information is not missed and the featuring of interactive devices or user interfaces that encourage corporeal engagement with story content. This phenomenon is on show across the book's many case studies but receives specific attention in Chaps. 2, 4 and

5. In Chap. 2, for example, I refer to the 360-degree stereoscopic video work *The Man Who Couldn't Leave* (dir. Singing Chen 2022), which adopts sound cues, theatrical staging and lighting techniques to reveal story material in a spatialised setting. Following the narrative of this project requires the full body participation of a viewer who must swivel left and right to avoid missing action. I've argued that this strategic staging of action contributes to the viewer's sense of embodiment and encourages a dynamic viewing experience.

In Chap. 4 I have examined the expressive environments of several projects through the lens of 'environmental storytelling', a concept that has received limited attention in the context of VR. Drawing upon approaches theorised by Jenkins (2004) in relation to video games, I have demonstrated how narrative elements might be embedded in objects and environmental structures that are decoded by the VR user. Moreover, I have explored the 360-degree VR storyworld as a space where narrative is enacted, a process that engages the user as a body positioned alongside depicted characters or participants. This phenomenon encourages narrative understanding that is based on physical discovery and embodied experience. The three case studies featured in Chap. 4 illustrate how VR, functioning as a narrative medium, is particularly adept at environmental storytelling, seeing as users can explore environments from various angles and perspectives.

Further to the enactment of narrative in space, Chap. 5 has examined the constituting role of the VR user's body in the represented 360-degree VR environment with reference to the VR game *The Under Presents* (Tender Claws 2019). This line of enquiry explores how the user's experience is mediated via VR technology, which as Flavian et al. note, 'offers a sense of embodiment since users see themselves as components of the virtual environment, feeling that the VR devices (HMD, gloves, etc.) belong to their own bodies' (2019, p. 550). This sense of embodiment that concerns the user's positioning *within* a storyworld, differs from that of film or video games, seeing as the interactor experiences events and actions directly with their own body, rather than through identification with a character that is projected on a screen or through an externally positioned avatar that is controlled via a keyboard or joystick. In this sense, a VR project's user interface and mechanics for interaction can enable fluid interaction with the virtual environment. On this subject, one can note VR pioneer Jaron Lanier's advice to aspiring VR designers to 'emphasize biological motion over rigid UI (user interface) elements that throw away most of what the body does' (2017, p. 36). This comment stresses the importance of considering the ways that VR software encourages the easy participation of the human body if one is to design an intuitive and engaging experience.

One such example of intuitive design is the 'scrunch teleport' mechanic that enables players to reach out their hand and literally 'pull' space towards their body in *The Under Presents*. As Chap. 5 has explored, this mechanic emphasises the player's navigation of space as an embodied activity that allows for rapid movement through the landscape. By this I mean that the real-life movement of the player's hands and arms and the swivelling of their body, mediated through a HMD and hand controllers, impacts upon the constitution of the virtual environment. This fosters 'coextensive space', wherein design elements enable the integration of 'concrete reality' (Saker & Frith, 2020, p. 1429). In other words, the user's physical body and real-world space influence or align with the virtual world portrayed in the project.

With reference to Ryan's notions of emotional and strategic space in digital narratives (2015b), I have proposed the term 'corporeal space' to encapsulate this simultaneous experience of the player as a physical body in real life and as a virtual avatar, creating and engaging with space in real-time rendered VR. While for Ryan, the concept of emotional space is connected to 'affective reactions', this idea does not seem adequate to capture a 360-degree space that is primarily experienced viscerally. Therefore, I embrace the term 'corporeal space' to characterise the space perceived by the player wearing the HMD as a physical body and virtual avatar situated within a virtual environment. As Chap. 5 has argued, this space may possess emotional or strategic attributes. Yet, it is a space governed by a player situated at the storyworld's centre, where bodily movements and actions—such as the twisting of their body or the motion of their head, arms, and hands—directly evoke and shape the space. As discussed in Chap. 5, this notion of 'corporeal space' seems apt when considered in light of other VR games, although further work is needed to evidence the concept's broader applicability to VR narratives.

Virtual Reality Narrators, User Positioning and Point of View

The book's various chapters have examined the ways that contemporary VR projects are narrated, considering the role of the user alongside other story agents. As a whole, the book demonstrates VR's status as a 'first person medium' (Laurel, 2014, p. 184), in which the user is positioned within a storyworld and experiences events as an invisible or physically represented avatar. This notion is explored in most detail in Chap. 3, which presents a taxonomy of user positioning within VR narratives. This taxonomy suggests that the user can assume either an 'observer' or 'explorer' role within a VR storyworld. These roles encompass variables that include the user's representation, perspective, levels of agency and ability to influence the narrative. Through the analysis of these roles in the three case studies, it becomes evident that user positioning in VR narratives is diverse and dynamic, allowing for the adoption of multiple positions within a single work. I note that the unfolding of VR stories, on a moment-by-moment basis, is intricate and involves mechanisms that encourage narrative immersion and self-reflection.

Across the book, one can note VR experiences that engage the interactor through direct address from unseen or physically represented narrators, or unspoken acknowledgement via characters' glances at the camera. The latter is evidenced in *Sorella's Story* (dir. Peter Hegedus 2022), an Australian project that recreates the last moments of Sorella Epstein and her family, all of whom were murdered during a Holocaust massacre that took place in Latvia in 1941. In this instance the young narrator's direct eye contact with the camera/user fosters a feeling of 'social presence' [the feeling of being present in a VR storyworld with another (Biocca, 1997; Nash, 2018)], which gives rise to the user's self-conscious reception of the narrative. Like the two other case studies in Chap. 3, this project also features voiceover narration that informs the user's understanding of visually represented events. As Chap. 3 explores, this narration produces a number of effects, but commonly serves as a means to engage the user on an emotional level.

The various approaches to narration that are outlined in Chap. 3 have been considered through the lens of focalisation (Bal, 2009; Genette, 1980). This narrative theory is concerned with the position or perspective from which a story is viewed but also takes into account the deliberate presentation of narrative information in relation to a character's experience and understanding within the diegesis. I have argued that VR works commonly feature 'internal focalisation', which occurs when events are seen from the point of view of a specific character, meaning that some story information is restricted (Genette, p. 189). More specifically, I have observed that the VR user can adopt a character role within the diegesis and therefore 'participates in the fabula as an actor' (Bal, 2009, p. 152). As such, narrative information may be deliberately limited to the user's visual field, and crucial story details could go unnoticed if, for instance, the user is not gazing in the correct direction at the appropriate moment. As Chap. 3 demonstrates, the concept of focalisation, as outlined by Gennette, is complicated by the positioning of the user within the VR storyworld as an observer or explorer character, seeing as they are technically the one 'who sees' (1980, p. 186) but their experience may also be aligned with the perspective of a story protagonist. This complexity points towards the specificity of VR storytelling as a first-person medium. As Bruni et al. point out, considering the VR interactor through the lens of focalisation 'can inform the design of both the interaction modalities afforded to the user, and the general form of the narrative representation according to the intentions of the author and the goals of the system that is being designed' (2022, p. 46). The case studies that are explored in Chap. 3 demonstrate creative approaches to user positioning within the virtual storyworld, which aligns their experience of the story with that of the represented protagonists.

Further to my interrogation of user perspective in Chap. 3, Chap. 2 has considered the impacts of physical body representation on the interactor's embodied experience of a VR narrative. Noting established links between the concepts of presence and embodiment in virtual reality environments (Biocca, 1997; Lee, 2004), this chapter has explored the way that the user's representation as an avatar (or conversely, their lack of representation) gives rise to a sense of embodiment. The case studies explored in this chapter demonstrate how body representation has consequences for the user's ability to interact with the story, as well as for their identification with a predetermined character. Notably, however, I suggest that a physical body representation is not required to foster a strong sense of embodiment for the user and rather, that a sense of 'self-presence' (Biocca, 1997), involving mental representations of oneself within a virtual environment, can be achieved through other means.

Virtual Reality as Interactive Digital Narrative (IDN)

The case studies featured throughout this book have demonstrated VR's specificity as a form of interactive digital narrative. This specificity relates to the affordances of VR technology, which gives rise to the interactor's immersion in a virtual environment. This ability of the medium to position the user *within* a virtual storyworld demands a full body engagement with narrative content and is implicated in the generation of feelings of presence. Such an engagement takes a variety of forms, but at a base level, involves the interactor's negotiation of 360-degree space through the turning of their head or the swivelling of their whole body so as to choose their field of vision of unfolding events, as they would in real life. The case studies in this book are varied, ranging from pre-rendered 360-degree videos to room scale works that react to user input, and projects featuring live actors; however, all of these works call for this base level of bodily engagement. In this sense VR can be considered an inherently interactive medium, even when in pre-rendered 360-degree video form. This is because an interactor's experience of a VR narrative is variable and dependent on their viewing direction at any given time.

Further to the interaction demanded by the VR as a spatialised storytelling medium, this book has explored additional devices that allow the user to interact with story agents and affect the narrative's unfolding or outcome (through, for example, branching narratives or manoeuvrable objects and/or avatars). One can note that such devices create more opportunity for the user to become an active participant in an unfolding scene, but may also require more sophisticated VR hardware. Game engine technology that enables the real-time manipulation of storyworlds presents opportunities for the user to personalise or customise their narrative experience, as evidenced in Chap. 6. Moreover, in the context of non-fiction VR narratives, interactive devices can encourage a user to relive the experience of story protagonists, as is demonstrated in Chap. 3's analysis of *Goliath: Playing with Reality* (dirs. Barry Murphy and May Abdalla 2021). This room scale work allows the user to assume the role of the online game-playing protagonist, Goliath, as he becomes debilitated by mental health problems. Further to depicting Goliath's struggles, the work's interactive devices encourage the user to experience his hardships first-hand, fostering understanding that is generated through corporeal engagement with story agents.

One can observe continued tensions between interactivity and the delivery of coherent narratives in VR, which has been a key challenge of IDN. Aylett and Lochart describe this problem as the 'narrative paradox' (2007, p. 116), observing that as users are granted greater freedom to influence a narrative, the challenge intensifies in crafting a story with definitive plot elements. This challenge for VR narratives has been explored in Chap. 6 in relation to 'storyliving', a concept used to describe the VR user experience that gained traction in 2017 following a Google News Labs study (Maschio, 2017). To emphasise the experiential nature of VR storytelling, this study called for a reimagining of narrative structure within a VR experience from traditional linear notions of 'beginning', 'middle', and 'end' to the three phases of 'initiation', 'exploration', and 'making sense' (Maschio, p. 10). Chapter 6 presents an analysis of these terms with reference to two VR narratives as interactive narrative systems, finding that the potential for 'storyliving' is linked to the user's ability to customise and/or personalise their narrative experience, thereby becoming active participants in the storytelling process. One can note, however, the highly structured and somewhat traditional plot structures that are featured in both of the case study works in this chapter, which means that only limited authorial control of the narrative is handed to the user. This is the case for many of the other chapters' case studies, which offer definitive narrative outcomes and linear structures. Works featuring multiplayer open-world structures and/or live actor scenarios, as seen in Chaps. 5 and 7 offer greater opportunity for the generation of emergent narrative but may require significant resourcing in their delivery to an audience. Developments in AI promise a solution to this problem in future, and might create fluid, individualised narrative experiences in virtual environments without the need for live actor input.

Having summarised these key themes that arise in the book, I return to the research questions listed in the introduction.

How do the experiential and immersive qualities of contemporary VR experiences support or reject traditional narrative structures?

To answer this first question, I note that the case studies that are explored in this book demonstrate a diversity of VR storytelling, encompassing scripted or factual works with pre-rendered or reactive story sequences, and a range of interactive devices. The common feature of all of the projects explored in the preceding chapters is the positioning of the user into the storyworld as observer or explorer, which impacts upon approaches to narration. This insertion of the user into a virtual storyworld creates new possibilities for intense and memorable interaction with fictional or non-fictional story agents.

As noted above, VR technology gives rise to a user's sense of presence in the virtual environment. Presence is a psychological state that fosters immersivity, and is experienced by the VR user as a body that interacts with a synthetic setting. This multidimensional perception that results from the user's cognitive processing of sensory data is 'what the technology delivers from an objective point of view' (Slater, 2003, p. 1). In other words, the immersive nature of VR is directly related to the affordances of the technology, which create a sense that the user is present within a virtual space.

Further to the psychological state of presence, the notion of embodiment encapsulates the tangible sensation of feeling present as a body in a virtual environment, and may involve a physical body representation. As Chap. 2 of this book has explored and the case studies featured in other chapters have evidenced, this embodied experience in the context of a VR narrative can shape the user's self-perception and sense of identity by fostering reflection about their positioning and role within the storyworld in relation to other characters and story agents. One can therefore conceive of VR as a narrative medium that harnesses immersivity to foreground affective encounters between the user and story agents. In this sense the affordances of the medium foster a specific type of narrative immersion in which the interactor's suspension of disbelief and emotional response results from their full body engagement with a storyworld.

Generally speaking, the VR narratives that are explored in this book are informed by Aristotelian patterns of narrative, featuring plots that are driven by cause and effect, and that attempt to create an experience of catharsis for the interactor. Regardless of their interactive devices, many of these projects tend towards linear plots, where narrative material is presented in an order that is controlled by the work's author. This linearity is a key feature of the 360-degree 'cinematic virtual reality' format but also extends to works with game-like interactive devices. For example, *Stay Alive, My Son* (dir Victoria Bousis 2022), which receives analysis in Chap. 2, recounts Pin Yathay's autobiographical tale of escape from the Khmer Rouge and does so by adopting a 'hero's journey' structure (Campbell, 1949). While the user can explore the work's computer-generated environments with six degrees of freedom (the ability to swivel to look around and to move their avatar somewhat freely, abbreviated as 6DoF) and manoeuvre some objects, this interaction triggers their progression through a narrative that is fixed to a scripted trajectory. Other projects, such as those profiled in Chap. 6 offer multiple story threads that unfold in non-linear fashion, meaning that the user can influence the progression of the narrative as well as story outcomes. However, both of these approaches (linear and non-linear) can be considered examples of what Ryan describes as a 'top-down' system of IDN, where 'the player's progression is a journey along a path that is already traced and that leads to a fixed destination, or to several destinations when the system offers branching points' (2009, p. 52). This top-down approach, she observes, is necessary for a project that seeks to implement an Aristotelian narrative pattern as this involves 'a strict control of both the characters' actions and the user's emotions' (2006, p. xviii).

Ryan's contrasting 'bottom-up' systems of IDN remain limited in the context of contemporary VR narratives, regardless of recent advances in technology. This category involves emergent narratives that are created 'during the run of (a) program' (Ryan, 2009, p. 51) and might perhaps feature plot events that develop based on the user's interaction with authored characters. The examples of 'bottom-up' systems that are explored in this book involve multiplayer games and works featuring immersive theatre elements (see Chaps. 5 and 7). The featuring of live actors within an open-world setting [as seen in VR game *The Under Presents* (Tender Claws 2019)] or within works staged in the social platform VRChat (see examples in Chap. 7) creates the conditions for emergent narratives that are derived from actor and audience/player improvisation. VR narratives that feature live actors present a solution to the problem of creating believable characters that respond intelligently and in a dramatically interesting way to audience input. However, as Bruni et al. (2022) observe, the multimodal representation of characters within VR creates additional challenges for the creation of realistically represented characters, and has resulted in approaches referred to as the 'uncanny valley'. As mentioned, advances in artificial intelligence (AI) show considerable promise in rectifying this problem. The development of believable, reactive characters that are controlled by AI algorithms is an ongoing project for researchers working in the context of IDN, and as such, current experimentations with VR drama connect with earlier digital media works, such as Michel Mateas' and Andrew Stern's interactive drama, Façade (2005), in which characters responded to text typed by the interactor, or David Cage's Heavy Rain (2010) a playstation game that also allows user input to influence the unfolding narrative.

Regardless of whether VR projects feature linear, non-linear, or fully emergent narratives, a key aspect of the medium is its ability to cast the user as a character with agency within an unfolding drama. This ability demands that VR creators who adopt the traditional and popular 'hero's journey' narrative model account for the presence of the user within the diegesis and even consider casting the user as hero. This notion has received analysis in Chap. 7's exploration of *The Severance Theory: Welcome to Respite* (Ferryman Collective 2021), a VR narrative staged in the VRChat platform with live actors. This project's narrative elements are distributed across onboarding and offboarding sequences, as well as an interactive 'main event', in which one audience member adopts the lead role in the drama (and a custom avatar) Other audience members become invisible allies of this protagonist (they are not granted physical avatars) and can respond to voting mechanics so as to influence the protagonist's journey. Regardless of the role and level of agency that the user is granted in *Welcome to Respite*, the result is a compelling journey during which the user leaves their ordinary world and 'real' physical reality aside. This foregrounding of the user within the virtual storyworld leads us to the book's second central research question.

> *How do contemporary VR narratives incorporate the user's body as a storytelling tool?*

The case studies that have been explored in this book demonstrate the specificity of VR as a storytelling format that foregrounds embodied encounters between users and story agents. Further to the notion of a VR user who adopts an observer or explorer perspective of unfolding events, and who may be granted agency to directly influence the progression of the narrative (as is the case with interactive digital narratives more broadly), one must note the full body engagement that narrative-based VR demands, which transforms the user's body into a storytelling tool. This is particularly evident in works that feature a physical body representation or avatar that functions as a replacement for the user's 'real' body. This digital avatar allows the user to contribute to narrative threads through bodily movement and engagement with story agents, meaning that actions unfolding in real-time can meaningfully influence the progression of narrative.

This process has been explored in Chap. 7's analysis of projects staged in the VRChat social platform. In my exploration of the chapter's key case study, the aforementioned *Welcome to Respite*, I have noted how the user enters the work alongside other audience members in a tailored avatar of their own choosing, which likely reflects their offline identity (Freeman & Maloney, 2021). In this context the digital avatar becomes a self-selected storytelling tool that not only provides cues for other participants in the storyworld but contributes to the user's perception of the environment. As an illustration, a tall avatar will perceive the world differently than a shorter one, and other participants may interact differently with a humanoid avatar compared to an alien avatar. In other words, the user's choice of avatar is a means of expression that impacts on their contribution to the unfolding narrative.

Moreover, a user occupying a system-controlled avatar (i.e. an avatar that they cannot customise) may enact narrative as a predefined character or generic entity. The former is observed in the main sequence of *Welcome to Respite*, when one audience member assumes the role of the lead protagonist, a child named Alex. Although this character's journey follows a predetermined trajectory, the participant embodying this role still possesses the capability to shape the unfolding narrative through their interactions with the live actors. In this way their improvised enactment of narrative shapes the live actors' approach and all other participants' experience of the story. The latter generic avatar is observed in Chap. 5's exploration of *The Under Presents*, a VR game that sees players adopt masked and voiceless avatars. This generic avatar allows players to contribute to narrative threads in the game's multiplayer area, an open world where narrative experience is underpinned by encounters with live actors, other players and programmed non-player characters (NPCs). In this context the player's use of their physical body to manipulate their avatar (the swivelling of their body to turn around or the use of their hands to grab and exchange objects) not only increases their sense of presence and immersion in the storyworld but foregrounds their corporeality in terms of how they experience and contribute to the unfolding narrative.

As Chap. 2 has evidenced, and is noted above, a virtual body representation or avatar is not, however, a prerequisite for a user's powerful corporeal engagement with a VR work. Projects that position the interactor as an invisible observer might also draw upon their physical body as a storytelling tool in the way that they demand user interaction with, and contemplation of an unfolding narrative. This is demonstrated with reference to the 360-degree video *The Man Who Couldn't Leave*, which fosters a sense of self-presence by positioning the invisible user at a human vantage point within the virtual environment, where they are directly addressed by the story protagonist. As Chap. 2 has argued, this direct address encourages self-reflection, meaning that the user not only views events and responds to stimuli based on their prior life experience, but might consider their positionality in relation to the various story agents.

In sum, one can note that the user's body, as a storytelling tool, has a variety of possible functions within VR narratives: as a selector or manipulator of content, activator of narrative sequences or generator of story material. This research underscores the significance of prioritising the user's physical engagement with story elements when crafting virtual reality narratives. In addition to shaping the user's narrative role, designers and storytellers must also contemplate the intuitiveness of user interfaces and how various bodily representations can enhance the thematic resonance of the narrative.

How do interactive devices and user interfaces grant the VR user agency and assist in the delivery of narrative?

Interactive devices and user interfaces allow the VR user to modify their environment (or in the case of pre-rendered video, their view of the environment) and to receive feedback related to their experience. Focussing on the technology, existing research has noted three broad categories of interaction that occur in immersive virtual environments: viewpoint motion control, selection and manipulation (Bowman & Hodges, 1999; Muhanna, 2015).[1] The former is an example of what Flavián et al. describe as low behavioural interactivity (2019) and relates to the interactor's ability to rotate or move their point of view. In the case of 360-video works, viewpoint motion control is limited to a fixed position from which the interactor can rotate their view, therefore selecting their field of vision within a 360-degree environment. By contrast, for room scale works, the interactor can move more freely in space (bending down or taking steps to their left or right, for example). Selection and manipulation, meanwhile,

[1] Bowan and Hodges also describe a fourth interaction task that they label 'system control', which encompasses other tasks that the interactor can undertake within a VR application, such as deleting material or loading a new location. They suggest, however, that at a low level these tasks can also be characterised as 'selection' or 'manipulation' (1999, p. 38).

offer higher degrees of interactivity. Selection involves the ability to touch or pick up a virtual object while manipulation involves actually doing something with the object, such as positioning or orienting it (Bowan & Hodges, p. 38). This type of interaction might be undertaken using hand controllers or via the activation of interactive hotspots.

In the case of narrative-based virtual reality, these forms of interaction contribute to the user's sense of presence and embodiment within the virtual environment and can foster a sense of narrative immersion. Moreover, the medium's interactive affordances are directly tied to the user's positioning and level of agency as an observer or explorer of narrative elements. A user who adopts an observer role within a pre-rendered 360-degree video work, for example, will have no ability to select or manipulate objects, but may still feel a sense of social presence when directly addressed by story agents. The lack of agency associated with 360-degree video can be harnessed as a means to generate a powerful emotional experience for the user, a phenomenon that is observed in Chap. 3's exploration of *Sorella's Story.* In the case of this work, the user's lack of agency fosters feelings of powerlessness, and parallels that of the protagonist, a Holocaust victim. Likewise, *The Man Who Couldn't Leave* (Chap. 2) positions the user as a witness to past atrocities but allows them no means to intervene.

A tactical limiting of agency as a narrative tool is also apparent in the more interactive work *Please, Believe Me* (dir. Nonny de la Peña 2022), a non-fiction project that explores one woman's experience and treatment of Lyme disease (see Chap. 2). At a key moment in this narrative, the user looks down at their generic white hands (which they can move using hand controllers) and sees that they have been bitten by a tick that remains attached to the back of their right hand. However much they flap this hand or attempt to brush the tick off, they cannot remove it and must watch as the hand turns red with infection. As Chap. 2 has argued, the user's sense of virtual body ownership and lack of agency to remove the tick gives rise to feelings of unease at this moment, which deepens the user's understanding of the narrative's themes. A tactical limiting of agency occurs more generally across the room scale works explored in this book when users are restricted from free exploration of a 360-degree environment in favour of traversing select passages or zones where narrative information is presented. This limitation ensures that narrative elements that are embedded in the environment are seen and/or that a linear narrative progresses towards its predestined conclusion.

Conversely, a user who is granted 6DoF as explorer might use hand controllers to rearrange objects and directly affect the storyworld. This has been observed in Chap. 3's case studies *Goliath: Playing with Reality* and *We Live Here* (dir. Rose Troche 2020), which offer interactive possibilities that are afforded by game engine technologies. In the first case, this interaction entails engaging in game play, an activity that immerses the user in the perspective of the protagonist, Goliath. In the latter case, it involves physically exploring the tent of a homeless protagonist to initiate story threads. Both experiences provide a simulation of experience that engages the user on a corporeal level, allowing them to walk in the shoes of the respective work's central characters. This approach to interactive devices is also apparent in the aforementioned *Stay Alive My Son*, which casts the user in the physically represented body of the work's persecuted protagonist. A key moment in this harrowing work that receives analysis in Chap. 2 involves the user's ability to pick up a torch and shine it to illuminate a dark passage full of destroyed objects and human remains. The torch light is dim, meaning that the user must move close to the various objects in order to see them, an action that encourages a strong emotional response to the abhorrent subject matter. A similar device appears in the 6DoF work, *Child of Empire* (Dir. Erfan Saadati 2022), when the user is encouraged to use an oil lamp to illuminate the bodies of massacre victims on a train (see Chap. 4). In both cases the interactive device cultivates a strong connection between the subjective experience of the narrators and the embodied experience of the user.

Further to the notions of 'selection' and 'manipulation' in the context of VR narratives, one can note the user's ability to activate branching narratives, or to move between scenes, using a project's user interface in some of the above-mentioned case studies. This type of interaction allows the user to directly affect the progression of the narrative but in the case of projects that are experienced for the first time, might be undertaken somewhat randomly seeing as the user cannot know how their choices will impact upon the events to come. This random selection is demonstrated in *Lustration VR* (New Canvas 2022) and *Fire Escape* (iINK Stories 2019), works that allow the user the ability to explore parallel narrative threads while also leading them towards predetermined narrative outcomes (see Chap. 6). In the case of *Fire Escape*, several parallel narratives that concern the tenants of an apartment building complement but are not essential to the project's overarching plot, meaning that users can engage with the project several times, obtaining new insights into character motivations each time.

Ryan's taxonomy of interactivity as inherent to the design of narrative texts provides a useful means to further consider user agency in the context of contemporary VR. Ryan proposes two dichotomies: 'internal versus external to the storyworld, and ontological versus exploratory' (2015a, p. 162). The internal position places the user within the storyworld where they might become a character in an unfolding drama, while the external user adopts a god-like perspective of unfolding drama and might control events from this position. The exploratory form of interactivity involves a user who can look around a world but has no creative power to affect the world or narrative, (this is not to be confused with the explorer user position that I have theorised in Chap. 3) while the ontological form of interaction grants the user agency to create lasting change through explorative actions. These two dichotomies give rise to four types of interactivity: external exploratory, external ontological, internal ontological and internal exploratory.

While the case studies featured in this book demonstrate that all four of Ryan's types of interactivity are possible within the context of VR storytelling,[2] one can observe that the internal ontological and internal exploratory forms are most common. The internal ontological variant is evidenced in VR games such as *The Under Presents* or works featuring live actors that are staged using online platforms. These works grant the user the ability to impact not only on their own narrative experience, but that of other players or audience members. Contrastingly, 6DoF works such as the aforementioned *Stay Alive My Son* or *Please, Believe Me* stand as examples of Ryan's internal exploratory form. Ryan considers this variant in which 'the user experiences the story world from the inside [...] and she is able to move around the world, play tourist, pick up objects, look at them,

[2] Further to the examples of internal ontological and internal exploratory variants that are presented, one can observe instances of the external exploratory and external ontological forms of interactivity within the book's case studies. In the opening of the room scale work *Child of Empire*, for example, the user views a paper theatre reenactment of India's partitioning (see Chap. 4). This experience, in which the user sits outside of the storyworld and has no creative ability to intervene in unfolding events, is an example of Ryan's external exploratory form of interactivity. The external ontological form is demonstrated in *The Under Presents* when the player removes her mask during the Time Boat experience. This grants the user a god-like view of the Aickman research vessel and allows the player to control the passing of time for characters (see Chap. 5).

even alter her perspective, but she has no power to change anything' (2015a, p. 164) as uncommon; however, I would argue that this approach to interactivity underpins the delivery of a linear narrative in VR. By this I mean that it enables the user to experience a scripted narrative as a series of embodied encounters with story agents. Discounting the ability to move around and pick up objects (as is typical of works featuring 6DoF), one could also consider 360-degree videos to offer an internal exploratory form of interactivity, as these works grant the user an ability to alter their field of vision within a virtual storyworld where they are located as physically represented or invisible avatar, but no ability to intervene in unfolding events. In the case of all of these room scale or 360-degree video examples referenced here, the user's position as internal to the storyworld is central.

Diversity and Inclusion

The centrality of the body as a storytelling tool for VR narratives raises questions as to how the medium might be designed for broad accessibility. One can note that a considerable portion of the population have accessibility requirements, a trend that is further amplified by the growing ageing demographic (Montagud et al., 2020). However, as Dombrowski et al. (2019, p. 35) regrettably observe, existing VR systems are generally crafted with a focus on core users. This means that controls frequently necessitate the use of both hands, the ability to manipulate complex user interfaces or tools, and the capacity to stand or move for extended durations. Creed et al. (2023) note that while VR and related augmented reality (AR) technologies have the potential to reshape how we collaborate and interact with others, recent research has underscored the significant accessibility barriers associated with these technologies, which can result in the exclusion of disabled individuals. Further to the potential requirement that a user operate two hand controllers simultaneously, the challenges that might be faced by people with physical impairments include difficulties in initiating a VR system (e.g. configuring play boundaries), donning and doffing HMDs and negotiating tethered systems that pose trip hazards (Creed et al., 2023; Mott et al., 2020). Moreover, VR systems present access barriers for the neurodiverse, cognitively impaired, or for individuals with sight or hearing issues.[3] In regard to the former, Boyd et al. (2018) identify challenges for individuals with autism spectrum disorder (ASD) that include a heightened sensitivity to sounds, feelings of fear and anxiety, deficits in visual processing, struggles in interpreting interpersonal spaces and prolonged temporal processing. On the latter, Creed et al. cite 'issues around the ergonomics of HMDs in relation to hearing aids, integration of other assistive tools, and a lack of synchronisation in group conversations' (2023, p. 1). These and other issues prevent differently abled individuals from enjoying or even experiencing entertainment-based VR narratives, and have the potential to further widen a digital divide (Macdonald & Clayton, 2013).

As Creed et al. point out, there have been limited efforts made to date to design and create immersive experiences that are more inclusive (2023). In relation to creative expressions of VR, one can note accessibility research that is emerging in the area of cultural heritage (Chong et al., 2021; Garzotto et al., 2018; Montagud et al., 2020), some of which is applicable to VR narratives more broadly. Montagud et al. (2020), for example, explore culture-related accessible VR360 content, drawing upon techniques such as altered presentation modes to support access services (e.g. subtitling, audio description and sign language), interaction modalities and personalisation features. As these researchers note, VR has the power to conquer geographical and temporal barriers associated with the enjoyment of a cultural event or performance; however, accessibility remains an ethical concern and therefore demands significant attention.

One answer to accessibility and inclusion issues in VR is the adoption of universal design principles, which aim to 'meet all user needs and maximize accessibility to the product or system' (Dombrowski et al., 2019, p. 34). Rather than designing a VR experience that works in a certain way for all people, this form of design relates to the 'composition of an environment so that it can be accessed, understood and used to the greatest extent possible by all people regardless of their age, size, ability or disability' (National Disability Authority, 2014). Dombrowski et al. propose the application of the seven principles of universal design to the development

[3] For a comprehensive summary of research that has identified AR and VR accessibility barriers in relation to various forms of impairment, as well as research that has investigated potential solutions to address these barriers, see: Creed, C., Al-Kalbani, M., Theil, A., Sarcar, S., & Williams, I. (2023). Inclusive augmented and virtual reality: A research agenda. *International Journal of Human–Computer Interaction*, 1–20.

of inclusive VR experiences as a means towards the creation of approachable and customisable experiences (p. 43). These principles relate to the equitable, flexible, simple and intuitive design of VR systems, in which information is effectively communicated while taking an interactor's sensory abilities and ambient conditions into account. Moreover, the principles encourage design that has a tolerance for error, that considers the size and space needed by a variety of users and that enables low physical effort (thus minimising fatigue). Dombrowski et al. explore audio guidance, haptic feedback, subtitles and other text cues as solutions to specific accessibility barriers but also suggest that VR controllers mimic real-world interaction for disabled users, such as the building of interfaces that might enable virtual tools such as prosthetic devices and wheelchair controls (p. 36). Such an approach might enable methods of interaction that are familiar and therefore comfortable, they suggest. Further research, and specifically, consultation with key stakeholders such as users, is needed to advance this research so that accessibility and inclusion might become a core consideration of the design of VR narratives going forward. As Creed et al. suggest, the adoption of a multidisciplinary and collaborative approach to the problem of VR accessibility can address technical challenges as well as wider ethical and societal concerns (p. 17). Such an approach might also breed creative approaches to storytelling that can advance VR as a narrative medium.

Future Directions

In recent years one can note a steady rise in consumer interest in VR. A reported 10.8 million VR HMDs were sold worldwide in 2022 (Katatikarn, 2024), and one can note the now affordable price tag for established models such as the Meta Quest 2, which is fostering further consumer adoption.[4] Looking forward, one can be sure that as VR technologies continue to develop, user experiences of VR narratives will become more fluid and sophisticated. The newly released Apple Vision Pro HMD, for example, is considerably lighter than its predecessors, offering a more comfortable (though perhaps prohibitively expensive) experience of VR entertainment.[5]

[4] In January 2024 a Meta Quest 2 HMD can be purchased for US$299.

[5] The Apple Vision Pro HMD, launched in February 2024 retailed at US$3499.

How technological developments will impact upon story genres and approaches to interactivity is less clear; however, one can expect narrative possibilities and challenges to remain closely tied to these advancements. As Bolter et al. (2021) note with reference to the development of film in the twentieth-century film, the relationship between technologies and narrative genres and styles is somewhat interdependent (e.g. narrative and stylistic approaches to cinema production changed with the introduction of sound in the 1920s) (p. 175). Similarly, VR narratives will continue to be shaped by the technological affordances of the medium.

Looking at recent trends, one can note developments in social storytelling as online VR communities expand their numbers. The popularity of VR gaming, in particular, has generated large user communities that engage in social activities online. Multiplayer game worlds (e.g. Epic Games' Fortnite or BigBox VR's Population One) and social platforms such as VRChat present exciting venues for emergent narrative. As I've noted elsewhere, such platforms and applications present a model for the metaverse, allowing users to enter alone or in a group and to explore and consume as they might in the real world (Dooley, 2021). Through these platforms, narratives can be created by individuals, small or large groups of people, in ways that complicate the notions of storyteller, narrator, character or audience member. Further research is needed to provide insights into the shape and effects of narratives that are constructed in these settings.

One can also observe the recent phenomenon of linear narratives that have been staged and recorded within VR social platforms. The 90-minute feature documentary film *We Met in Virtual Reality* (dir. Joe Hunting 2021), for example, was filmed entirely within the VRChat platform, and featured five social actors portrayed using avatars. Following the screening of this film at the high-profile 2022 Venice Immersive festival, the 2023 edition of London's Raindance Immersive festival featured an entire new category of two-dimensional (2D) films shot in VRChat, evidencing the popularity of this emerging genre. This category of projects demonstrates the strong ongoing influence of cinema on the development of VR narratives and conversely, the remediation of VR back into 2D filmmaking. This remediation is also at play in virtual production film techniques that have allowed cinema directors to pre-visualise scenes using HMDs and game engine technology in recent years. As is the case for the VRChat films, VR as an immersive technology is used in this instance as a tool to generate cinematic content.

The case studies that have featured in this book constitute a broad range of entertainment-based VR narratives but are by no means representative of all VR narratives. Care has been taken to examine projects that adopt a variety of approaches to narrative representation across fiction, non-fiction and hybrid genres. The majority of the projects that are included in the book are award-winning works that have been featured at high-profile festivals, or that can be purchased and downloaded from online platforms. It must, however, be noted that the author's ability to attend festivals and/or visit other venues for VR storytelling in-person has impacted upon the inclusion of location-based projects as case studies. The challenge of researching VR narratives, which relates to the limited geographical reach or time-frame for experiencing some projects, is acknowledged in this respect. While this book offers insights into a range of works, further work is needed to catalogue and examine projects created at a range of budget levels and by diverse creators located around the globe. Advances in technology that enable more numerous, equitable and democratic opportunities for the distribution of VR entertainment in 3DoF or 6DoF formats are welcome in this regard.

The featured case studies evidence the increasing sophistication of VR narratives that draw upon a range of interactive devices to grant agency to the interactor. Writing on interactive narratives in 2015, Koenitz et al. suggested that advances in graphical representations were yet to give rise to more compelling stories. They write that 'the virtual environments used for many contemporary interactive narratives are realistic, dynamic and feature high fidelity in terms of their visual presentation and physical mechanics. However, the narratives and characters they host remain shallow, static and lacking in believability, dramatic engagement, and narrative development in comparison' (2015, p. 2). One can observe that in the several years since this comment was made VR technologies have continued to develop at rapid speed, and now feature even more impressive high-fidelity environments as well as advanced haptic devices. This has resulted in more compelling stories, and created new conditions for dramatic engagement; however, there is still some distance to travel in terms of reaching the full potential of VR storytelling. While the narratives of the last five years are considerably more mature than those that emerged at the beginning of VR's latest wave, further experimentation is needed to reconcile the affordances of the medium and its interactive potential with specific narrative goals. Research in this area might further explore the impacts of interactive devices on narrative immersion in a virtual environment, as well as creative expressions of user agency within the design of a narrative system.

Lastly, considering the role of the user's body as a storytelling tool in VR, it will be important to further examine the impacts of VR narratives on the bodies and minds of the user. VR's status as an 'empathy machine' (Milk, 2015) has been hotly debated in recent years; however, it is clear that the medium's immersive qualities have the potential to change attitudes and could therefore be used for the purpose of indoctrination (Bruni et al., 2022). This might involve the harnessing of affective experience in a virtual environment as a tool to foster strong emotions. Further research is needed to explore the ways that VR narratives have and can be used for rhetorical purposes, considering the design and reception of projects. This research area highlights VR's capabilities as a narrative medium that can immerse the user in another reality and powerfully engage their whole body in the experience of unfolding events.

References

Apple. (2023). *Apple vision pro*. https://www.apple.com/apple-vision-pro/

Aylett, R., & Louchart, S. (2007). Being there: Participants and spectators in interactive narrative. In *International conference on virtual storytelling* (pp. 117–128). Springer.

Bal, M. (2009). *Narratology: Introduction to the theory of narrative*. University of Toronto Press.

Biocca, F. (1997). The cyborg's dilemma: Progressive embodiment in virtual environments. *Journal of Computer-Mediated Communication, 3*(2), JCMC324.

Bolter, J. D., Engberg, M., & MacIntyre, B. (2021). *Reality media: Augmented and virtual reality*. MIT Press.

Bowman, D. A., & Hodges, L. F. (1999). Formalizing the design, evaluation, and application of interaction techniques for immersive virtual environments. *Journal of Visual Languages & Computing, 10*(1), 37–53.

Boyd, L. E., Day, K., Stewart, N., Abdo, K., Lamkin, K., & Linstead, E. (2018). Leveling the playing field: Supporting neurodiversity via virtual realities. *Technology & Innovation, 20*(1), 105–116. https://doi.org/10.21300/20.1-2.2018.105

Bruni, L. E., Kadastik, N., Pedersen, T. A., & Dini, H. (2022). Digital narratives in extended realities. *Roadmapping Extended Reality: Fundamentals and Applications*, 35–62.

Campbell, J. (1949). *The hero with a thousand faces*. Pantheon Books.

Child of Empire. (2022). Dir. Erfan Saadati. Project Datsaan.

Chong, H. T., Lim, C. K., Ahmed, M. F., Tan, K. L., & Mokhtar, M. B. (2021). Virtual reality usability and accessibility for cultural heritage practices: Challenges mapping and recommendations. *Electronics, 10*(12), 1430.

Creed, C., Al-Kalbani, M., Theil, A., Sarcar, S., & Williams, I. (2023). Inclusive augmented and virtual reality: A research agenda. *International Journal of Human–Computer Interaction*, 1–20.

Dombrowski, M., Smith, P. A., Manero, A., & Sparkman, J. (2019, July 26–31). Designing inclusive virtual reality experiences. In *Virtual, augmented and mixed reality. Multimodal interaction: 11th international conference, VAMR 2019, held as part of the 21st HCI international conference, HCII 2019, proceedings, part I 21* (pp. 33–43). Springer International Publishing.

Dooley, K. (2021). *Cinematic virtual reality: A critical study of 21st century approaches and practices.* Springer.

Façade. (2005). Developers: Michael Mateas and Andrew Stern. Procedural Arts.

Fire Escape. (2019). Writers Sam Butin, Navid Khonsari, Vassiliki Khonsari, Andres Perez-Duarte. Director Navid Khonsari. iNK Stories: USA. Three episodes.

Flavián, C., Ibáñez-Sánchez, S., & Orús, C. (2019). The impact of virtual, augmented and mixed reality technologies on the customer experience. *Journal of Business Research, 100*, 547–560.

Freeman, G., & Maloney, D. (2021). Body, avatar, and me: The presentation and perception of self in social virtual reality. *Proceedings of the ACM on Human-Computer Interaction, 4*(CSCW3), 1–27.

Garzotto, F., Matarazzo, V., Messina, N., Gelsomini, M., & Riva, C. (2018, October). Improving museum accessibility through storytelling in wearable immersive virtual reality. In *2018 3rd digital heritage international congress (DigitalHERITAGE) held jointly with 2018 24th International conference on virtual systems & multimedia (VSMM 2018)* (pp. 1–8). IEEE.

Genette, G. (1980). *Narrative discourse.* Cornell University Press.

Goliath: Playing with Reality. (2021). Dirs. Barry Gene Murphy and May Abdalla. Anagram, UK.

Hachman, M. (2022). Horizon Worlds isn't the killer VR app Meta wants it to be. *PC World.* Published October 11. https://www.pcworld.com/article/1346768/metas-horizon-worlds-vr-chat-is-facebook-fake.html.

Heath, A. (2022). Meta's flagship metaverse app is barely used by the employees building it. Published October 7. https://www.theverge.com/2022/10/6/23391895/meta-facebook-horizon-worlds-vr-social-network-too-buggy-leaked-memo

Heavy Rain. (2010). Dir. David Cage. Quantic Dream.

Jenkins, H. (2004). Game design as narrative architecture. *Computer, 44*(3), 11.

Katatikarn, J. (2024). Virtual reality statistics: The ultimate list in 2024. Published January 11. https://academyofanimatedart.com/virtual-reality-statistics/

Koenitz, H., Ferri, G., Haahr, M., Sezen, D., & Sezen, T. I. (2015). Introduction. In Koenitz et al. (Eds.), *Interactive digital narrative: History, theory and practice* (pp. 9–21). Routledge.

Lanier, J. (2017). *Dawn of the new everything: A journey through virtual reality.* Random House.

Laurel, B. (2014). *Computers as theatre* (2nd ed.). Addison-Wesley.

Lee, K. M. (2004). Presence, explicated. *Communication Theory, 14*(1), 27–50.

Lustration VR. (2022). Dir. Ryan Griffen. New Canvas, Australia

Macdonald, S. J., & Clayton, J. (2013). Back to the future, disability and the digital divide. *Disability & Society, 28*(5), 702–718.

Maschio, T.. (2017). *Storyliving: An ethnographic study of how audiences experience VR and what that means for journalists.* Google News Lab. https://newslab.withgoogle.com/assets/docs/storyliving-a-study-of-vr-in-journalism.pdf

Milk, C. (2015). *Chris Milk: How virtual reality can create the ultimate empathy machine.* [Videofile]. https://www.ted.com/talks/chris_milk_how_virtual_reality_can_create_the_ultimate_empathy_machine

Montagud, M., Orero, P., & Matamala, A. (2020). Culture 4 all: Accessibility-enabled cultural experiences through immersive VR360 content. *Personal and Ubiquitous Computing, 24*(6), 887–905.

Mott, M., Tang, J., Kane, S., Cutrell, E., & Ringel Morris, M. (2020, October). "i just went into it assuming that i wouldn't be able to have the full experience" understanding the accessibility of virtual reality for people with limited mobility. In *Proceedings of the 22nd international ACM SIGACCESS conference on computers and accessibility* (pp. 1–13).

Muhanna, M. A. (2015). Virtual reality and the CAVE: Taxonomy, interaction challenges and research directions. *Journal of King Saud University-Computer and Information Sciences, 27*(3), 344–361.

Nash, K. (2018). Virtual reality witness: Exploring the ethics of mediated presence. *Studies in Documentary Film, 12*(2), 119–131.

National Disability Authority (2014). *About universal design.* Centre for Excellence in Universal Design. https://universaldesign.ie/about-universal-design

Please, Believe Me. (2022). Dir. Nonny de la Peña. United States.

Ryan, M. L. (2006). *Avatars of story.* U of Minnesota Press.

Ryan, M. L. (2009). From narrative games to playable stories: Toward a poetics of interactive narrative. *Storyworlds: A Journal of Narrative Studies, 1*, 43–59.

Ryan, M. L. (2015a). *Narrative as virtual reality 2: Revisiting immersion and interactivity in literature and electronic media*. JHU press.

Ryan, M. L. (2015b). Emotional and strategic conceptions of space in digital narratives. In *Interactive digital narrative* (pp. 106–120). Routledge.

Saker, M., & Frith. (2020). Coextensive space: Virtual reality and the developing relationship between the body, the digital and physical space. *Media, Culture & Society, 42*(7–8), 1427–1442.

Slater, M. (2003). A note on presence terminology. *Presence Connect, 3*(3), 1–5.
Stay Alive, My Son. (2022). Dir. Victoria Bousis. United States.
The Man Who Couldn't Leave. (2022). Dir. Singing Chen. Taiwan.
The Severance Theory: Welcome to Respite. (2021). CoAct productions and Ferryman collective, Los Angeles.
The Under Presents. (2019). Dirs. Danny Cannizzaro & Samantha Gorman. Tender claws, Los Angeles.
We Live Here. (2020). Dir. Rose Troche. Afrobel/ Oculus VR for Good/VR Playhouse, United States.
We Met in Virtual Reality. (2021). Dir. Joe hunting. Painted Clouds Productions.

Correction to: Virtual Reality Narratives

Correction to:

K. Dooley, *Virtual Reality Narratives*,
https://doi.org/10.1007/978-3-031-64965-3

The last name of May Abdalla, the person quoted in the chapters, was unfortunately published with an error.

The credit for the work co-directed by Abdalla (cited on page 69) is missing from the reference list for chapter 3.

The correction chapters and the book have been updated with these changes.

The updated versions of these chapters can be found at
https://doi.org/10.1007/978-3-031-64965-3_3
https://doi.org/10.1007/978-3-031-64965-3_8

K. Dooley, *Virtual Reality Narratives*,
https://doi.org/10.1007/978-3-031-64965-3_9

Index

NUMBERS AND SYMBOLS
3D cinema, 10
360-degree video, 7, 22n8, 42, 63, 73, 86, 96n2, 97, 164, 219, 225, 226, 229
 See also 360-video
360-video, 6, 7, 75, 160, 225

A
Affect, 18, 19, 22n8, 27, 40, 44, 47, 53, 57, 62, 64, 65, 74, 80, 121, 122, 158–160, 179, 180, 193, 208, 219, 227, 228
Agency, 15, 16, 27, 29, 42, 43, 46, 46n3, 48, 53–57, 60, 63, 73, 75, 76, 81, 89–91, 102, 109, 116, 120, 122, 128, 136, 173, 177, 179, 180, 205, 213, 217, 223, 225, 226, 228, 233, 234
AI algorithms, 12, 222
AltSpace, 4
Architecture, 8, 144
Aristotle's Poetics, 13
Artificial intelligence (AI), 18, 29, 45, 143, 162, 182, 214, 220, 222
Audience participation, 19, 133, 147, 148, 186
Augmented reality (AR), 6, 7, 128, 164, 229, 230n3
Authorial control, 16, 24, 26, 122n9, 150, 158, 182, 206–208, 220
Authorship, 17, 162
Avatars, 1, 2, 29, 43, 46, 46n3, 47, 63, 70, 73, 80, 81, 130, 131, 133, 137, 142, 143, 149–152, 185, 188, 192, 193, 195–198, 200, 201, 203, 206–209, 215–219, 222–224, 229, 232

B
Body ownership, 43, 45, 47, 53, 54, 56, 57, 60–62, 62n7, 226
Body representation, 30, 39–65, 218, 221, 223, 224
Branching narratives, 32, 75, 158, 163, 164, 174, 176, 181, 196, 197, 219, 227

K. Dooley, *Virtual Reality Narratives*,
https://doi.org/10.1007/978-3-031-64965-3

C
Camera angles, 24
Catharsis, 20, 221
CAVE environment, 3
The Changing Same, 98, 104–110, 121, 122
Character, 1, 9, 11–16, 19, 21, 25, 26, 30, 40, 44, 48, 51, 56, 63, 64, 72–77, 82, 88, 90, 91, 98, 102, 104, 107, 110, 112–116, 118, 121, 122, 132, 135–138, 141, 144, 145, 149–153, 158–160, 163, 165–167, 169–171, 173–181, 193–195, 198, 199, 201, 202, 204–208, 215, 217, 218, 221–224, 227, 228, 228n2, 232, 233
Child of Empire, 98, 111–116, 120, 121, 227, 228n2
Cinema, 3, 5, 10, 12–14, 17, 24, 27, 28, 70–74, 122, 134, 164, 165, 232
Cinematic codes and conventions, 5, 14
Cinematic virtual reality (CVR), 5–7, 25, 51n5, 73, 74, 160, 164, 192, 221
Classical film narratives, 12
Computer games, 14, 16, 138
Convergence, 2
Corporeal space, 31, 138–144, 153, 216
COVID-19, 3, 4, 97, 133, 152, 153, 186, 193, 195, 209
Crowdfunding, 3, 129

D
Delivery platforms, 2, 30
Digital media, 11, 12, 17, 27, 48, 139, 162, 222
Diversity, 3, 75, 220
Diversity and inclusion, 32, 229–231
Docu-drama, 30, 43, 97, 100n5, 111
Documentary, 7, 17, 30, 31, 42, 43, 43n2, 60, 95–123, 180, 181, 232
Dome screens, 3

E
Embodied sensemaking, 45, 47, 54, 65
Empathy, 40, 57, 90, 97, 202
Environmental storytelling, 31, 95–123, 139, 139n3, 165, 215

F
Facebook, 3, 6, 214
Film festivals, 5, 6, 71, 157
Fire Escape, 31, 158, 159, 176–181, 227
First-person testimony, 30, 69–92, 98
Focalisation, 13, 14, 30, 70, 71, 76, 77, 85, 91, 217, 218
Formal analysis, 28

G
Game design, 7, 144
Game engines, 25, 26, 54, 83, 91, 97, 159, 161, 165, 194, 219, 227, 232
Game mechanics, 32, 39, 127, 144, 187, 209
Goliath: Playing with Reality, 69–72, 78–83, 85, 86, 91, 219, 227
Google Cardboard, 4, 95, 95n1, 97

H
Haptic feedback, 56, 231
Haptic technologies, 151

Head mounted display (HMD), 3, 4, 4n5, 9, 18, 29, 31, 39, 54, 72, 78, 97, 128–130, 139, 142, 152, 160, 165, 172, 177, 190, 192, 193, 195, 198, 200, 215, 216, 229–232
Hero's journey, 12, 13, 16, 204, 205, 221, 223
Heterodiegetic narration, 83
Hollywood, 6, 13, 102
Homodiegetic narration, 91

I
Immersive theatre, 2, 19, 26, 31, 127, 147, 148, 152, 185–209, 222
Installation, 147, 190, 192
Interaction design, 151
Interactive devices, 7, 27, 30–32, 40–43, 47, 57, 58, 63, 64, 69, 71, 73–75, 84–86, 98, 99, 115, 116, 121, 134, 143, 152, 158, 161, 173, 179, 180, 182, 194, 199, 203, 214, 219–221, 225, 227, 233
Interactive digital narrative (IDN), 12, 17–19, 22, 23, 134, 160, 162–166, 177, 180, 213, 214, 219–229
Interactive drama, 17, 164, 222
Interdisciplinary, 8, 11, 17, 28, 30

J
Journalism, 5, 6, 95, 95n1, 96, 157

L
Live action, 5, 6, 31, 48, 71, 83–86, 96, 99, 100, 100n5, 161, 192
Live actors, 1, 12, 26, 29, 32, 128, 130, 131, 138, 146–152, 187, 193, 195–200, 204, 206–209, 219, 220, 222–224, 228
Liveness, 29, 187–188
Live theatre, 5, 7, 133, 134, 186–189, 194–204, 209
Locomotion, 58, 130, 142
Ludology, 15, 15n7
Ludology *vs.* narratology debate, 14, 15n7, 101, 101n6, 135, 135n2
Lustration, 31, 158, 159, 167–170, 179–181, 227

M
The Man Who Couldn't Leave, 42, 46–55, 57, 63, 215, 225, 226
Meta, 3, 4, 71, 167, 214
Motion tracking, 9, 190
Movement dynamics, 104, 110
Moving image, 3, 23, 28, 51, 89, 214

N
Narration, 13, 19–21, 30, 69–92, 101n6, 115, 120, 158, 189, 214, 217, 221
Narrative representation, 23, 24, 213, 218, 233
Narrative theory, 10–15, 17, 22, 24, 31, 128, 138, 162–166, 217

O
Oculus Quest, 1, 4, 7, 97, 133, 185, 193, 194
Oculus Rift, 3, 4n4, 4n5, 133
Oculus Story Studio, 6
Oculus TV, 5
Omnidirectional cameras, 6, 95
Onboarding, 32, 79, 130, 167–169, 179, 187, 197–201, 203–207, 223

On the Morning You Wake: to the End of the World, 98, 116–122
Open-world games, 10, 140, 191

P
Participatory drama, 1
Personalisation, 32, 158, 159, 162, 181, 230
Perspective, 6, 11, 14, 20, 24, 26, 28, 29, 31, 40, 43, 45, 46, 60, 71–74, 76, 77, 79, 82–85, 90, 91, 99, 118, 122, 127, 139, 151, 163, 171–173, 179, 181, 189, 207, 215, 217, 218, 223, 227–229
Phenomenological analysis, 28, 128
Phenomenology, 28, 98
Please, Believe Me, 42, 57–64, 226, 228
Production studies, 28, 29

R
Real-time, 20, 24, 32, 54, 99, 132, 144–147, 158, 159, 161, 163, 186, 188, 190, 194, 208, 216, 219, 223

S
Screen production, 28
Screen studies, 5, 28
Screenwriting, 5
Self-presence, 45, 47, 50, 53, 55, 64, 218, 225
Sensory modalities, 8
The Severance Theory: Welcome to Respite, 32, 186, 187, 197–209, 223, 224
Simulation, 10, 72, 90, 91, 99, 107, 110, 181, 227
Six degrees of freedom (6DoF), 4, 7, 25, 53, 57, 58, 71, 72, 74, 75, 83, 97, 104, 104n7, 105, 111, 120, 160, 161, 169, 193, 222, 227–229, 233
Smart phone technologies, 4
Social presence, 45, 47, 50, 53, 55, 60, 62, 64, 88, 169, 176, 217, 226
Social storytelling, 232
Social VR, 1, 143, 185, 187, 207, 208
Software applications, 7
Sorella's Story, 71, 85–91, 100n5, 217, 226
Spatial storytelling, 99, 104
Spotlight Stories, 6
Stay Alive, My Son, 39, 40, 42, 53–58, 63, 64, 221
Stereoscope, 9
Stereoscopic view, 9
Storyliving, 31, 32, 157–182, 220
System, Process, Product (SPP) model, 18, 32, 159, 165, 166, 172

T
Tactile interfaces, 9
Telesphere Mask, 9
Television, 3, 14, 15, 44, 60, 78, 99, 99n4, 187
Theme park, 31, 99, 101
Three degrees of freedom (3DoF), 5, 18, 25, 48, 71–75, 83, 84, 86, 104, 104n7, 160, 161, 164, 176, 179, 233
Tribeca Film Festival, 5

U

The Under Presents, 31, 127–153, 193, 194, 215, 216, 222, 224, 228, 228n2

Unreal Engine, 54, 55, 97

User customisation, 18, 29, 31, 157–182

User positioning, 30, 64, 70, 72–77, 85, 90, 217–218

V

Venice Immersive, 7, 48, 71, 232

Virtual actors, 32, 186, 196, 208

VRChat, 1, 4, 7, 32, 147, 147n5, 185–209, 222–224, 232

W

We Live Here, 71, 72, 82–86, 91, 227

GPSR Compliance

The European Union's (EU) General Product Safety Regulation (GPSR) is a set of rules that requires consumer products to be safe and our obligations to ensure this.

If you have any concerns about our products, you can contact us on ProductSafety@springernature.com

In case Publisher is established outside the EU, the EU authorized representative is:

Springer Nature Customer Service Center GmbH
Europaplatz 3
69115 Heidelberg, Germany

The manufacturer's authorised representative in the EU is Springer Nature Customer Service Centre GmbH, Europaplatz 3, 69115 Heidelberg, Germany. If you have any concerns regarding our products, please contact ProductSafety@springernature.com

Printed and bound by CPI Group (UK) Ltd, Croydon, CR0 4YY

01/10/2026

02225953-0010